Dark Night of the Soul

Pamela Kribbe

Published by BookLocker.com, Inc., Bradenton, Florida.

Printed on acid-free paper.

BookLocker.com, Inc.

2015

First Edition

Translation by Maria Baes and Pamela Kribbe

Cover design by Janet Witte, www.janetwitte.nl

Cover art and illustrations by Elles Grzybek

Contents

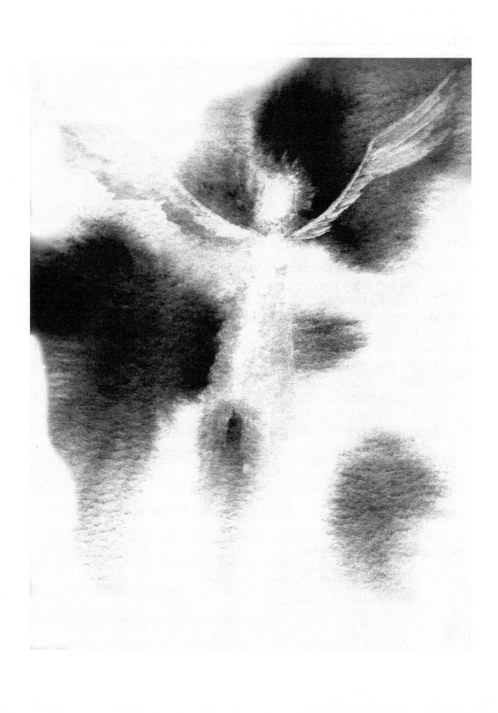

Introduction

On March 11, 2010, I found myself physically restrained in an ambulance that was taking me to the psychiatric ward of a hospital. Through the window I could see the streets of my hometown pass by me, streets where I had lived happily for years. Here I had built up a thriving professional practice while living with my husband and our beautiful daughter. Now I felt rejected and spit out by life. I was closed off from contact with others, and my only wish was to disappear; I just didn't know how. I was at the lowest point of my dark night of the soul.

This dark night had begun much earlier, in the spring of 2009, when I started to experience severe stomach problems, and I was overcome by violent fears. Gradually, I sank into a downward spiral of fear, pain, insomnia and eventually depression and psychosis. I experienced states of consciousness that I didn't know existed. I felt completely alienated from life and shut off from the merest glimpse of light, hope and perspective. It was a journey through hell. The recovery was eventually to be miraculously quick. A month after my stay in the hospital, I woke up from this horrible nightmare, and I felt reborn. It was as if the lowest had to be reached before I could rise up again. I had hit rock-bottom, as they say, and I could never have imagined how gruesome it was down there. Spiraling upward from this low point, however, something miraculous and deeply valuable travelled with me: the seeds of true love for myself and a sense of joy that felt divine.

Looking back on this horrific experience, I can now perceive the contours of an underlying spiritual logic. This journey through the underworld was not without meaning. At the time itself, the logic behind it eluded me completely. I felt utterly lost and desperate, without any sense of direction. This book, written some years later, has been a search for meaning, an attempt to interpret and integrate what happened to me. Part I is a personal account of my dark night of the soul. It is the story of how the downward spiral took hold of me, despite my connection with Jeshua and my intimate knowledge of psychology, therapy and spirituality. This account contains several inner dialogues with my soul and my guides that I recorded in my journal. In a separate chapter, my husband Gerrit speaks about his confusion, powerlessness and insights during my dark night of the soul.

In addition to telling my personal story, I also address the question of what role psychiatry can play in certain manifestations of the dark night of the soul. My personal experience with regular psychiatry has not been negative, although my initial attitude toward it was distinctly hostile. My stay in the hospital and the medication that I was given played an essential role in my recovery. Nevertheless, I often found the psychiatric approach one-sided and unnecessarily cold and clinical. In this book, I argue that both the spiritual and the modern psychiatric approach contribute valuable insights that can be reconciled and co-exist in treatment of psychiatric disorders. The first part of this book ends with a chapter on the excesses that may occur from a one-sided spiritual perspective, such as a naive faith in clairvoyance. These excesses confirm prejudices that exist towards modern spirituality (i.e., that it is vague and lacking substance) and can even lead to mental imbalance. A mature and well-grounded spirituality does not isolate itself from earthly reality, but rather connects itself with earthly reality and keeps both feet solidly on the ground.

The second part of this book consists of a series of channeled messages on the dark night of the soul. Channeled messages are received through inner (telepathic) contact with a spiritual guide. The inner contact is established as the receiver (channel) opens up to the energy and wisdom of the guide who is beyond the earthly sphere. To open up to the guide means that you enter a state of alert receptiveness and let go of your own thoughts, allowing the guide to speak. When I channel, I feel peaceful and inspired. I remain present, and I am aware of everything that is said through me. Thus, I am not 'taken over' when a guide speaks through me, which is an experience I would not choose to have. I see channeling as collaboration between channel and guide. The channel's job is to give earthly form to a wisdom that lies beyond the earthly. The message has to be put into words, and the channel is the one providing the words, even if the channel is not 'making them up'. As I receive messages from Jeshua (and others) I do not invent the words; they come to me fluently. However, the guide speaking through me has to make use of my vocabulary, which is shaped by my personal and cultural background. Even when a channel is completely open and receptive, the message that comes through her or him is put into human words and concepts which are the product of an historical setting and which can be interpreted in different ways. It is important to be aware that all channeling is influenced by the psychological and cultural background of the channel. I have written extensively about this in my previous books and on my website, so I will not elaborate here.

With me, channeling began in the year 2002, when the energy of Jesus spontaneously came to me during a healing session I was doing with my husband Gerrit. From my youth, I had felt familiar with and attracted by the energy of early Christianity, although I did not have a religious upbringing. However, I was completely surprised by the fact that Jeshua - this is how he introduced himself to me, as *Jeshua ben Joseph* - appeared to me inwardly and told me that he wanted to pass on a number of messages. I felt moved, honored, frightened, skeptical and, above all, amazed and intrigued. In *The Jeshua Channelings*, my first book, I have described in detail how the channeling process began for me (*The Jeshua Channelings* pp.251-262).

In one of our first conversations Jeshua introduced himself as follows:

I am the one who has been among you and whom you have come to know as Jesus. I am not the Jesus of your Church tradition or the Jesus of your religious writings. I am Jeshua-ben-Joseph; *I have lived as a man of flesh and blood. I did attain Christ consciousness before you, but I was supported in this by powers which are beyond your imagination at present. My coming was a cosmic event – I made myself available for this.*

It was not easy. I did not succeed in my endeavors to pass on to people the immensity of God's love. There was a lot of misunderstanding. I came too early but someone had to come. My coming was like throwing a stone into a fish pond: all the fish flee and the stone sinks into the deep; the ripples on the surface of the water, however, remain noticeable for a long time. You could say that the kind of consciousness I wished to convey did its work underground after that. On the surface of the pool there were constant ripples; well-intended but misguided interpretations rose to meet and fight each other in my name. Those who were touched by my energy, moved by the impulse of the Christ energy, could not really integrate it into their psychological and physical reality.

It took a long time before Christ consciousness could really set foot on Earth, but now the time has come. And I have returned and speak through many, through all and to everyone who wants to hear me and who has come to understand me from the quietness of their hearts. I do not preach, and I do not judge. My sincerest hope is to speak to you of the vast and unfailing presence of Love, accessible to you at any time.

I am part of a much larger consciousness, a greater entity, but I, Jeshua, am the incarnated part of that entity (or field of consciousness). I do not like the name Jesus much, for it has become so caught up with a distorted version of what I stand for. 'Jesus' is owned by the Church traditions and authorities. He has been molded to fit the interests of the Church patriarchs for centuries, so much so that the prevailing image of Jesus is now so far removed from what I represent that it would truly please me if you could just let it go and release me from that heritage.

I am Jeshua, man of flesh and blood. I am your friend and brother, familiar with being human in every way. I am teacher and friend. Do not fear me. Embrace me as you would embrace one of your kin. We are family.

(From: The Jeshua Channelings, pp.7,8)

From this contact with Jeshua, a number of books have emerged. The channelings touched a much larger group of people than I had ever thought possible. Years later, I also began to feel with me the energies of (mother) Mary, mother Earth and Mary Magdalene. Since then I have also received from them channeled messages. In part II of this book you find a selection of channelings from several sources. All the channelings have to do with the theme of the dark night of the soul, some directly and others indirectly. The aim of the channelings is to provide clear, loving information about inner growth and awareness. At least as important as the words is the energy that can be felt while reading the channelings. If you feel inspired, comforted and encouraged by them, their true goal has been reached. It means that the channelings have helped you connect with your soul, the source from which you can find your own answers.

The final part of this book contains two articles by my husband and soul mate Gerrit Gielen. They both shed light on the dark night of the soul, i.e. intense experiences of crisis and self-loss, from the perspective of the soul and its many past lives. In the Appendix, I share my own experiences with regression to past lives.

I would like to thank a number of people from my heart, both for their love and support during my dark night of the soul, as well as for their invaluable assistance in the creation of this book. First of all, my gratitude goes to my life partner Gerrit and my daughter Laura. I feel infinitely blessed by your unconditional loyalty and love. Our being together in everyday life is for me a source of fulfillment and joy. From this inspiration I could write this book. I thank my parents Amelita and Frans Kribbe for their loving support and background presence. Many people kept offering me friendship and encouragement during my journey through the underworld. In particular, I would like to thank my dear friends Anne Marie de Vrieze, Franca van der Linden and Christel Schulz. Your sincere love and commitment have deeply touched me. I am very grateful to Maria Baes, Martha Mason and Frank Tehan for helping me translate this book, which was originally written in Dutch, into English. They gave generously of their time and energy and I am very appreciative both for their language skills and their dedication. Finally, I would like to thank all of the participants in our workshops for their inspirational presence. The channeled messages in this book were received during various workshops and they derive their content in part from the energy and awareness of the participants. Together we have repeatedly created a field of love and compassion; from this fertile soil the channelings in this book emerged.

Part I

My Dark Night of the Soul

1. Pain and Fear

In the spring of 2009, I had to deal with stomach complaints. It was a busy time in my practice. I found it hard to say no when people asked for a consultation, so I scheduled too many appointments per week. Realistically, I felt I could not do more than three or four consultations a week. Because of the intensity of each consultation, I needed a lot of time to recuperate. During a session, I intuitively attuned myself to the energy of the client, and I was inclined to sympathize with the pain, fear and loneliness that I encountered. In addition, I tended to do my best and wanted to be as completely present as possible. I was a perfectionist. The readings were mostly well received, and I usually felt very inspired afterward. Following the readings, however, I also felt drained and tired and was able to do very little for the rest of the day. I then needed to take a day off to become properly grounded and to regain my inner strength.

In addition to the readings I gave, my husband Gerrit and I offered workshops that demanded a lot from me as well. It was the combination of my sensitivity and being anxious to succeed that ultimately lead to my breakdown. On a Saturday morning in April 2009, I was sitting in a playground with my daughter Laura, then seven years of age, when I experienced a sharp burning sensation in my esophagus. I guessed that it was acid reflux from my stomach, but it became so strong that a couple of antacids – or even an entire package – could do little to assuage it. This scared me, and the following Monday I went to my family doctor (my 'GP'). He gave me medication that would reduce the acid production in my stomach and advised me to rest. I started to cancel some workshops and appointments. After ten days, the drug seemed to take hold, and I felt somewhat better. However, there was still an undercurrent of anxiety, tension and agitation present in me.

I was afraid to say no and to create space for myself. I told myself that, after all, the work I did in my practice was my heart's passion, and three or four readings per week were not that many anyway, or were they? I had all sorts of judgments about what I should and could do. Beneath lay the fear of rejection: suppose I took the space I needed for myself; would people not turn away from me?

I also had deep fears about doing channelings for a large audience. There was a lot of interest in my work, and often things went very well during the gatherings. During the channelings, there was a flow of inspiration that carried me, and there was the shared, warm energy with the attendees that always gave me a great feeling afterward. But one or two weeks prior to each public channeling, I experienced a lot of anxiety, tension and resistance, which was grueling. Performing for a large public does not come naturally to me; I had found that frightening already during my internship at the University. I am naturally introverted and withdrawn. There was also a deep fear of rejection; what I was doing (channeling) was still very unusual. Would I not encounter skepticism and ridicule? Yet I had the sense that I *had* to do this. I felt authentically inspired. In addition, there were less valid reasons: people were asking for the channelings, and I did not want to disappoint them. Also, I assumed that as a writer I was supposed to give public talks and channelings. In retrospect, it was a combination of my fear of rejection and false images of 'how it should be' that prompted me to ignore my own rhythm and to exceed the limits of what I could handle. Looking back, offering channelings to large audiences was probably something that I should have built up slowly and calmly, so that I could overcome my fear gradually.

In May 2009, I still felt shaky, and my stomach was still sensitive. In addition, I then received the message that my mother had breast cancer. I remember that I heard the news from her over the phone. It was as if at that point something snapped in my nervous system. My usual capacity to hold myself together seemed to have been lost. I tried to prevent myself from feeling too much compassion and sympathy, which my mother did not expect from me and which would not have helped her, in any event. This setting of my emotional boundaries worked out better than I expected, perhaps because I simply did not have the capacity for experiencing those emotions at that point. It was helpful that, in this period, I had inner contact with my grandpa, my mother's father whom I had never known, because he died before my birth. From him, I received very positive, encouraging messages which I relayed to my mother. She was very open to this communication and experienced a wonderful and much deeper connection with her father, even though her personal relationship with him had not been easy. In the end, my mother's surgery was successful, and she traversed her illness with great courage and a positive attitude. She recovered well from cancer.

However, that spring things went downhill with me. I again got violent stomach upsets, and the medications seemed to work less effectively. I tried to eat as carefully as possible and to avoid everything that produced stomach acid. Because of that, I began to eat less, lost weight, and had more trouble sleeping. My nerves were overwrought, and I had a continual, violently burning sore throat at night because of the reflux of stomach acid. This pervasive pain kept me from sleeping and got progressively worse. I could no longer offset the sleep deprivation with an afternoon nap, something I was used to doing. Never before had I had trouble sleeping. I was someone who always fell asleep easily and slept through the night. Now there was this constant tension in my body that made it hard for me to cross that boundary into sleep. I tried alternative remedies such as Valerian root, Melatonin, and certain herbal mixtures, but they hardly made a difference.

In the summer of 2009, I also had to deal with anxiety and panic attacks, which also were new experiences for me. I was used to experiencing fear related to something specific. For example, when I was afraid before a reading, I felt a fear relating to that specific event, but the fear would disappear when the session was over. Now, however, I was faced with anxiety attacks that were more general in nature and that seemed to come out of nowhere. Suddenly, I would be overcome by waves of fear that manifested themselves in my body as violent stimulation and tension in my stomach, chest and throat. This happened several times a day. After a while, I could feel the fear even between my shoulder blades and in my arms and legs. It was a very physical sensation which was extremely unpleasant.

I received from the family doctor a prescription of tranquilizers (benzodiazepines) that also promoted sleep. These pills actually helped me to relax. One pill provided me with three or four hours of rest, which was a relief. What upset me, however, was that I felt terribly guilty about taking such a pill. The doctor cautioned restraint in the use of this medication, and I felt weighed down by the idea that the pills could artificially veil the fear and become addictive. All kinds of spiritual judgments came to the surface and were also confirmed by the people around me, such as: 'You need to go through this and not artificially suppress it.' 'With the pills, you fight your symptoms and you do not get to the underlying cause.' In short, 'Taking pills means you fail spiritually'. By this type of prejudice, which I internalized, I felt ashamed and weak when I took a pill. The positive effect of the pills – the receding anxiety and tension - became undone by the self-recrimination that went along with it.

In retrospect, I could have swallowed those pills without remorse and in a higher dose rather than a lower one. The adverse effects of taking the pills were nothing compared to the advantage that they would have given me of more sleep and relaxation. The lack of sleep would eventually lead to a severe psychosis and depression, leaving me completely incapacitated. I had not hit rock bottom yet, however. Looking back on this period, I still see the summer of 2009 as a positive time, in which, despite the anxiety attacks, insomnia, and continuous physical pain, I still had hope and a meaningful connection with others. During that time, I had cancelled all channelings, consultations, and workshops and did nothing anymore in terms of work. It was more a matter of day-to-day survival, and what was worse, getting through the night. I also began to suffer from hyperventilation, a chronically rapid (chest) breathing in which you ingest too much oxygen, but you have the sense that you lack oxygen. Some weeks the experience became so debilitating that I could no longer walk outside. I found this terrible as I love walking in nature. My breathing was enormously erratic, and I could no longer breathe deeply into my belly. Only when I lay flat on the ground did I find some peace.

During those months, I still had contact with my spirit guides and with Jeshua. I opened up to their energy and their positive, encouraging words. I also received help from people around me, primarily from my husband Gerrit, who patiently talked with me and encouraged me. In addition, I received occasional readings from a friend and fellow therapist, and I received a weekly massage, all of which made me feel somewhat better. Even though the upset stomach, the fear and the tension, the insomnia and the hyperventilation did not lessen during this period of time, I still felt hope and encouragement as a result of these helpful interactions.

During July and August 2009, I kept a diary in which I attempted to better understand my fears through writing. I often wrote in dialogue form, by posing questions to my spiritual guides or to my soul. The next chapter contains a number of excerpts from my diary at the time.

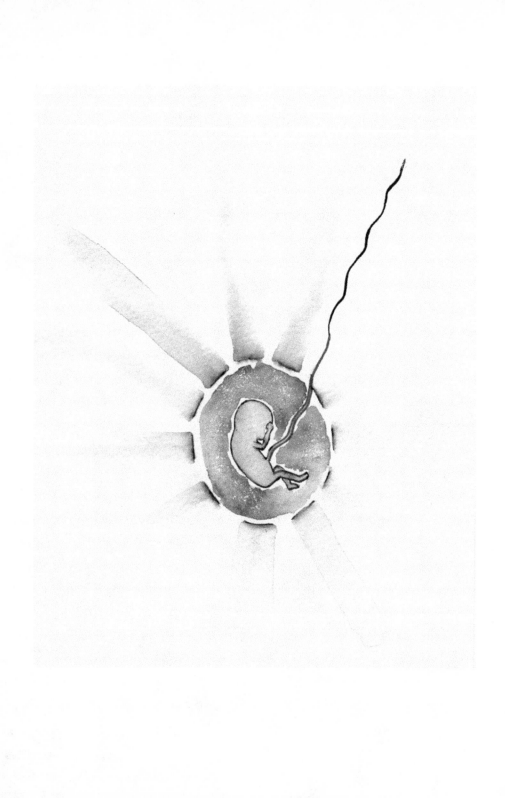

2. Diary Excerpts

I have received a healing by Franca and afterward the following images come up spontaneously. They are accompanied by a lot of emotion.

I see myself before my birth in an atmosphere of light and love. At one point there is the decision that I will incarnate again. There is a guide with me. He feels very familiar and is called Bartholomew. His charisma is loving and wise. He says that I cannot keep my birth from happening. It is part of the rhythm of life that I now will be born on Earth. There are things that want to come to completion in this life. Old grief and old fear want to be resolved. Life on Earth can help me. It wants to invite me to let go of my old mistrust, and to believe again in what is beautiful and amazing about life in the material realm.

I oppose the decision. The decision comes from life itself, from the womb of the cosmos. It is not Bartholomew who compels me. I need to give hearing to the call. The hand that nudges me is gentle, but I resist and cringe. *I do not want to go.*

Why do I refuse? I do not want to be caught in the veils of the Earth, this place which I associate with violence, threat, aggression and ultimate rejection. I want to be free, taste the perfect harmony of the spheres, and float around there in happiness and ecstasy. Kicking and screaming I find myself taken up in a vacuum that sucks me towards Earth. Something in me wants to exclude the light that accompanies me. I am angry, I am resisting.

I see an image of a circle of women in the spiritual world who prepare me for life on Earth. I see myself as a baby as they carry me, sing to me like angels and envelop me with gentle love and words of confidence. The child wants it, but a part of me is cut off, angry, on the sidelines, and does not want to listen. This part in me does not want to incarnate. This part of me is bitter, furious and full of disillusionment. It is cynical and critical in a sharp kind of way. It wants revenge. It wants to be right, but there is no one around her. She is alone. A prison so dark and bare, worse than a material prison. When your own mind becomes your prison, you let go of life. You no longer give it a chance to surprise you, offer you new avenues, or make it up to you.

I was closed off when I incarnated. The healing women could not reach me. When I descended to Earth, I felt like a brittle autumn leaf that swirls to the ground slowly and lifelessly. I had no desire for it. To become an embryonic body felt to me as distressing as being smeared with tar. As if the last shred of hope was taken away from me: the freedom of the heavenly spheres. I felt suffocated in this body, petrified. Chilled to the bone. I did not want to incarnate, but it happened to me: I became flesh and blood. Powerless, I turned and shifted in the womb, not wanting to be or to be born. But the tiny body grew and developed even if I did not want it to. It happened anyway. The energy of my mother felt strange and remote to me. I had no connection with it. I was turned in on myself, angry, hurt, and resistant. Apathy overcame me. I kept life at a distance; there was a fog between me and everything else.

Then came the birth. Violent movements in the womb. I got scared, panicked, did not want to leave the womb. I had become accustomed to living inside. Even though it did not feel good, it had given me a certain security. The birth took a long time; I did not help the process, because deep inside me something was opposed to life on Earth. This prolonged the birth process. When I came out, the light overwhelmed me. I also became aware of the emotions of my mother, her fear and panic about the difficult birth. I felt guilty and selfish, because my inner resistance had damaged her somehow.

July 3, 2009

Dialogue with Mother Earth

Why is my stomach so upset?

You have too much stomach acid because you want to defend yourself against something. The acid is a repellent. You feel bombarded by impressions; this you cannot integrate well. The acid acts as an internal regulator. It tells you 'This far and no further'.

I cannot set my own boundaries and because of that, the acid does it for me?

Yes, that's right.

Why is it so difficult for me to remain centered, and simply to allow energies around me to pass me by, so that they cannot cause me to lose my inner balance?

You desire to do your best for others. You want their approval and appreciation. There is a little girl in you who is desperate for affirmation. When, in your early childhood, you decided to orient yourself to your mother as the one who fed you at various levels, you moved away from your center. This has never been completely resolved.

You wanted her approval above all, everything else was secondary. You have repeated this habit in subsequent relationships. In this tendency you always put the judgment of another above your own needs. 'What does the other think of me? Am I doing well in his or her eyes?' is much more important than: 'What do I think of this, what do I really want?' This pattern is deeply ingrained, and it repeats itself in your practice. You want to do well for others and you rarely ask yourself: 'Is this really what I want, is this good for me?'

So I automatically regard the opinion of the other person as the criterion by which I measure myself; they are my judge so to speak. Is this the survival mechanism that I have chosen to avoid feeling my loneliness and sadness too directly?

You might put it that way. As a baby you came in with a deep grudge against life. You did not want to live on Earth. You had no trust in life, and trust is the foundation for the ability to stay true to yourself. When you were born, and became overwhelmed by the stimuli from outside, there was no trust present from which you could integrate these new impressions. Everything seemed scary and dangerous. There was no inner grounding, and thus you grasped onto something extraneous, for what seemed to promise a certain degree of certainty. This exterior compass was your mother.

You were without a center when you were born. You might say that you did not have a true self, because the part of you that could have said yes to life, and could have provided the foundation for independent observation and experience, was closed off from life. Your consciousness, filled with fear and panic in the beginning of life, was looking blindly for a beacon, something to hold onto. Inwardly it was not there, because your soul's light did not truly descend on Earth. You have only discovered your soul later in life.

Was there a kind of separation between my soul and my earthly personality?

The soul could not be consciously experienced. The resentment and disappointment set up a screen. However it is only by incarnating again into earthly life that one can eventually break through this screen. This cannot be accomplished in the higher realms, because there you do not experience life as a separate personality (ego). You are much more in touch with the whole and with your soul there, but precisely because of this you can never truly connect with old emotional burdens and resolve them on the feeling level.

Yes, I understand. I would like to get a better grasp on this automatic response of putting the other above myself. What happens when I meet people is that I easily become identified with them. It seems as if something in me 'jumps over' to that person and starts to see life from their perspective. Is that empathy? In any case, I then also see myself through the eyes of the other. I feel their expectations and I am afraid of not fulfilling those expectations; there is a fear of inadequacy, *not quite being able to erase myself and be completely like they want me to be.* The idea of a boundary, possibly even a conflict between us seems unbearable. I tend to merge with the other; I want to be liked, while at the same time I am anxious that this will not succeed. Is this the automatism I need to let go of?

The automatism is that you give up yourself in favor of the other. The other is for you dominant, so they may determine what you feel and see and you adapt to their wishes. That's the survival mechanism. You adapt.

In adapting to the other, I lose myself, I lose my center.

Yes and the crux is that you consider that loss of self to be desirable. Then you are a 'good girl'. Then you will be appreciated. The fallacy in your head is this: self loss is good and okay and solves all my problems.

The tempting part of self loss is that you then feel harmony; you feel that you have a right to be, because the other approves of you. Now, in your current life as a channel and writer, many people are looking to receive your affirmation, your empathy and understanding. The pressure on you has risen, and you cannot answer all needs. You have to find your own anchor, your independence, because needy people will not stop you in that mechanism of losing yourself. They often do not know that you are giving up yourself in relation to them. It just feels good for them to be with you.

So how does one start to realize that loss of self is not good, that it is a false (survival) mechanism?

*That realization comes when you have given up so much of yourself that you begin to suffer. You can lull yourself to sleep for very long, for example in a romantic relationship, but there will come a point at which you will realize that you are not happy. In the case of your relationship with R. (*a previous relationship that lasted four years*) there came a wake-up call for you because you fell in love with M. That seemed to be just happening, but it was your soul attracting this to you. You felt safe for a long time with R., but falling in love with M. made you aware of how much of yourself you had been denying in the relationship with R.*

I remember how I struggled when I was in the process of making the decision to leave R. I was very attached to him energetically. Just after I had decided to bite the bullet and leave him, we were together in the kitchen, and for the first time I refused to comply with his expectations. I said loud and clear: 'I'm leaving.' Right at that moment something happened on the energetic level that struck me deeply. There was a bubble of energy surrounding R. that in a flash shifted back to me. I believe that was my energy, my empathy and identification with him, everything that belonged to me, and that I literally had given him in an attempt to acquire his approval. With great vigor it returned back into my body. Suddenly I felt very strong and powerful. It was as if I had abruptly awakened from an anesthetic, conscious of myself and no longer afraid to go my own way. Everything became crystal clear. My decision was final, and I left him that same day.

Later I had the same experience in a somewhat lesser degree when I walked out from some volunteer work that I was doing. I said openly to an employee who treated me in a very meddlesome and unpleasant manner, 'I am quitting.' It was wonderfully liberating.

Yes, you then felt what it is like to be in your center: 'I think, I feel, I want' - and to act accordingly. That is healing for you. Sometimes you need to deny yourself for a while before coming to such a breakthrough. In that sense, such a self-denying phase fulfills a useful function. It leads you to a point where you see that this cannot continue any longer. Such a moment of deep self-awareness is very valuable. It could be a breakthrough for the rest of your life. Leaving R. has been crucial for your inner development. From that time on you have not attracted a dominant partner who automatically took the lead. You have met up with gentle, introverted partners, who through their character, invited you to stand up for who you are rather than to identify with a strong figure next to you.

Have I stepped into the same trap of losing myself in my practice in relation to my clients?

Yes, to a certain extent. You have given too much of yourself. You wanted to do well. You also have something of the perfectionist in you that causes you to give more than is necessary. You need not do as much as you think you have to do. You often think that you should give people precisely the answers that they are looking for in order to solve something. But that's not what they really need. What they really need, and what you can offer, is to facilitate a shift in their energy from fear to trust, from uncertainty to inner knowing, from self-rejection to self-understanding. From this new space of trust and self-appreciation, they can see their problem in a different light and find the solution themselves. You offer the possibility of helping them make an energetic shift, not providing the solution to their problem.

And if I do that consciously, will I have less pain in my stomach? Because then I do not put as many heavy requirements on myself?

Yes, precisely.

Is it really that simple?

Yes, because you then keep your energy close to you. If you want to fix something for someone else, you make a move toward them that causes you to lose yourself. You start doing your best by considering strategies through your mind, or you try to see with your third eye what direction they have to take. All this trying, doing your best and making such effort draws from your stomach, where your third chakra is located. You suffer along with them at that moment, and you want to solve the problem with them. But you are not there to solve their problem; you are there to show them that they can solve it themselves.

I find it annoying to be approached as a clairvoyant who sees for others what they cannot see for themselves. If they see me as a clairvoyant, or psychic, who knows objectively things that they themselves do not know, it means that the solution to their problem lies in something extraneous. One example, is when they ask, 'Can you tell me whether I should resign or not, break off a relationship or not?' The real solution always lies on the inner plane, and I want to work on that level.

Precisely. You should explain to people that you are not going to tell them what to do or not do, and you will not give them objective guidelines about their lives. You are working on the inner plane. Your work is about how to deal with fear and negativity, how to deal with emotions, how to be more grounded, to set boundaries, to make contact with your intuition and your soul. And so on. That's your area of work.

Indeed. Exactly. I am sick and tired of being called on as a kind of oracle!

Okay. Feel that carefully again. You're sick and tired!

I am angry too.

Why?

I think it is childish that people want to know all those things from me. At the same time I feel also that I am falling short if I cannot give them those answers. Then I am overcome with a fear of failure. 'Say, you are not a real psychic.'

Would you like to be a true psychic?

No. Essentially no. I want to help people find inner liberation, the light from within. I think I have sometimes helped people through clairvoyance (by giving objective answers) something with which they were quite happy. I have found their gratitude wonderful, and maybe I became attached to that? Perhaps I have subconsciously set myself up to meet the requirement of being a good clairvoyant, while my original interest did not lie there at all. My whole life long I have been interested in philosophy, psychology and spirituality, in the workings of the inner life. My work with Jeshua fits in so well with that.

Yes. That's what you really want and where your self-realization lies. You don't have to be a clairvoyant for others. Relieve yourself from that duty. You have bought into other people's expectations that you should play that role for them. You have been half-hearted about this point for fear of failure. On the one hand, there was fear, and the feeling of wanting to do your best, to work harder. On the other hand, there emerged this anger and irritation that caused you to find it stupid that people were asking you these kinds of questions. But people are often filled with fear and often come to you in despair with an urgent life question: 'What should I do?' Precisely then it is very necessary to stay grounded in yourself and not to allow others to draw on and deplete your third chakra by their urgent need for concrete, objective answers. That's not your job.

Often I feel a kind of paralysis come over me as people make such a desperate, urgent appeal to me. When Jeshua then responds through me, his answers are always focused on creating that energy shift, not on giving concrete advice. So that part is going well. But I still feel that I am falling short and that I should give more specific answers. I feel uncertain, like I'm disappointing someone.

The fear and uncertainty you feel are an attack on the third chakra. Jeshua's answers throw people back on themselves, while you want to embrace them so to speak. His energy creates a space through which you can keep centered. But the frightened inner child in you thinks you are not allowed to be in a calm and peaceful state while the other person is suffering and desperate for some answers. 'I cannot be that powerful! And also keep my energy all to myself? I will be punished.' That's how the inner child reasons. It is used to staying small and adapting itself.

So when I want to make a new beginning in my work, I have to transform this inner child part, right? I have to dare to be great and independent.

Yes. The inner child part is caused by the way in which you incarnated: with much resistance. The inner child that denies itself and tries so hard to do its best for the approval of others can only exist from the lack of confidence that you felt at the beginning of your incarnation. You solve this and you find renewed trust in life on Earth, you say yes to your life here and now on Earth, and take your strength from there. This inner strength ensures that your inner child will find peace, an anchor in yourself, so that it no longer has to reach out to others for security and warmth. You see?

Yes, thank you. A nice thought that I can overcome the problem through something positive, by building trust instead of something negative such as having to fight against my fear, or by correcting my inner child. How do I build trust?

By knowing and feeling that you are okay just as you are. You need not change yourself. It is not about trying to convince yourself that you should let go of your resistance because things are all well and fine here. Such reasoning, such an attempt to convince yourself is a form of struggle. Accept the resistance, envelop it with understanding and say, 'I understand very well that you are feeling resistance. I do not condemn you; I love you and take you in my arms.'

I have done that recently when I started to write this piece. I felt such an intense sadness about myself, about my loneliness and abject misery right before entering this lifetime, and I could only say, 'Oh my dear beautiful girl.' I said that to the dark, rigid figure that I was when I incarnated. I felt the need to cry terribly then, and I saw with my inner eye a bright turquoise light emerge from that dark figure. There seemed to be something touched and resolved. I felt it physically, too, in my stomach.

Something broke open in you, yes, and that was good. You have resolved some of the pain. And the rest you solve by looking at yourself with understanding. Fighting with your problem, your fear or your resistance is never the solution.

This issue of trust and the survival mechanism of self-loss that is based on it, will only gradually solve itself, or not? Can I start working again? How long of a leave of absence do I take?

You cannot know that yet. Allow it to take its course. You don't have to work before you feel good again.

The past few years I've always had a lot of fear and tension prior to workshops, and certainly before large gatherings. Will that become less?

It will be less. Trust. You are growing on the inner level during this period.

July 8, 2009

Today I have felt contact again with Jeshua! He had seemed so far away. I was afraid of his energy since it is so powerful and direct, and I feared that he would condemn me because I feel so dejected and tearful on account of my illness. I was taking a walk, and then I felt him so close, like a brother, not at all judgmental. He told me that he does not condemn anything in me, that I may be all of it, scared, lonely, sad, that he accepts me as I am totally and completely, in my humanity. That gave me such a good feeling. He was close to me at last.

I also felt a glimpse of how it could be in the future. Twice in succession I have drawn the tarot card, Death, a card that shows that there truly is change at hand. Jeshua's calmness and self-awareness allowed me to feel that I have to meet my own work with serenity and self-awareness, focusing on what feels good, what flows naturally, and letting go of everything else. No more fretting, worrying, doubting, and all that hassle. To be myself authentically, and let go of what others do with it, or like about it. Really believe in what wants to flow through me instead of thinking that I have to create it myself. That has been my fear, that I did actually make it all up, and that I should make every effort to do it right. But that is not the case. There is an energy present during the channelings and workshops which is greater than I am. I can follow that and let go of everything else.

At the last public channeling on May 16, I felt so strong. During the process I felt truly carried by the Christ energy; I surrendered. But the week leading up to the meeting I had fears so overwhelming that I almost felt like dying.

Dear Jeshua, why am I sick?

There has been a long process preceding your illness in which you received signals – via your stomach and your emotions – that things were too much for you, and you could not carry the load. There was a lot of stress in your energy system, fear of failure, fear of not being good enough. You were pulled away from your center, you lost your grounding and your third chakra became disordered, crippled. This chakra (solar plexus) relates to self-care, to standing in your own power and truth, and not being swayed by the many influences from outside. The third chakra is the center of I-power. It is what you need when you channel a transpersonal power, when you need to stand simultaneously firmly in your own shoes, in the sense of being grounded and remaining yourself. You are the channel, and all those fears that you are dealing with are demanding that you see them in order for you to address and heal them. You have exceeded your boundaries for too long, even though your fears have called you to return to yourself. Your illness has literally forced you to do so, but you now also intuitively feel the need to withdraw. You have had that feeling for months, but you did not follow its call. The voice of your heart was drowned out by ideas from outside: to plan more new workshops, to take on all kind of things. In your heart you desired rest; now you are getting it.

I thought it was bad to want that peace, a flight from reality.

The desire for peace is a natural desire for balance. What you desire deeply and sincerely is never a flight from reality, but rather indicates the direction towards which your soul wants to go.

Autumn 2009

Dialogue with my Greater Self

I am afraid of the pain, that I will not able to bear it.

There is always a choice Pamela. You can choose a positive or negative approach to pain. In the positive approach you say yes to it and give purpose and meaning to the pain. It that way it becomes more relative, and not so overpowering. Look what purpose you can give the pain. Does it have a function for you?

It forces me to be very much in the moment, to always remain present to myself. In this way I become more patient and thoughtful. My eyes are open for the good things that are out there, the love of the people around me. I am now less critical and suspicious of people. I am more open to them.

What can I do if despair overtakes me and I think I cannot take it any longer?

Go into the despair, crawl into it with your consciousness. Your consciousness has a healing effect on the despair. Don't forget who you are, you are made of God. You are an angel, see your light radiate. I am with you.

Are you my larger Self?

Yes, I reach beyond your earthly existence. I am you but I also transcend you. I am your soul and you are one of my manifestations.

Did I choose to have this illness?

You have allowed it into your existence because you wanted to learn something. You want to learn to be more present in the body, to deepen your grounding on Earth. You want to learn to be present in your love, and overcome your fears of being here.

You would prefer for the pain to go away. Do not focus so much on the pain. It is going away. Fear not. There is help and love around you and inside you. Work is being done; feel the constructive forces around you. Join us in the process; do not place yourself outside of it by asking: 'When is this going to stop?' Stay in it; it will give you something of value.

Does the pain open up a way for me?

Your surrender to it paves the way. If you surrender, you say yes, and you trust in life, that it takes you somewhere, to something new and valuable.

Last night I felt so full of confidence. I looked at the stars in the night sky, and I was quiet and calm even though I had a lot of pain.

Yes, you then were connected with me very strongly. I can help you to keep your perspective on the totality, on the whole, because I can see further than you. Not because I am higher up, but because I am in a different dimension than yours. I am not bound by space and time. Last night you made contact with that grander perspective, and that allowed you to feel free. Now you feel again somewhat restless and frightened. And that's totally okay. That is part of the human experience. Allow it to be. You are allowed to be afraid.

But what is the value of that experience? It feels so rotten.

Go deep inside. The fear feels rotten to you because you oppose it. The fear is a cry for help that comes from within. If you are open to it, you simply hear someone cry or moan. You can go to that person, that part of you. Listen. What do you see?

Yes, I see a crying woman in a dungeon. There are windows above, just below the roof, but she cannot see through them. They are too high up. She always looks up to those windows. She is very lonely and crying out for help.

That's your fear seen from the inside. It is a part of you that is lonely and wants to be freed. Now go to that prison. Descend down into it. You are an angel and you can do that.

I light up the room from the inside. She looks at me frightened, eyes wide.

She is still not sure who you are. Tell her who you are.

I am your angel. I have come to help you.

How does she react?

I see hope in her eyes. I offer my hand. She grabs it.

Hold on tightly to her hand. Allow your light to flow into it.

I feel it. But as an angel, my feet do not touch the ground. Does that matter?

No, that doesn't matter. You are a being from another dimension. She is the part of you that makes full contact with Earth; she gives form to your feet.

How? She is very tired and brittle. She lies broken in my arms. It seems she wants to die.

Ask her about that.

She says: 'I want to be with you.' She wants to be included in my heart, no longer separate from me.

Now try to let your light shine through her entire body.

(…)

Yes, I have done that. In my head and shoulders, arms, hands and heart it flows easily. But in the third chakra, there is something that blocks it. There I see a grey area which holds resistance. There is a longing for death.

Yes, that is right. Now feel it from within. What does it say?

I see a room, dark, dusty and full of spider webs. I believe I see skulls. It is garish and clammy in there. It is awful. I hear the words, 'Start cleaning.' I begin to wipe at the dust and I have a bucket with suds. Then I ask if there is any help. Three women appear in work clothes! They make a joke, something like 'angels may also appear as cleaning ladies'. We go to work. I notice that the windows at the top are clouded and covered. Slowly the windows become clear until they shine like crystal. Oh, how wonderful that light now is in my room; the walls are clean now, too. A beautiful wooden door shows up in the room. A fireplace appears and a fire burns, the fire of my solar plexus. There is now a red carpet on the floor in front of the fireplace, and there are three wooden rocking chairs with cushions. From above, a clear soft light falls on the room. In this place, I feel that I am very old, but I feel good here. I see gray tiles on the floor. The room is now clean and my own.

Now I can also come in. Here I am together with you. See if you can allow the light to flow through the third chakra.

It flows better, channels have been opened. It is still not quite right, but I do see the light flow through to my belly and root chakra and legs. There is flow.

That is very good.

What is still stuck?

Let's get to that next time.

Later that day

Here I am again. I feel like one day lasts a week, so much happens and time goes so slowly.

You complain.

Yes, that's true. Is that not allowed?

Yes, everything is allowed. But it keeps you away from a positive flow. Indeed there is much happening now. You find yourself in an intense period of time. That's not bad. Much wants to be resolved now. It can also be beautiful, when you observe clearly what happens. You are building a new paradigm for yourself. You want to release much of the old, a kind of big spring cleaning. There are parts of you that really want this. They desire more freedom, joy and a deep, fulfilling manifestation on Earth. Recognize those parts in yourself, and it becomes less troublesome to take in the fear and pain.

Okay, I feel that. This morning I have seen even more things that I want to tell you about.

After cleaning the room I went to lie down on a bench, and in my mind I allowed my broken self to sit down into a rocking chair by the fire. That gave me a good feeling. I then started to massage her right foot. I saw it clearly, and the skinny, old foot became nice and white, with red painted toenails. However, when I started on the left foot, I noticed I wasn't getting hold of it. The left foot escaped me, and suddenly I saw a black cloud of anger on the left side. In it I felt the energy of an old incarnation in Atlantis, a man whom I have seen earlier in regression therapy. He had the typical arrogance of the mentally highly developed Atlantian. I felt he made a covenant to act jointly with a group of souls prior to entering life on Earth. It had to do with 'advancing Earth and bringing it to a higher plane', but there was also an element of manipulation and coercion. We were actually megalomaniacs, but we did not think of ourselves that way. There was a covenant, an agreement between groups of souls. I heard that. (For more on this lifetime, see Addendum, and for more on Atlantis see the channeling 'The Legacy of Atlantis' in *The Jeshua Channelings* or on www.jeshua.net).

I go to a profound point in that life, the pinnacle of my power. I see that I and others manipulate Earth; from the third eye we call on great spiritual forces by which we influence the elements on Earth. But everything goes wrong. There are earthquakes, and we perish. I die by drowning. I'm baffled when I die. This should not have happened. I am completely taken by surprise. That bewilderment and the arrogance that accompanies it – that we knew better and assumed we would accomplish our purpose – is apparently still present in me, otherwise that anger on the left side would not be there. Because of that bewilderment I do not want to connect to Earth on the left side.

I realize that in my present life I have often felt exalted above the earthly reality, as if I am too refined for it, as if I am more evolved than others. There is a false sense of superiority in that feeling, and I know this is not right. I'm just as human as anyone else, and now that I am sick, I sense that truth more clearly.

During this flow of images you were there also, my greater Self, and you told me to go to the time before the incarnation, when that man still had to start that life. There was a moment of clarity, when he realized he was going to Earth, not to force and manipulate, but to really connect with Earth and human life from the heart. The actual intention behind that life was to give up the arrogance, the ego-centeredness, to learn to live in surrender to the ignorance and to the naked experience on Earth. That was the aim. I see this now, and he will see it too.

I should release this arrogant part of the ego. That was the purpose behind the Christ energy: the absolute unity and equality of every living being. Each being is a unique unfolding of God's beautiful creation. Every living blade of grass is infinitely precious and cherished. That is the truth we did not see in the Atlantian lives. We set ourselves up as masters of the universe.

I look at myself as that man now and I ask, 'Do you see it?' He says, 'Yes, I have a feeling of falling into a big empty space. My certitudes are falling away.'

Ask him how that feels, that loss of certainties.

Awful. I feel small and afraid in a large and unfamiliar universe.

Ask him how that universe feels, what the atmosphere of it is.

Grand and powerful and uncertain.

It is bigger than he, but is it also powerful in the sense that it wields power over him?

No, I don't feel that power is being exercised over me, I'm quite free, but that freedom feels like Emptiness; too much freedom maybe?

Feel that freedom completely, that Emptiness.

There is no judgment, only development. There is openness.

Do you feel a connection to it somewhere?

I see a tree to which I cling. I feel a connection, but the tree seems to rest in a kind of security and safety from which I am locked out.

You are the tree. Go within, to the roots.

I feel his surrender there. Can I ever surrender like that? How can all those fears go away?

Let the fears be. Surrender to the fears. Be like the tree. Don't go against the fears. The tree trusts and always says: 'Whatever comes, comes.'

Therefore, the tree surrenders to life. Whether it rains, storms, or is sunny. See your fear as a severe thunderstorm. Allow it to break out, let the great forces of life unfold and do their work in you. Let things be cleaned up. All you need is to surrender. To be.

I only need to say yes.

Yes is the word that unlocks all doors. Yes is life. Yes is beautiful and grand; it brings you home to yourself.

Should I now try again to massage the left foot?

Yes.

I sense that I cannot touch the foot as yet. It still stands there, very pale and half in the shadows. There is still some resentment and reluctance there.

I can move my hands around it if I keep some distance. I see a fresh green lawn in front of me. The foot sets itself down on it gingerly.

That is great. It has set foot on Earth at last.

Conversation with a Chinese guide Piang No Jo

Here follows a dialogue with a guide, whom I began to meet with some years ago but did not write about on my website.

Piang appears as a somewhat older Chinese man who radiates an Oriental energy that is clearly palpable.

About his identity he reported the following at our first meeting in 2005.

Autumn 2005 - Piang No Jo

Can you say more about who you are?

Maybe you will get to know me best by what I say if I don't talk about myself.

Have you ever lived on Earth?

Yes, I have lived on Earth many times.

You look like a Chinese master.

Ha ha, I do not want to be a master. It is dead boring to be a master. It's much more fun to be a student. The feeling that opens up when you have a new insight dawning upon you, isn't that wonderful? I always want to be a student.

To be a master is highly overrated in spiritual circles, ha ha. Mastery is the death of the master. He no longer expands as he becomes 'master'. The urge to achieve mastery is a death wish.

If you love life, you always want to learn and be open to the new. You do not rely on what you know, but you look forward to finding out what you do not know as yet.

You do not enjoy being questioned about your identity?

No, I don't like it very much. It is not important. The temptation for self-aggrandizement is always lurking, for people as well as for spiritual entities.

What?! I wouldn't have thought you were susceptible to that anymore?

Who knows? Who will tell you that? Me? That would not be very reliable.

This is a funny conversation.

Yes, I agree. But there is an undertone of seriousness in what I tell you. Talking about your own identity, your achievements, and your so-called degrees in mastery does not lead up to any interesting truths, and it's actually quite boring if you ask me.

It leads the attention away from what really matters, which is your message. Look, there has been a philosopher you know well, Ludwig Wittgenstein, and he made the distinction between that which can be spoken or expressed in words, and that which only can be shown (in German: sagen *versus* zeigen). *Mastery in the only true sense of the word 'shows itself' (zeigt sich), it cannot be articulated or proven by means of words. So if you ever wonder when you read a text or speak with a person if you are witnessing a true master, then take a look at what that text or person radiates. Forget the words, and notice what you feel.*

Does it feel loving, does it feel gentle, does it feel joyful? Does it strike you as having integrity, as being sincere? Does the energy make you feel light and happy, and does it instill a zest for life in you? Then there must be a touch of truth in it. That is all you need to know.

Questions to Piang about pain and fear (Autumn 2009)

I am afraid and I have pain. How can I deal with it?

The very words 'to deal with' *have a connotation of doing. There is nothing to do. You can only allow it to be. Life has a natural tendency toward the good, to flourishing and health. You can only resist this temporarily. Life always regains its strength. I am speaking about eternal life that flows. Trust in that flow. You cannot go wrong.*

By trying to fix your suffering, you unwittingly go against the current. You condemn the suffering and want it to lift. You swallow painkillers to ease the pain and not to feel it, but in that you confirm the reality of the pain or the fear. Pain and fear are only shadows. You can look beyond these; there is a wide world around them. If you focus on them, however, you make them into walls that turn into a fortress from which you can no longer see the blue sky. But no matter how thick the walls are, they exist only in your head. There is real beauty, goodness and truth around you, and these knock constantly at your door. They want to lift you up and embrace you. Give them a chance by not resisting them. You resist them if you want to organize and steer the process too much, if you focus too much on doing your best to get well.

Your body knows how to get well. Just ask it what it wants.

It wants peace and simplicity, to be alternately moving and resting, and an occasional bath. It wants to walk in nature, wants me to expect nothing, to focus on the positive, and that I hold onto courage.

Question your body about what is going on with your stomach.

My stomach says: 'I am upset because of all the stimuli that have been there. There is too much that I have not been able to digest, mainly impressions of fear and uncertainty.'

Then ask your stomach what it needs to be able to process these impressions well.

Not wanting to achieve too many things at once, quietly building up my reserves, no hasty decisions, and a firm reliance on my intuition.

Clear, right?

I'm learning to let go of my impatience.

Impatience means that you are not going along with the flow of life, and it betrays a kind of rigidity in your energy. Impatience is saying no, saying no to the natural flow and unfolding of things. Look at your body. It needs time to heal. You have difficulty accepting this. You think that you have understood the lessons of your illness by now, and you feel like moving on. But perhaps the disease still wants to give you something that you have not been aware of yet or have not felt very deeply. Allow the illness to bring you its gift. There is a gift in every illness. The secret is to believe in this, and to trust that the disease is the messenger of something good, pure and true.

That is a beautiful thought. But how do I stay positive and trustful when I feel so much pain?

Physical pain is less horrible than you think. You create a lot of thoughts around it that produce fear, and these extra thoughts make the experience of pain unnecessarily heavy. Pain is just a place in your body that hurts. No more. You can deal with it in different ways. One is to enter into it with unbiased awareness and say yes to it without reserve. If you do so, you stop being divided. You are one with the pain and do not place yourself outside of it. You stop fighting or resisting it, and so the suffering lessens because fighting causes suffering.

Another way is to respect the pain and yet to shift your attention somewhere else. You will experience the pain as a sensation while you are at the same time focusing your attention elsewhere, for instance on breathing, walking, writing (like you do now) or anything else you like to do. It does not matter much which activity you choose, but make sure that the activity pleases you and that you are not using it as an instrument to avoid or get rid of the pain. The pain must be allowed to be present with you. As soon as you try to escape it, the pain will start to interfere and upset you. It will make you angry and frustrated and thus you will suffer more.

So either way it is about staying present with the pain?

You are right. It is about saying yes to what is there. This can be tough, because you are used to being away from yourself often, away from the Now. If you are ill, it seems as if you are involuntarily glued to the Now. You cannot escape what is there. But herein lies precisely the solution. Through the Now flows not only pain, but also love, kindness and healing. If you surrender to what is there, and stop fighting it, one layer of suffering is automatically dropped. Resistance is one of the strongest pillars of suffering. If you remain present in your pain without resisting it, you open yourself to healing. It comes to you by itself.

Then it is a matter of waiting?

It is a matter of trust. 'Waiting' is bound up with time. Trust isn't. You can wait for healing to come, but you can also ask life what it wants to tell you right now. 'What would the universal force of kindness and truth want me to know right now?'

If I ask this, the answer I receive is: you are very courageous and you are not giving up.

So receive that answer on the inner level. Can you experience your own courage?

Yes, somewhat, but I sense fear simultaneously.

That is okay. Perhaps you are afraid of your own courage, your greatness.

Why would that be?

Because you might take up more space and you have been told that this is not right.

Am I ashamed of my greatness?

You hold yourself back.

I am afraid that dark forces might swallow me up if I stand tall and be who I am.

The opposite is true. Dark forces can only touch you when you feel dark and bad about yourself. Showing your true colors chases the darkness away and brings light, beauty, and goodness into the world. And you will not damage or hurt anyone else in doing so. This is a lie that has been impressed on so many people. Have faith in who you naturally are. Do not hold back. You are a unique expression of the universal intelligence and radiant joy that is God.

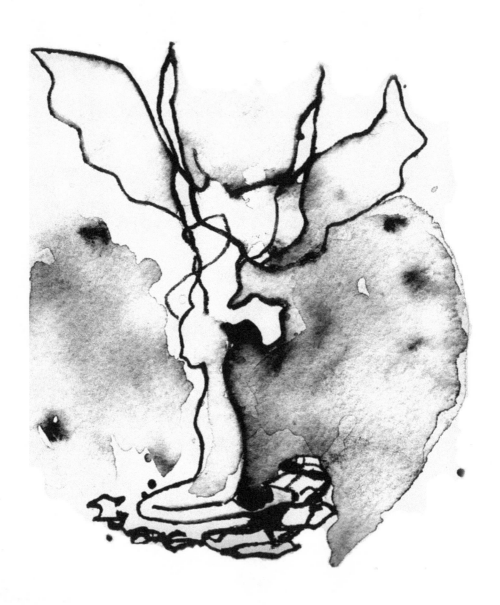

3. Depression and Psychosis

What caused me to break down in the end was the sense that nothing I tried helped. My stomach remained extremely vulnerable despite the drugs that I took in ever higher doses. In the hospital, after an internal examination of the stomach, the official diagnosis was that I had inflammation of the stomach (gastritis). Through my GP I had received and tried every possible antacid medication. Alternative remedies gave me almost no relief. Readings and healings by others, or through my journaling, did provide me with something positive, but I could not retain the positive effects because of the persistent pain, anxiety, and the maddening fatigue caused by chronic insomnia. In November 2009, I began to slip into a clinical depression, with a total lack of perspective or hope for improvement.

In early September of that year, I had given a final workshop to a group of women who had been taking a course with my husband Gerrit and me for almost a year. By that time, the women had become friends, and for that reason I decided to offer that last workshop. It was a very beautiful day, in which I experienced much understanding and support from the group, and I received another beautiful channeling from Mother Earth. ('From Heart to Belly', published in the second part of this book). For days afterward, I felt the warmth of our being together. Then I fell into a dark hole. I no longer had the prospect of being able to work and the inspiration it would give me, leaving me only with constant and unremitting pain, fear, and the torture of insomnia, which had lasted already for over four months. I felt I had exhausted every therapeutic instrument available: making contact with my inner child, conversations with my guides, massage, painting, regression therapy, yoga, swimming, herbal supplements, medications, canceling all of my engagements, giving up coffee, tea and alcohol, and only eating those foods that were safe for me.

I felt empty and numb inside. I was passive and talked very little anymore. Slowly the fears subsided and made room for a depressing deadness, making everything feel meaningless. I did not even experience as positive the fading of the fears that had constantly plagued my body and mind. I had no feeling at all anymore. I was completely cut off from myself and others. I had never gone through anything like this. Usually, I cry easily. Beautiful music or touching movies make me reach for a tissue in no time. Now however, I could no longer cry. It seemed as if I could no longer feel any emotions. It felt as if I were dead.

Even though on the one hand I had become passive and lifeless, on the other hand my thoughts increasingly became more and more frenzied and feverish. Thoughts raged through my head at an excruciating pace and were becoming ever more negative in tone. The crux of my thoughts was that I was a bad person who lived merely from my ego and who had always done that. Everything with which I had ever been happy or content was based on my vanity and arrogance. My whole mind seemed to be focused on one goal: to destroy, through my reasoning, everything positive that I had ever accomplished and to prove that I was an inferior creature who did not deserve to live.

An outside observer would have thought that my mind was degenerating. I could hardly focus on anything outside of myself, such as a newspaper article or a movie on TV. It took an enormous amount of strength and effort simply to understand the subject matter and extreme concentration to allow two paragraphs of text from the newspaper to sink in. My memory also seemed blocked. I remember playing a memory game with my daughter and not getting even one card right. I could not hold on to anything in my memory. The whole experience was like cycling against a strong wind, where each push on the pedal takes tremendous effort, and forward progress is hampered and slow.

I remember that I had a kind of philosophical astonishment about the fact that I could barely read two paragraphs in the newspaper and yet my brain was still able to argue flawlessly in two minutes why I was a perfect ignoramus with extremely low motives. I would take an event from the past, which before had made me feel good about myself, and would convince myself that instead I should feel horrible about myself. One example was the memory of how I had the courage to start a private professional practice and how I had to overcome a lot of fear in order to do that. My mind diligently set to work to reason all of that away. It told me that I had deceived people during my consultations, and they had been naive enough to believe me. It was all a display of vanity, and it was worth nothing. My entire past was being examined from this unstoppable, compulsive, critical thinking, and everything about which I had ever been proud or happy was levelled to the ground by a bulldozer of destructive prejudice. The books I had written in the area of spirituality, about which I had received warm and grateful responses from many people all over the world: it was all a sham, all of it derived purely from ego.

During this period, I became psychotic. A psychosis refers to an abnormal condition of the mind, and is a generic psychiatric term for a mental state often described as involving a 'loss of contact with reality'. It was *not clear* to me at that moment that I was becoming psychotic. I did not even know what that meant then. I still remember very well that one morning, after another bad night with only little or very light sleep, I felt very awake. It was an unnatural form of being awake. In the preceding months, I had felt broken and decrepit, a normal reaction to sleep deprivation. However, now I felt bright and alert, but in a tense, frenetic way. That morning I visited a friend whose job it is to accompany psychiatric patients. Coincidentally, she also had trouble sleeping during that period, and we talked regularly about it. That day she asked me, 'How was it last night, did you manage to get in some hours?' I remained silent, or merely uttered something vague. I did not talk about that strange feeling in my head. I was ashamed of it. I kept it to myself, and I realized that I was keeping something important from the people around me. I was aware that I had crossed a boundary and that there was something very wrong.

The unusual vividness in my head, and the strange absence of fatigue continued. The border between waking and sleeping faded completely. I still did sleep a few hours per night. However, it was a strange, light sleep with regular, horrible, vivid nightmares. I faced two phenomena, for which I only learned the official psychiatric names after my recovery. At that time I did not realize that these were psychiatric disorders. The first was *flight of ideas*. This is a ceaseless flow of frantic thoughts that through associations become completely entangled with each other. The thoughts in your head are fired off like bullets from a machine gun. You have no control over the speed. *Flight of ideas* often occurs in people who suffer a form of mania. In a manic state you can be very positive (euphoric) as well as very negative (depressed). With me the mania was colored with negativity. The contents of the high-speed train that thundered through my head were without exception negative. I had thoughts of doom and disaster, arguments why everything in my life would go wrong, thoughts full of fear and suspicion.

In addition to *flight of ideas*, I was dealing with the phenomenon called *relational delusion* (delusions of reference). Relational delusion is a compulsive tendency to see everything that is happening around you as

41

related to you. You are obsessed with the notion that everything you see and think is caused by you, or that it is a sign for you. According to the definition on Wikipedia, relational delusion is a psychopathological condition in which a series of mostly ordinary and everyday facts and events are interpreted in relation to one's own person. Relational delusion is almost always paranoid in nature, that is to say that the purported meaning and how it applies to oneself is interpreted in a negative, disadvantaging way. For example, I was walking on the street and saw that a cyclist suddenly got a flat tire. He cursed out loud and had to walk. Immediately I was convinced that I was the cause of the flat tire. My wickedness and toxic energy had influenced the bike as it passed me by. I had been selfish to go and walk outside. I should stay at home, so that I would not do as much damage.

Another example. I was lying on the couch and heard the siren of a police car outside, which I interpreted immediately as a sign, a warning that I wasn't allowed to sleep. If I would go to sleep anyway, I reasoned, I would abandon my daughter. When after a while I nevertheless closed my eyes, it proved once again how bad and selfish I was.

This compulsive explaining of everything around me as a sign was very exhausting, and it weakened my self-image. At the same time, it was a desperate attempt to find meaning in a life that seemed to have become utterly meaningless. Everything that had made my life purposeful and fulfilling seemed to have disappeared. My work lay dormant, and my relationships with my loved ones suffered heavily under the depression and psychosis in which I had landed.

The relationship with my husband Gerrit, once filled with mutual recognition, love and joy, had now become outright hostile on my part. I lived within the prison of my confused, psychotic mind. It was no longer possible for me to talk coherently about myself and what I was going through. My behavior became incomprehensible to Gerrit. I no longer communicated, ate hardly anything, did not take good care of myself, and I became completely inaccessible to others. I was severely emaciated and struggled with suicidal thoughts. I was convinced that my family was better off without me. The relationship with my then eight year old daughter Laura also became a struggle. It was often argumentative and unloving. I could no longer function as a mother, a role in which I continually had to make choices and decisions.

I could no longer make the simplest decisions and became paralyzed when I had to make choices. For example, the decision just to take a shower became an extremely complicated one. I would sit on the edge of my bed for fifteen minutes thinking about how I would do that: what clothes I would choose, and what the symbolic meaning of that choice would be, if I would turn on the hot or the cold faucet first, what color of bathing cap I would pick, and what that would signify, and so on. The minutest action created insurmountable dilemmas for me. For someone with a normal operating mind, this is extremely hard to imagine. However, for a psychotic person, this is a living reality which they are unable to handle. The possibility of 'just doing it' was not available to me. The basic ability to act, to do something on autopilot, had vanished.

Along with the relational delusion also came the fear that I would infect others with my symptoms. I saw that my memory and intellect were crumbling, and I was afraid that I would likewise contaminate my husband and my daughter. In the example of the memory game that I mentioned above, I noticed that, like me, Laura did not do well in selecting the right card. Although she was probably just tired at the time, I was certain that I had infected her mind, and that it would also be damaged now, like mine was.

In this way I was spinning round and round in self-recriminating, self-condemning thoughts. The normalcy of everyday life no longer existed, and the house was in chaos. Gerrit tried to maintain some level of order and structure as much as possible, but in the course of January and February 2010, the situation became intolerable for me. I felt deeply miserable, and this state appeared not so much as an emotion, but as the sensation of being completely cut off from life. It was actually the *lack* of feeling, positive or negative, that struck me most deeply in the depression that I experienced. To me, a depression does not mean that you are sad, feel bleak or dejected. In a real depression, you cross a crucial boundary; *you feel nothing at all* anymore, so your very humanity is at stake. I remember that I sometimes experienced a sensation of cold in my body (it was a very harsh winter), and I would feel warmth when I came inside. 'Hey,' I would say to myself, 'I feel something!' But these were only physical sensations, not emotional ones.

Life then no longer made sense or had any meaning for me. During the day I would wander aimlessly around in the city. I had a kind of surreal fantasy that I had to walk away, and then at some point behind a hill somewhere I would lose my life. I had thoughts of suicide, but at the same time I felt too weak to carry them out. I did not speak to anyone about these thoughts.

By this time, I was very emaciated and faced with a serious eating disorder. Before my depression I weighed fifty-eight kilos (hundred twenty-eight pounds), and in the course of one year I lost sixteen kilos (thirty-five pounds). Initially, I lost weight because my stomach gave me so many problems, and there was little that I could actually eat and digest. When I sank into the depression, however, an old demon reared its ugly head: a persistent eating disorder that had haunted me since my teens. It started around my twelfth year. I was unsure about myself, and although from an objective viewpoint, I was not too heavy, I considered myself to be fat and by extension ugly. I tried to lose weight through many diets, but this turned out not to be so easy. While at first I had never thought about food, it now had a mysterious attraction for me, because it was forbidden. The weight loss did not happen fast enough in my view; I kept up with the diet, until I started to reach again for food, especially sweets. My mind became consumed with food: counting calories, setting up the ideal diet, guilt about my lack of self-control, binging followed by another diet. I was caught up in a vicious circle of dieting and overeating which held me captive for about fifteen years.

When I began my academic studies at the age of nineteen, I discovered the literature on eating disorders. It was very liberating not to approach this tormenting obsession from the perspective of dieting, but from a psychological point of view. I read the feminist-oriented books by Susie Orbach, in which becoming heavy is explained as a twisted attempt by women to take up space. Sensitive, empathetic women who are inclined to give too much try to take back their space by (over)eating. I even discovered a channeled book (by Dutch author Sun van der Meijel) that gave me a lot of insight on eating disorders. In this book, the ambiguous, strained relationship with food is interpreted as an ambiguous, tense relationship with life in the body on Earth.

Someone with anorexia (who systematically refuses to eat) has major problems in surrendering to the earthly, physical self. Someone who eats compulsively and then diets again, goes back and forth between saying yes and no to the physical. I recognized both patterns in myself. Later an astrologer told me that, based on my horoscope and her own clairsentience, my eating problem could not have been prevented. It had to do with a 'heavy karma' that I had taken from a past life, she said. Only when I went in regression therapy in the year 2000 did I discover that, in the life before this, I was a Jewish woman who starved to death in a concentration camp (see annex for a report of my regression experience). I am convinced that part of the explanation of my eating problem indeed lies in that past life.

Toward the end of my twenties, my eating problem became less disruptive; it disappeared somewhat into the background. I began to accept myself more as I was, and I was engaged with my studies in philosophy that fascinated and fulfilled me. Although my relationship with food remained an issue for me, it was no longer such an obsession.

At the end of 2010, in the middle of the depression in which I found myself, I no longer wanted to live. I decided that the best thing for me to do would be to stop eating, which was the only strategy for ending my life that occurred to me that I could actually accomplish. This 'decision' was not well-considered, but rather came from a mind affected by psychosis. I was sure that my husband and daughter would be better off without me. An angry, compelling voice in my head convinced me that I no longer needed to eat and drink. Taking in food testified to my weakness and selfishness. In fact, this was the same old, chilly voice that had admonished me to lose weight before and who now told me that it would be better if I ceased to exist. I ate and drank nothing for two days. At the end of the second day I ate some pudding, not because I was hungry, but because I felt very tense, and eating something sweet relieved the tension. I was used to deriving reassurance from food; it played the role of nourishing and warming me emotionally and psychologically. During that time, I did eat intermittently but only furtively when no one was there to observe me. After all, it was forbidden; it was a sign of weakness and cowardice to reach for food, because it was clear as day to me that it was better not to eat.

The inner command not to eat, and the evil compelling voice that accompanied it, ran against all advice I was receiving from the outside world. Gerrit continuously urged me to eat. I was skin and bones and had not menstruated during a span of over eight months. Often, I responded angrily and with denial when Gerrit confronted me with my disturbed eating behavior. Rightly or wrongly, eating was the only thing over which I felt that I could exercise control, and I became furious when someone else wanted to interfere with my ability to exercise that control. As a result, this issue became the source of grueling fights between Gerrit and me.

Finally, Gerrit decided to intervene and with the help of the GP, it was arranged that I would be involuntarily admitted to the psychiatric department of the hospital. I resisted enormously. I was convinced that no one could help me and that I would disappear forever in an institution. By this time I had also become paranoid: I interpreted everything that people said to me with suspicion. Because of that, I had to be taken by physical force to the hospital in an ambulance.

I experienced the admission to the hospital as surreal and humiliating. Suddenly, a complete panel of medical experts was sitting opposite me. There were blood tests, and as in a daze, I looked at the clearly visible blue veins on my thin left arm where the nurse inserted a needle. I no longer experienced myself as truly in my body. The psychiatrist diagnosed me with 'psychotic depression'. This dumbfounded me. I had no idea that my behavior corresponded to a specific psychiatric clinical picture. I simply thought that I was extraordinarily bad and sinful and that my behavior was not caused by a disease, but rather by my incorrigible sinful and selfish nature. I was surprised that the psychiatrist did not see that. My paranoid mindset faltered at this point: what advantage was it for them to treat me? It would be more fitting that they throw me out in the street and not look back at me. But no, I received a room to myself, medicine to help me sleep and three meals a day.

4. Recovery and Rebirth

Although my admission to the hospital had filled me with horror and shame, and during those initial days all I could think of was how to escape, it created a sea change in me. Despite the surreal environment, the first thing that I experienced as a positive was that I did not have to accomplish anything anymore. Here it was clear to everyone that *I was sick* and I could do nothing. My living space was reduced to a room with a bed. That was a huge relief because as long as I was unable to do anything, I also could no longer fail time and time again as a mother, as a wife, as a human being. All the pressure was off of me. On top of that a miracle took place: I was prescribed a sleeping pill, and on that first night I slept six hours straight through. I was drunk with delight. I no longer needed to worry endlessly over whether or not to take a pill. It belonged to the daily routine, and I thought that best. To return to a more or less normal sleep pattern was truly a gift from God. I could finally experience drowsiness and sleepiness again before I went to sleep, whereas before there had been too much tension, and the little sleep I did get had felt unnatural and nightmarish.

To have been admitted to the hospital was clearly a positive turn for me. Here began my recovery. That doesn't take away from the fact that I found it horrible, especially during the day. A psychiatric ward is a strange, unnatural environment where you spend the day tinkering aimlessly in company of people who, just like you, are pretty lost. The days dragged on endlessly. There was no therapy, as treatment focused primarily on medication and the restoration of a normal daily routine. Yet it was a suitable environment for me to recover at a basic level. Beside my sleeping pills, I was also prescribed an antidepressant that caused unpleasant side effects such as drowsiness, heart palpitations and a dry mouth. It was unpleasant to have to swallow those pills, but in retrospect, I think it is certainly possible that the medication helped me recover. I am now convinced that a depression and a psychosis go together with malfunctioning processes in the brain, and that treatment on a chemical level may be appropriate and even highly desirable. I have let go of the prejudices I had against the use of meds to treat psychiatric problems.

In the beginning of my confinement, I was still strongly under the influence of the relational delusion that had taken on an especially paranoid character. So I experienced the nursing staff as hostile and accusing. As the weeks progressed, I began to think more normally. I could again cry and feel sadness. I was still very scared that I would never be able to go home from the mental hospital, and I felt a lot of grief for all that I had lost: my family, my work, and the walks in nature. My thinking was still obsessive, suspicious and negative. Yet there was improvement: I did not want to flee anymore and had no more thoughts of suicide.

A sense of rebirth

A defining moment took place when I began to experience life again. One morning, after about two weeks in the hospital, I felt the desire to live again. This feeling just bubbled up in me, and it was stronger than the shame that I felt about all that had happened to me. Even though other people could see openly what was going on with me, that I had become 'crazy', I nevertheless wanted to connect again to life and to people once again. The pure desire for life that I felt welling up in me was unconditional and shamelessly joyful; I experienced it as a rebirth.

To my recurring self-critical thoughts, I said: 'Too bad!' To my remaining feelings of not being any good and of failing again and again, I said, 'That may be, but I want to live! I choose to be human, a human being who has qualities that are good and not so good, a mixture of ego and heart, a human being who is not perfect, but who must grow and learn.' During the psychotic depression, my deepest self-condemning thoughts had come to the surface, and I had long believed in them. Now that I was getting my head above water a little, I could gain some perspective and choose more positive thoughts about myself. But this choice for positivity and gentleness towards myself was not so much a consciously willed decision. Rather, it was a deeply-felt insight that somehow broke through in me. The choice for life was like a wave of grace that washed over and through me.

How this turnabout happened exactly is difficult to reconstruct. On the one hand there were the physical aspects to the recovery process of my brain. Going back to normal sleeping and eating patterns and taking medications made it possible for me to land back on Earth and to reenter my body, so to speak. I had lived very strongly from the head for a long time, away from my body almost entirely. My body had felt stiff and unreal during the depression. My movements had become no longer fluid, but rather, wooden and rigid. (This is actually a symptom of clinical depression). Through the restoration of sleep and a regimen of nutrition, I reinhabited my body again in a natural way.

In addition to these physical aspects, I experienced a spiritual breakthrough. What I found incredible was that people remained true to me throughout my collapse. My relatives came to the hospital nearly every day, and a circle of friends around me remained faithful, always showing me sincere and concerned interest. It was very special and revealing to experience that people truly cared for me, even if I could do nothing. Free of the roles that I had fulfilled, that of therapist, of wife, of mother, friend, spiritual guide and author, I could see clearly that they saw *me*, they valued *me*. Through their loving gaze I learned that there was *something* about me that was valuable, even when at the same time I still doubted if that was the case. The genuine love and interest of people around me have helped me to move past the shame and to believe again in the beauty of life and the possibility of true friendship.

I awoke from a nightmare of mistrust, fear and self-loathing. The grey, heavy veil of depression was pulled back. From the perspective of the people close to me, the recovery was miraculously quick. After just three weeks in the hospital, I was doing so well that I was discharged and went home. My own sense of time was different. During the depression and psychosis, time passed terribly slowly. The minutes crawled by, and one day seemed to last an eternity. The people around me at the time were more aware of my rapid improvement than I was.

After I got home, I felt well enough during the day, and soon I began to take an active part in everything. During the night, however, I was still overcome with dark thoughts: that my recovery was only an illusion, that the whole thing was deceptive, and that I was still very bad and sinful. Why did people not see that? Were they really so naive? During the psychosis I had a kind of reversed worldview. Feeling good about myself and taking care of myself was the right thing according to other people, but according to my psychotic logic, that was selfishness, self-delusion and vanity. In that same vein, I still felt that I was not worthy enough to warrant self respect and my life, as I perceived I had lived it to that point, was evidence of that unworthiness.

Hypomania

Even with the strong remnants of the negative feelings remaining, now the positive flow was winning out. It was even so strong that for awhile I lived in a somewhat euphoric state that in psychiatry is called *hypomania*. I felt reborn, intensely grateful and very energetic. I had a tendency toward a manic type of consciousness whereby you have an enlarged feeling of bliss, and you busily keep on a high-performance. In a true mania you lose your grounding completely; you lose your sense of reality and become prone to delusions and hallucinations. The term hypomania is used for people who tend to a mania, but who are still in the safe zone: they function normally and do not show any excessive or extreme behavior.

I had experienced a real mania once, although it had not been officially diagnosed as such. This was in 2001, when for the first time in my life I had been involved in a profound regression therapy that released an immense amount of buried material in me. Because of the intense experiences with past lives and deep trance states, I lost my connection to the everyday, earthly reality. Initially this did not feel bad at all; in fact I had never felt so completely blissful and elevated above earthly gravity. I was in an ecstatic and euphoric state of happiness which I believe resembles the high you feel after taking certain drugs. I would have preferred to remain in this state, until I began to have a huge amount of fast-moving thoughts through my mind (here also the *flight of ideas*, but then with positive content). And I started to hyperventilate terribly. Later I will come back to this experience, in particular about the question of whether, when you have such euphoria, you may regard it as a spiritual experience, i.e. an authentic experience of unity consciousness and enlightenment.

In the wake of my recovery from depression, as I landed in a hypomanic state during a few weeks, I enjoyed it, but I realized immediately that something wasn't right about this level of joy. I remembered how I had felt very euphoric at one time earlier in my life, and how this state of consciousness was quite appealing, but ultimately not grounded and authentic. I had learned from my previous experience with mania. Because of that, I could regain more stability and inner peace after a short few weeks.

Advantages and limitations of the psychiatric perspective

When I look back now on that period when I was depressed and psychotic, it is frustrating to see how much I could have had benefited from knowledge I did not have at the time. With what I know now, I would have understood at a much earlier stage what was happening to me, and I would have intervened much earlier. I would also have been less ashamed, and therefore I would have asked for help much sooner. I remember well how during a talk with the psychiatrist afterward, I was introduced for the first time to the term *relational delusion*. He was explaining this phenomenon to me, and I recognized it immediately. This was exactly what had terrorized me over the past few months. It was wonderful to hear that there existed a word for it, and I suddenly understood much better what had happened to me. I had lived for a long time in a bizarre world of delusion, and here was someone who explained to me that this is a known and recognized phenomenon that is characteristic of certain psychiatric disturbances. Had I understood this earlier, I might have attached less weight to my own delusions, and maybe I would have been able to view them from the perspective of a recognized mental illness. I say maybe, because once you enter into a psychosis, you are never sure if you will still have sufficient objectivity to recognize your delusions for what they are. Nevertheless, I believe sincerely that now, with some knowledge of psychiatry, I am better armed against a recurring psychosis or depression than before. Nowadays you often hear people say that psychiatry overzealously labels people, and fails to recognize the individuality of patients. This will undoubtedly occur and even be reinforced by a purely clinical, scientific way of thinking. Nevertheless it can also be quite liberating to recognize that, whatever you are going through during a deep crisis, is not just your individual madness, but a widely recognized syndrome, one that can be treated. At least for me this was very liberating. Diagnoses, labels and knowledge are not always narrow and limiting; they can also make you more conscious, and offer you a wider perspective on your unique experiences.

Does this mean that I regard my individual experience of the dark night of the soul solely in terms of a psychiatric disorder, i.e. the *psychotic depression* that affected my brain and from which I was cured with the help of chemicals? I feel clearly that this is a too narrow and reductionist interpretation of what happened. After my recovery, my life and my consciousness have been permanently changed. There is more gratitude, joy, less anxiety than ever, and a deep sense of fulfillment. The whole experience has been cathartic and liberating on a profound level. I feel that I am in touch with my soul on a much deeper plane now, and I am genuinely grateful to be on earth and to be living the life that I lead.

My dark night of the soul, the total collapse of my certainties, has freed me from some very old burdens. Can this spiritual outcome be understood through a purely psychiatric approach? Although I would never want to experience the hell of depression again, I cannot deny that this profound crisis has led to a rebirth on the inner level. This inner rebirth, or transformation, I can only describe in spiritual terms. The vocabulary of psychiatry falls short; it contains no words for the soul, for that elusive source that we call the Self which is central to the very meaning and purpose of life. We have two very different vocabularies here and so the question arises how one should interpret extreme states of consciousness such as depression, mania and psychosis. Should one regard them as psychiatric disorders only, or is there a way of conceiving them as transformative, meaningful or even illuminating experiences? By speaking of the 'dark night of the soul', I am already implying that my experience cannot be reduced to a mental illness. I recognize that there is another perspective, that of the soul, from which this experience can be understood in a different way, and not merely as something negative, an illness, an aberration.

What then is the perspective of the soul? How should one look upon the extremes of our consciousness from a spiritual perspective? In the next chapter, I interpret my dark night of the soul as a journey of inner transformation, in which the unknown and obscure come to fore and the familiar is released. This journey leads to a new birth, but not without labor pains that touch you to the core, and force you to let go of all you held certain. This perspective on my experience with depression and psychosis unfolded for me through an inner dialogue with my soul. In this dialogue I asked questions from my human, everyday awareness, and I then attuned myself to the level of awareness that belongs to my soul. I received answers that surprised me and led to new insights. As evidenced by the dialogue in the next chapter, my human personality feels that by means of certain knowledge, or certain actions, I could have prevented the falling into the deep. My soul however offers a different perspective, and regards the fall into darkness as something that belonged to my inner path.

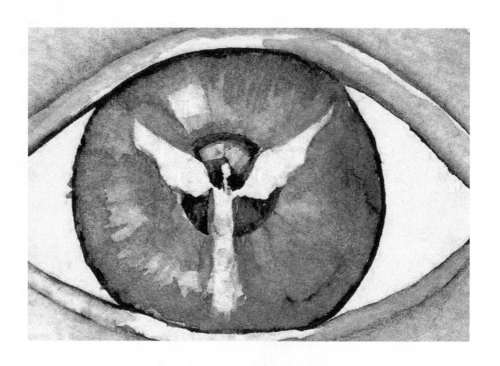

5. Perspective of the Soul

When I ask my soul why I had to go through all of this, the answer I receive is that sooner or later *everything that is dark and unconscious must be brought to light*. Fears and negative judgments slumber in the human unconscious. These may long continue to be hidden, and sometimes have to remain that way, as there is a time and a place for everything. It is not the purpose of the soul to confront us all at once with everything that lives inside us by way of deep anxiety, despair and desolation. But the intention is that, in the course of your life, you will get in touch with these hidden layers in your consciousness, so that they can be healed and transformed in the light of the present. The purpose of the soul is to make the unconscious conscious, and thus to grow into greater self awareness and a more deeply felt connection to the One, to Spirit.

The soul does not limit its perspective to a single life; the soul is connected to all the different incarnations that it has in the past, present and future. This is beyond the grasp of human understanding. However, it is possible for us humans to be in touch with the soul and to sense that there is a larger perspective to our everyday life which guides and directs us toward certain people and situations that we may *seem* to experience randomly. From an interior perspective, we attract these events, and they are anything but random. Our soul draws them to us because, in the interaction with these people and situations, we are invited to gain deeper self-understanding. Those exterior stimuli are not necessarily pleasant. Events that are not so enjoyable can be an incentive provided by the soul that can challenge you to let go of distorted beliefs and to look deep fears in the eye and transcend them.

When I asked my soul about the ordeal I went through, my soul told me that sooner or later I would have had to face my fear of rejection and my fear to live. How exactly this would happen was not predetermined. By doing work that really inspired me (writing books and offering workshops about spirituality), I had demonstrated my intention to live on Earth and connect with people from the soul level. However, this work at the same time activated my old fear and resistance to being here on Earth. If you decide to follow your heart and do what truly inspires you, something stirs in the depths of your being. On the one hand, there will be more lightness and joy in your life. Paradoxically, on the other hand, taking that leap of faith awakens the dark parts inside, the parts that are filled with fear, doubt and distrust. Dark and unconscious energies (e.g., old fears of being visible, of being violently rejected, mistrust of people, cynicism about life in general) were driven to the surface by my choice to go and do what my heart most deeply desired. To do what my heart was prompting me to do had felt enticing, like falling in love, and even inescapable, yet it also forced me to confront my deepest fears.

Was it therefore inevitable that I would be faced with anxiety attacks, depression and finally psychosis? Did it need to be so violent and was there no other way? I put this question to my soul, and here I offer the literal conversation that ensued.

SOUL: The way things transpired was one possibility, one potential way to process and transform old trauma that originated from other lives.

Pamela: Could it have gone otherwise? From my human perspective it was horrific; that is why it is important for me to know if it could have been different.

SOUL: It could have happened in a different way, but it still would have been very confrontational and intense.

Pamela: What was the most difficult part I would have had to come across in my life in one way or another?

SOUL: Your unwillingness to live, your resistance to being on Earth.

Pamela: Did it express itself in my depression, in which I felt dead, totally cut off from life? Did the part of me that did not want to live manifest itself in that?

SOUL: Your depression consisted of a solidified rage, a refusal to live as the result of a deep fear of surrendering to life. You cannot live without trusting life on a basic level. Trusting life means to say yes and to surrender to everything that life brings with it: pain, joy, sadness, pleasure, fear, but also courage and inspiration. At some point, when you were completely shattered and exhausted by the emotional traumas that you sustained in multiple lives on Earth, you said No to life. This No existed before you were born in your current lifetime. It is older and yet it wants to be healed and transformed in this life.

Pamela: I understand and recognize it. But I still wonder very specifically if I could have done certain things differently, so I would not have sunk so deep. For example: Had I taken it easier with my work earlier on, would my stomach upsets have been less severe? Perhaps the fears and insomnia would have been less serious also. Could a lot of it not have been prevented if had listened to the everyday signals of my body and emotions, thus making the fall less deep?

SOUL: Why did you not do that? Why did you not listen?

Pamela: I received clear signs from my body that I could not handle what was coming at me by way of public attention and demands for help. I felt a lot of pressure on me and wanted very much to have some peace and space for myself. I did not take that space, or took it too late, because I felt obligated towards people. Hidden behind that sense of obligation was, I think, fear of rejection. Apparently, this fear was bigger than my ability or my courage to listen to my body.

SOUL: What could you have done differently?

Pamela: Deal more consciously with my fears and see through them, and not allow them to take over and dictate my behavior. I could have chosen to trust the language of my soul instead of the language of fear.

SOUL: Were you in a position to do so?

Pamela: Good question. I don't know. Do you mean to say that I was not able to rise above my fear, that I did not as yet have the awareness and self esteem to do so, and that first I had to experience what happens when you ignore your intuition and listen to fear? That only after this fateful experience I could rise above the fear, recognize the language of the soul and live by it?

SOUL: Good summary! And how are you now? Has it become easier to listen to the language of your soul?

Pamela: Indeed, it has. It is now easier for me to say No. I am also less bothered by being different or not living up to people's expectations. After going through my Dark Night, I have become more placid and face things with more equanimity. I accept myself more as I am, and I compare myself less with some ideal image. That is incredibly liberating. I enjoy life much more now. I am not constantly 'working on myself', trying to become a 'better person'. And I have continued to do the work that really inspires me, but with more boundaries in place now. I don't do so many individual readings anymore. It takes a lot of energy. I love to write, and I like to do occasional workshops with groups that are not too large. I am by nature solitary; I need a lot of time spent alone. At first I had a lot of trouble admitting this and tried to be other than who I was. Now I understand that I can be who I am, and that this is exactly where the language of the soul is pointing, by way of my uncensored emotions and body signals.

SOUL: So in retrospect the experience of the dark night of the soul has lifted you above old fears, with the result that you can now hear and trust the language of your soul more clearly?

Pamela: Yes. The language of fear has lost some of its power over me. I now live more from the soul. This brings deep joy and gratefulness. But I wonder: it is said that spiritual growth doesn't necessarily need to take place through suffering, but that it can happen in a joyous way. Is that true? Can the dark night of the soul be avoided?

SOUL: At this moment, you are growing through joy. Because you listen more carefully to the language of the soul, you are quicker to notice when you are thrown off balance and you are less afraid to act upon your intuitions. You are still growing and learning about who you are, but now you are growing through joy.

Growth through suffering is, however, part of human life. There are dark and fearful parts in each human being which cannot always be dealt with and transcended in a peaceful or joyful way. The dark night of the soul occurs when a human being is faced with pain and suffering that are overwhelming and incomprehensible to them. They resist what is happening in their life and this resistance causes the greatest suffering. It makes you lose touch with your soul, with a perspective of hope and meaningfulness. The resistance comes from the anxious, uncertain or suspicious part in you and this part needs to be released for the Night to end.

The night becomes day again once you trust the changes in your life, even though you cannot yet grasp their meaning or see where it will all end. In theory you would not have to experience a dark night of the soul if you could trust directly and surrender to whatever is happening in your life. Practically speaking, however, almost all people have to deal with fear, anger and mistrust. Almost everyone resists experiences of loss and pain. If the resistance remains, then it is often only through a dark night of the soul that you can be reborn and begin to experience life in a different way. During this night, your fear, distrust or bitterness are magnified. This offers you the chance to fully face these states of mind, and to enter deeply into them, until at some point you decide that it is unbearable and you open up to change. The night cannot last forever. Ultimately the part of you that resists bends before something greater than itself. It opens up to love.

Pamela: Then awakens a new dawn.

SOUL: Resistance gives way to surrender, the dark dissolves into the light of a wider and greater awareness that is not based on fear. You experience this as a moment of grace. It is the moment when the old self, which was governed by resistance, lets go.

Pamela: For me this moment of grace occurred when I decided I wanted to live again. However, this decision felt like something that was birthed in me, as if the resolve took place without me exercising my will power. It was something that revealed itself to me rather than something I decided. It seemed to happen beyond my power or control.

SOUL: Beyond the power and control of the old self.

Pamela: The old self let go at that moment. But it seems that one cannot force it to do so; it just happens at some point?

SOUL: Yes and no. You cannot force that moment of release, but you prepare for it by sinking deeper into the darkness, moving away from your own essence. At some point - and this time is not predictable or within your control- you have reached the summit of self denial and suffering. The resisting part of you surrenders and you return to your center; you open up to the light of the soul. This happens spontaneously. Once you let go of struggle and fear, your inner space immediately becomes filled with the natural light and joy of your soul. You experience this as a moment of grace. People who are religious in the traditional way may experience his as an intervention of God, or as a divine miracle. But in fact, for this moment of grace to occur, a deep inner struggle had to take place first, and you are clearly involved in this.

Pamela: Can the dark night of the soul be prevented or shortened by taking psychiatric drugs (like antidepressants)?

SOUL: Medications can be helpful when you are already on the way back, so to speak. When you have reached the turning point, and you are ready to let go of resistance, medicine can help with your recovery. That was the case with you. You took prescriptions in the hospital at the right moment. At an earlier stage, they would have been less helpful, because you were not ready yet for real change.

Pamela: It is very weird, but in hindsight I no longer see the element of coercion during the forced admission (to the hospital) as something negative. Something had to be done, and deep inside I knew that. Things were getting out of control, there was an ever growing turmoil in me, and I often said to Gerrit, 'I need to get away'. With that I meant 'out of the house' and from my psychotic brain I thought that I simply needed to leave the world, be eliminated. My ego, my proud self, opposed itself in the extreme to being admitted, and so there literally had to be physical coercion. Now I feel, however, that I attracted this on a deep inner level and that inwardly I gave permission to this forced admission. Because the suffering became intolerable, I was prepared to undergo the humiliation of an involuntary admission. It was horrible, but less so than a continued persistence of an intolerable situation in which I dragged myself, and my loved ones, into an increasingly destructive downward spiral. I see that now, but I did not experience it that way then. Still, it explains why I surrendered fairly quickly, after only a few days, to the intervention, the food they wanted me to eat and the taking of drugs. Does it also explain why I recovered so quickly?

SOUL: When you were admitted to the hospital, something lethal happened to the ego. What had been secret came out in the open and became public. You were admitted to a locked psychiatric ward of the hospital, you went to the 'madhouse', and you were diagnosed as psychotic and depressed. This was openly and clearly visible to others. From the perspective of the ego, which was the frightened, distrustful, resisting part of you, the worst possible thing had happened: her proud and tenacious resistance was broken. Then came the redemptive experience of not being judged by others, but rather to be supported and to be appreciated authentically and sincerely by your loved ones. It was not the ultimate rejection that took place, but an experience of being received as you are. The fear-based assumptions of the ego were disproved by what really happened. This old, traumatized, inhospitable ego died then. There was room for something new, a rebirth.

Pamela: What was decisive then: that others approached me lovingly, which encouraged me to embrace life again, or that I decided to embrace and value myself (despite what had happened and the damage I had done to the people around me) and that I could subsequently accept the love of others?

SOUL: The decisive step was that you gave up your resistance. That happened in the hospital. The presence of others approaching you lovingly assisted in the process, but the crucial step was that you *opened up to them. This surrender could only take place with your inward permission. Other people can cheer you on, and their presence can give you a helping hand, but you decide. That's free will. This also means that you cannot give a general recipe for the most appropriate way to approach people during a psychosis. For every person, the unique moment of surrender, of return to the true self, takes place in their own way and at their own rhythm.*

6. Perspective of Those Close to Me

In this chapter my husband Gerrit shares his perspective on my dark night of the soul. He describes how it affected him and the struggle he went through. How do you deal with someone who is beyond the reach of normal communication? Gerrit also discusses how he now looks back on what happened to me from his perspective as a past life regression therapist.

Perspective of Gerrit (by Gerrit Gielen)

Writing about the psychosis and depression of your partner is difficult. So much happened that I do not know where to start. Pamela's illness started very gradually; occasionally I noticed something abnormal, weird and unreasonable behavior. There is no fixed boundary between the normal and abnormal. By the end of Pamela's psychotic episode, shortly before the forced committal (to the psych ward), it was almost the opposite: on rare occasions a normal conversation would take place between us. She would suddenly be a bit more reasonable, but mostly not. It seemed as if her soul itself, the good and beautiful in her, withdrew very slowly. Only the bad characteristics remained. What remained was a dismal, evil shadow of the personality that she had been once, as if something dark had completely taken over. Every character flaw was magnified to the extreme. That was horrible for Laura, our daughter, and myself, but above all it was Pamela's life that for her became a living hell.

In the end, every day became a struggle from start to finish. It started in the morning during the preparation of our Laura's school lunch. Pamela took issue with everything I did and when I gave in, she changed her mind immediately. At times, it degenerated into a physical tussle. So it went throughout the day, she was against everything I did. She could do nothing herself any more. As soon as she tried to do something, she thought that she did it wrong and tried to do it another way, and so it went on and on. There was something paradoxical about her self-image. On the one hand she felt very bad and inferior; on the other hand, her ego was so big that she thought everything that happened was related to, or caused by, her and her alone. She perceived herself as the negative center of the universe: little things that she did, she thought would cause disasters elsewhere. She perceived innocent things I did as being intended to hurt her because she was so bad.

One major problem was that Pamela hardly wanted to eat anymore. She became extremely thin, but no matter what we did, how much we tried to talk her into eating something, it did not help. Food was also an obsession for her in other respects. In the kitchen she had a drawer full of moldy leftovers that she preserved as if they were a priceless treasure. She was furious when I tried to throw them away.

The question then is: how can you help someone who absolutely refuses to be helped? Someone who interprets everything you do as hostile? My answer now is that you cannot do anything until the situation is so severe that a forced committal becomes necessary. Empathy or attempts at reasonableness are of no use at that point; they only exhaust you and lead to frustration. Having gone through the experience, I would now say that the best thing you can do is to go about your own business as much as possible. *Take care of yourself and try to keep things running at a basic level.* That is the best you can do.

Below I share some emails that I wrote to a mutual female friend and which show how I felt and struggled on during that difficult time.

December 12, 2009

You ask how things are with us. To be honest: not good. Pamela has a severe depression. She says very little and what worries me the most is that she barely eats at all. Still, she takes good care of Laura.

December 19, 2009

I have downloaded the text that you recorded for Pamela. A loving gift from a dear friend. Thanks!

I hope I can convince Pamela to listen to it. At the moment she is totally incapable of being open to anything positive. Everything is dark and negative in her world. Tonight, she called herself a monster. It is strange that Pamela, who has helped so many people around the world, is completely unable to help herself. She is also not able to write. It seems as if her consciousness has closed itself off from everything beautiful, good and positive in order to experience the negative to the extreme. It is as you write: she now experiences her heaviest emotions. If I try to speak with her, she looks away and says that it is no use to talk, because everything has already been said.

I am increasingly convinced that she has an eating disorder such as anorexia nervosa. She eats hardly at all, and she can't or won't explain why. I spend all day every day trying to convince her that she should eat. I have a feeling that when the winter is over, and spring comes again, things will be better here. But she needs to eat in order to get through this phase.

January 9, 2010

Thanks you for your best wishes. Yes, our little girl is already eight years old now. The birthday was a nice day for Laura, but not for Pamela. Even under normal circumstances she doesn't like all the commotion but presently not at all.

She is becoming very thin. Today I finally managed to get her on a bathroom scale (during these past months, she always refused) and she weighed only 41 kilograms [90 pounds]. That is, of course, far too little for a woman of her height (1.67 m) [5'5']. It does not surprise me. Her strength does not seem affected yet.

I constantly try to get her to her eat something, but she usually responds very defensively and sometimes even aggressively when I do that. Yesterday she even said to me, 'I know you hate me', when I tried to make her eat something. Maybe it would be better for the atmosphere in the house if I let things be. But of course this is very difficult if you have to watch the person you love the most starve herself.

I knew from the start that Pamela also had a dark side. I remember when I saw her eat a cookie for the first time; all of a sudden out of nowhere the thought came to me that she had anorexia. And now, nine years later, it shows up. Shortly after our first meeting I noticed she could at times act in an unbalanced way that clearly wasn't normal. I remember I was quite relieved when I first saw her parents: they were so normal and friendly to me, which they still are.

But when I got to know her better, I became more and more aware of her good and special qualities: her beautiful angelic energy, her kindness and modesty, her deep spirituality. Although she still had trouble really enjoying life. But now, now the darkness has returned and she is completely swallowed up by it.

Despite all of that, I have noticed small signs of improvement these past few days, as if she begins to open up to me a bit. This morning I sat next to her. I said nothing and rested my hand on her back. I thought of all the beautiful things we had experienced together. I remembered how she looked when we got married: so incredibly beautiful. There was a sudden jolt that ran through her body, something happened; I felt positive energy flowing into her body.

Later that day we finally had a real conversation, the first one in a long time. She told me how terrible she felt. I tried to comfort her, I told her that all would be better in the spring, and that we would again go hiking together in the forests we love. But winter is so cold now.

January 16, 2010

Thank you for all that you do for us. I hope your energy reaches her from distance. A few days ago my sister and I had a very confrontational conversation with Pamela. Until now she has denied that she has an eating disorder. But now I believe that she is slowly beginning to admit it. She looked at a slice of bread, and I asked her, 'Why don't you eat that?' She replied: 'I am afraid I will still be hungry afterward.' This is how bizarre her thinking is. I tried to explain to her how irrational her thoughts were, and she seemed to understand me a bit. She ate the bread and afterward we went to a cafeteria where she still ate some more.

Today there was another battle about eating (at one point she was so mad at me that she began to hit me), but before she went to bed, she promised me to try to eat some. Personally I have the feeling that Pamela's depression and eating disorder have a lot to do with her previous life as a Jewish woman, in which she died in a concentration camp. I am sure that the voice in her head telling her she should not eat has something to do with that. She has the delusion that other people – particularly Laura – will be shortchanged when she eats.

A friend of ours who is an energy reader attuned herself to her and described how she felt: 'a grief too big to be carried by someone alone, a sadness that comes from so deep'. That is how Pamela is at the moment.

I will take a look at the holistic remedies you mentioned. But I don't think I can convince her to take them.

January 28, 2010

Of course, Pamela needs help, especially professional help, but the problem is that she refuses to accept help. She stands alone in her darkness and refuses all outstretched hands. If she would be willing to accept help, the biggest problem would be solved; the healing process could then begin. But she indicates time and time again that she does not want to, and she becomes aggressive when I mention it to her. I have a feeling that it is a race against the clock. On the one hand, she begins to open up very slowly to me; on the other hand, she eats far too little. I don't know how much longer an involuntary intervention can be avoided. I'm afraid that she will experience the environment of a hospital, or psychiatric facility, as very hostile and that it will do her no good.

Slowly she starts to see that she has an eating disorder. Today she even said that food is an obsession for her, and sometimes she makes comments that confirm my suspicions about the influence of a past life. She told me, for example, that she is embarrassed when people see her eat. That she is afraid that there is not enough food, and that when she eats there is not enough for Laura.

Another suspicion that I have, that there are strange energies in her aura, has been confirmed. When I told her about my suspicions, we did a short session and she became aware of it. In a follow-up session we discovered that it is a man. He is now driven back but not yet removed.

Pamela's parents are aware of the situation. Her mother has had several conversations with her. She is obviously very worried; she tries to trust Pamela and encourages her to get help.

I think it is a good idea if you write to her. Your energy is good for her and I think she will read it. I just do not know if she will reply.

March 1, 2010

The situation here has changed little. Pamela still eats hardly at all and she refuses to see a doctor. Her behavior is sometimes very confused and irrational, borderline-like. It's obvious that she is going through a deep psychological crisis. The good news is that she has started writing e-mails, to you among others. She has also started to edit a channeling. I hope these things help clear her mind.

I hope she will finish the email to you quickly, but I don't know for sure.

Today I called our family doctor again to inform him of the situation and to ask his advice, but he was away this week.

I am preparing for a life without Pamela, because if things get worse, a forced committal cannot be avoided. But spring is not far away anymore and I hope things will get better then.

March 14, 2010

I am afraid I have more bad news. At this moment, Pamela is no longer at home but on the psychiatric ward of a hospital. Her behavior became increasingly disturbed the last few weeks. Against her will, I decided to contact the family doctor. He came, along with Pamela's parents and my sister. She refused to listen to his suggestion to go to a special clinic. After this refusal, he decided to engage a crisis team. They came on Friday (March 12). They spoke with Pamela and when she refused to go along voluntarily, they contacted a judge and were given permission for an obligatory admission.

It was awful. Until the ambulance came, we had to keep her caught in the house while she tried to escape. My sister had all the keys, while I held firmly on to Pamela. She begged me to let her go and called out: 'Let go of me, let me go, I'll go away and you'll never see me again. Never again!' Of course I did not let go of her.

When the ambulance arrived, she was more quiet and seemed to accept her fate. I stayed with her in the ambulance and left her behind in the secured psychiatric ward of the hospital. Now I'm home alone with Laura and I don't know if Pamela will ever return to me. But deep in my heart I feel that on my birthday (May 26) Pamela will be with us again. Thank you for everything.

March 27, 2010

Pamela has been in the hospital for two weeks now and there are clear signs of recovery. She is eating more and starting to gain weight. She is more quiet and clear. She has started to do some editing work on a channeling. During the next weekend she is allowed to come home. Compared to the situation two weeks ago, there has been much progress.

If it continues like this, I expect her to come home in a few weeks, perhaps even sooner. Then our little family can start to heal. Laura is doing very well, under the circumstances, even though she is a bit tense at times.

Afterward

Pamela would remain in hospital for a total of three weeks. Soon after her return home she stopped taking the medication prescribed by the psychiatrist, and I experienced her as completely healed. Thus, I concluded that her recovery was miraculously quick.

My hunch, that in the spring of 2010 everything would be fine again, had surprisingly become a reality. It was as if I woke up from a dark nightmare, and all of a sudden everything was back to normal in the bright morning light. Not only I, but also Pamela's parents, felt that a miracle had occurred.

I knew from the start that we would be open and honest about what had happened. We're all human; we all have our difficult periods, our moments of fear and doubt. Precisely because we do work in the area of spirituality, it is important to be forthcoming about it.

By talking and writing about this excruciating experience, we can perhaps offer some assistance to others who are going through the same thing. We understand people who have gone through a psychological crisis better than before.

Meaning

After Pamela's dark night was over and our lives were back to normal, it was natural for me to ponder everything that had happened, and I tried to give meaning to it from my perspective on life.

I believe in reincarnation. People have had many past lives along with all kinds of experiences. Every life is unique: an immersion in a new personality and a unique culture with its own worldview. In every incarnation, different problems are encountered, some of them quite intense. In this way, the soul gradually matures and evolves. However, some lives are dedicated to integration rather than solving new problems. These are lives of relative outward prosperity and good general development, which offer ample opportunity to reflect about oneself and deal with unresolved issues.

This is what many people are doing at the present time: integrating the past and making themselves whole. They do this by forging different energies from past lives into a single whole, balancing all these aspects and healing old trauma. As a regression therapist, I try to guide people on this inner path, and I offer workshops called *'Becoming Whole through the Integration of Past Lives'*. I see many people struggle with this process of integration, as it brings up many psychological problems and tensions.

Some of our past lives ended very badly. If we die feeling deeply depressed or desperate, only a shadow of us is left after death. Think of someone who dies in a concentration camp and who has lost all self-respect, all faith in humanity, in God, in the good. Imagine such a wandering, empty shell who does not even remember what light is.

How do you integrate trauma like that? How do you bring such a shadow back into the light? Pamela did it by becoming that shadow all over again. Step by step she descended into the dark to reclaim this lost part of hers. Whereas from our perspective she was losing herself, from her soul's perspective the errant shadow was being filled again with the light of consciousness. This is my explanation of what happened during Pamela's dark night of the soul: a lost part of her personality was recovered and integrated.

Looking back, I feel that on a deep level there was a soul agreement between the three of us, Pamela, Laura and me, to experience this process at this time. Laura was old enough to handle it, and for a child she remained remarkably stable throughout the whole period. She understood that mommy was not normal, and she went about her own business as much as possible without concerning herself too much with Pamela's bizarre behavior. I had stopped working outside the house, and I could be totally present at home. Although neither of us had any paid employment anymore, in one way or another there was always enough income. And despite all my fears, in the background I always had the feeling that everything would turn out right.

7. Dark Night of the Soul: Spiritual or Psychiatric Experience?

Psychiatry would no doubt describe what I experienced as a mental illness, a disease of the mind caused by disturbed brain functioning. From a spiritual perspective, however, there is much more to it. This experience was part of an inner process of growth and transformation, and it arose from the inner need to propel what was dark and unconscious into the light of consciousness. From a purely psychiatric point of view, my 'illness' can be attributed to an unfortunate genetic sensitivity and/or unfortunate external events which caused me to break down. From a spiritual perspective, the breakdown is a meaningful part of a bigger story: a tale about inner growth and gradual awakening to the reality of the soul.

Which perspective is true, and are they really contradictory? I will argue that both approaches are valuable and helpful in understanding extreme states of consciousness. Twice in my life I have experienced extreme, transgressive states of mind. The first was mania (more than ten years ago) and the second was psychotic depression. Although both can be described in terms of deviant brain processes and be treated medically this way, they both also coincided with a rebirth on the inner level, initiating new chapters in my life and thus constituting meaningful and in the end positive experiences of transition. I do not object to viewing mania and depression as partly physical in nature (having to do with brain chemistry), but I think we should recognize that there is a spiritual dimension to these phenomena that cannot be reduced to mere biological processes. I will now illustrate this by reviewing both situations in my life in more detail.

The experience with mania happened in 2001 and was the result of a regression therapy which introduced me to my past lives. When I started this therapy, I discovered that I could easily slip into the trance state and I received a lot of impressions from past lives which affected me deeply. I felt that I entered the *dimension of my soul*, because by reliving my past lives, I became aware that I, Pamela, was only one of the selves in whom my soul was expressing itself. The anchor to which all those selves were attached was *my soul*, and during the trance state, I felt like I was *becoming* my soul. I felt much bigger and more spacious than usual, which was a very liberating and impressive experience. By connecting with multiple past lives, I learned a lot about why I am the person that I am now, and it was like puzzle pieces falling into place.

Although the regression therapy was transformative and empowering, I was hurled so strongly into the dimension of my soul that I began to lose touch with the practical reality of life on Earth here-and-now. For example, time and again I would ask myself the question: 'Who am I?' I was confused about whether I was Pamela, or rather my soul whose reality was so much vaster than Pamela's human personality. 'Pamela' did not encompass who I was anymore, but being my soul felt so grand and cosmic that it blew my mind away. WHO AM I? It wasn't an abstract philosophical question, but a violent, urgent need to know. All the while, I was in a state of intense joy and euphoria, like I had been lifted out of the density of Earth life. I was in ecstasy. It felt like a homecoming to my true self and a release from the heaviness I experienced before.

During that time, I miraculously came to know Gerrit, who later became my husband. I discovered his website on the Internet, and we started to write each other via email. I experienced a deep and unexplainable sense of familiarity with him, and a lively correspondence ensued. One month later, I met Gerrit in person for the first time, and I knew in advance deep down that he would be my life partner. I was still in a constant state of heightened awareness and my intuition played out to be true afterwards. It was not an impulsive idea coming from a confused brain. We have been together now for more than twelve years and have a happy, stable relationship. The state of ecstasy I found myself in did not lead to insane decisions. I also believe that I did not experience a false bliss in the sense that it was illusionary. Still it eventually became untenable: my thinking was becoming fast and uncontrollable (flight of ideas) and I began to hyperventilate violently. I had uncontrolled kundalini experiences (burning energy along my spine, especially in my heart), and once I had an unpleasant hallucination where I heard a metallic voice that was not real from my balcony through the night. It was obvious that the spiritual ecstasy that I found myself in was derailing my mind and my body.

Looking back at it, I believe that I went through an accelerated process of awakening, during which I could not sufficiently integrate what was happening into my human personality. I lost it, so to speak. Enraptured by the sensation of freedom and lightness, I often told myself: 'This feels *amazingly great;* I never want to come down again.' 'Down' was the drab, heavy reality of Earth. From the perspective of psychiatry, I was probably suffering from mania. I did not know the word mania back then, but later I discovered that it applied in part to what I had experienced. However, there was also an element to it that cannot be described in terms of a disorder, or as a pathological phenomenon. On the spiritual level, an authentic, inner step toward more insight and deeper connection with my soul had been made. The experience also marked an entirely new beginning in my personal life. After I met Gerrit and we were both strongly attracted to each other, I moved quickly to the city where he lived, which was quite far from where I had lived before. One month later, I was pregnant with our daughter Laura, and this radical change brought me down from the mania back to Earth.

Although the experience of ecstasy that I had lived through was neither well balanced nor grounded, I still regard it as a genuine breakthrough to a new level of awareness and a new phase in my life. I feel that the connection with my soul that I made during the regression into past lives drew Gerrit into my life, and he is a life partner who feels like a soul mate to me. Not only did our coming together bring us both the joy and healing of being recognized on the soul level by another human being, but we also shared a keen interest in spirituality and philosophy, which we had both pursued independently all of our lives. After our daughter was born, we started to work together in our spiritual practice and very soon I started to receive channeled messages from Jeshua, supported by Gerrit. I was finally doing the work of my heart. In short, the experience of 'mania' was much more than a derangement. It initiated a spiritually meaningful and powerful transition into a new life for me, and it was more like a rebirth than an illness. The extreme states of consciousness I experienced may be compared to birth pangs. When you observe a woman in labor and regard the birth contractions as an isolated event, you see a woman who is apparently ill and crying out in pain. But when you see the contractions in the light of the impending birth, they are not symptoms of illness, but rather the gateway to a new birth which brings something magnificent into the world.

My experience with psychosis and depression, about eight years later, also initiated a spiritual rebirth. During this period, there were no states of higher awareness or transcendent consciousness. On the contrary, I became completely shut off from my soul and from spiritual guidance. Yet something essential happened in this process: the part of my ego that was full of fear and mistrust against life rose to the surface. It took charge of my consciousness in such a way that I drowned in it. There seemingly wasn't any growth anymore because I had no inner space left to observe or reflect on my negative emotions. I *was* them. Now, however, a mechanism occurred that was described earlier in the dialogue with my soul: if you are not growing, even if you're completely stuck, life does not stand still. Life keeps on moving. If you don't go up, you go down. If you go down, as I did, the suffering intensifies, until there is a moment when it becomes unbearable. This is the time when change and growth are possible again. In my case, at that moment a part of my ego let go, a part filled with shame, pride, and need for control. I surrendered, and it resulted in a rebirth.

The diary excerpts in Chapter 2 show that I started this incarnation with a deep aversion to life on Earth. Because of that, I could not connect with Earth and with life for a long time. In the background there were always emotions such as anger, fear, cynicism and arrogance. Ultimately, these emotions stemmed from painful past life experiences that festered as unhealed wounds and stood in the way of true joy and fulfillment. Through the experience of my dark night of the soul, I feel that this past life incarnation pain has in part been resolved. I say *in part* because I have become careful about claiming that any deep-seated emotional issue has been resolved definitively and completely. A rebirth is not a one-time event; rather we constantly go through life cycles in which we alternatively visit our own underworld and then rise to the surface and integrate what we have learned, so we can grow from it and enjoy it. After having experienced this second rebirth, I feel lighter, yet I am well aware that this is not the end of the road. I do feel closer to Spirit, the One, the core of our being, and to my soul, the part of me that transcends my human personality.

The first rebirth initiated me into the realm of the soul. For many years afterwards, I was very interested in exploring past lives, reliving and healing old trauma, and it felt like I was finding the pieces of a large puzzle and could finally put them together. Now, ten years later and after the second rebirth, I feel less attracted to past life exploration and even to the whole idea of 'working on myself.' I am more inclined to accept myself, the whole package so to speak, with the dark and the light aspects. Falling so deeply into the abyss of depression, after having experienced significant inner growth in the years before, has made me realize that it is not realistic to look upon yourself as a 'spiritual project' that can be handled by the human personality, to be worked on and gradually perfected. Even though inner work and things like regression therapy can be extremely valuable, we should not underestimate what we still do not know and the depth of the emotions that we hide from ourselves. Life is a wild ride. It is much more uncontrollable than our personality would like it to be, yet there is meaning behind it, which one can often only understand and appreciate later on. I am actually relieved by this realization, because the ambition to make yourself a better person is often fraught with struggle and judgment. Life is lighter now. I feel more drawn to seeking stillness, trying to surrender to what is and embracing the mystery of that which surpasses our human understanding.

My main point in this chapter is that the sense of liberation and growth that I experienced with both rebirths cannot be adequately described in terms of the vocabulary of psychiatry. That medical model makes no room for the transformative, cathartic qualities of extreme states of consciousness, which depression and psychosis are. Having enjoyed the benefits of anti-depressant and sleeping medications, I do not want to push aside the achievements of modern psychiatry (more on this in the next chapter). I do, however, believe that to look at mental illness solely from a scientific, neurobiological viewpoint unnecessarily impoverishes and limits our understanding of the phenomenon. The spiritual perspective can and should coexist with the psychiatric one and add a kind of depth and meaningfulness that our current science can never provide.

8. Advice for Cases of Severe Depression or Psychosis

Having experienced clinical depression and psychosis first hand, I would like to offer some advice to people who find themselves in a similar situation. This advice is based on *my* experience and cannot replace the advice of a doctor, psychiatrist or other professional. Also, this counsel is aimed especially at people who have an affinity for spirituality and who therefore will probably read this book.

My experience is that people who come from a spiritual perspective have a certain way of looking at phenomena such as psychosis, depression and psychiatric disorders in general. In short, they tend to view the occurrence from the perspective of the soul, and there is an aversion to reducing the phenomenon to a mere disorder, to see it strictly as some type of illness. Now, as I argued in the previous chapter, it can be very valuable to look at psychiatric disorders from the perspective of the soul. A purely neurobiological, scientific approach (which reduces the spiritual to chemical brain processes) is unnecessarily limiting, and therefore also can be harmful. On the other hand, I notice that people with a strong spiritual bent sometimes neglect the physical component. They go to the other extreme, concluding that the spirit is not determined by the body, but rather that the body is completely ruled by the spirit. I think that this is just as much a one dimensional view as is a pure medical approach. I am (now) of the opinion that psychiatry with its labels of illness and medication can be truly helpful. You can approach a psychic imbalance from multiple levels, and the physical level is, especially during serious imbalances, of great importance to address.

To offer one example here, suppose someone has delusions or hallucinations in which he thinks he is an angel who is not restricted by the laws of space and time. The extremely neurobiologically oriented psychiatrist says, 'Easy. This person suffers from a chemical disorder in the brain that generates these visions. It is a purely clinical picture that is separate from the individual personality; it is a physical abnormality like diabetes or liver failure.' Now, the interpretation from a one-sided spiritual view would go something like this: 'The delusions and hallucinations indicate that this person is in fact highly sensitive and psychic. The upper chakras are opened all the way, and because of that this person is in contact with higher-other-worldly dimensions. The visions that he has contain an important core of truth, and it is questionable whether we actually must see it as a disorder. This is a special gift that we should not flatten out with medication.'

Here are two opposite interpretations that both do injustice to the phenomenon of psychological imbalance through their one-sidedness. Prior to my own experiences, I tended toward the second form of one-sidedness. I had a firm bias against psychiatry and chose unconditionally the perspective of the soul. Now I find that approach pretty naive, and I am much more inclined to adopt a middle position. I would now say that someone with the above mentioned delusion might be having valuable intuitive perceptions, but that it is especially important that this person get grounded and firmly anchored into his body. There are several ways to achieve this result, and the methods used by psychiatry should certainly not be excluded.

During my psychotic depression I was beyond reach of any spiritually oriented help. I still believed in the existence of the soul, life after death and so on. I was so overcome by the idea that I was bad and sinful, however, that I became closed off from any spiritual help, either in the form of therapies offered by others or of inner work that I could do myself. In the months before I completely drifted away in depression and psychosis, I could get myself out of the low points every now and then by, for example, getting in touch with my inner child, my higher self or Jeshua. But when I sunk even deeper, I lost all contact. I was petrified inside and appalled at the fact that *nothing* worked. As I look back on it now, I would say I was in need of a *different type of help* and had been for quite a while. I needed help on a physical level (i.e., a minimum number of hours of sleep and rest for my erratic mind) that would restore a basic sense of well-being. I could have received that kind of help only through a psychiatric evaluation and a prescription.

I was too far gone for any other form of assistance. My brain was on a runaway course, and alternative means no longer helped. I was filled with distrust and paranoia toward other people; when Gerrit came home with a bouquet of flowers for me, I wanted to hurl them away and destroy them because I interpreted this gesture as a taunt towards me. Also, I could not bear to see the beauty of the flowers anymore; their beauty just confirmed the contrast of my deadness and ugliness. The idea that someone at this stage could actually have helped me by giving me a massage or otherwise treating me therapeutically is not realistic. I suspect strongly that committal to a mental hospital and medication were the only avenues for me then that could offer any hope of true help and healing.

If you have never experienced a serious mental imbalance, it is hard to imagine how strange, cut off and insane your thinking is in that condition. Deep down you realize this yourself, yet you cannot escape from it. As I look back now, I would give myself the following advice.

1. Recognize when you are crossing the line

The following symptoms may indicate a psychiatric disorder. These are the symptoms I have experienced firsthand. There are more, and you can get a more complete picture via a psychiatric manual or by consulting an expert. What matters is that you recognize when you are crossing the line.

Relational delusion

To see a *sign* in everything that happens to you; little, mundane things are deeply meaningful and are all related to you. They contain a secret language that you understand but other people do not. Everything that occurs is a mirror or signal for you: everything is caused by you or is your fault. Interpreting everything as related to you becomes an obsession; you cannot stop even though it makes you very tired.

Paranoia

Being deeply distrustful of other people's motives. They are out to get you. Even if they say nice things and seem to want to help you, they are actually hostile towards you and have secret motives to hurt and destroy you. Suspecting there are conspiracies against you. Also called persecution complex.

Flight of Ideas

Your thinking is very fast and agitated and you are unusually clear in your head. The brightness does not feel normal; it is an alertness that does not want to recede. It is causing sleeplessness and the inability to feel tired, sleepy or drowsy. You are not able to get out of your head and relax.

Numbness

Feeling inwardly dead, petrified or rigid. No longer being able to be happy or cry. Your emotions are flat, or you no longer feel them. As a result, you feel very strange and alienated. You feel closed off from other, *living* people.

Euphoria

Euphoria is a great feeling of bliss that occurs in a mania (a manic psychosis). This symptom is different from the foregoing in the sense that (initially) it is perceived as very positive. It is similar to intense romantic love. You may feel enlightened and able to understand everything. What is not is right about it is that you lose your grounding and become disconnected from everyday reality and other people. You fly too high and usually you do not land very softly. True enlightenment does not remove you from earthly reality; it reconciles you with it and makes you kind and friendly towards other people.

If you are having any of these symptoms, take it seriously and find help in a timely way.

The line between a psychological and a psychiatric condition, between a 'dip' and a depression cannot be drawn tightly. When do you cross the boundary into madness? I suspect that in many psychiatric disorders, you can perceive a magnified version of behavior that is displayed by many people, but the milder variety does not really constitute a disorder. For example, many people are suspicious about the motives of other people. They easily can tend to think that someone is talking about them in a negative way, while that's not the case at all. In its extreme form, distrust becomes paranoia, where you consistently interpret the behavior of other people as an attack on you. Then there clearly is a psychiatric disorder. But where do you draw the line exactly?

Another example is the belief in *synchronicity* that many people who come from a spiritual perspective have. Apparent coincidences are considered to be highly meaningful. For instance: 'My train was delayed so I could not be on time; the universe must be telling me something meaningful by this.' I do think that sometimes the universe wants to tell us something through a seemingly chance event that is quite telling. Synchronicity exists. But the way this is applied in spiritual circles is, from my perspective, going overboard. You cannot find a dime in the street, or see a peculiarly shaped cloud in the sky without regarding it as having an important message for you. I now consider the tendency to look for the hidden meaning behind every little thing that happens as a mild form of relational delusion. It is a delusion, because a lot of things that happen around you have nothing at all to do with you, and the 'larger meaning' that you see in them is often not at all correct. In the mild variant this delusion is not harmful. However, when you really suffer from relational delusion in the psychiatric sense, this is damaging to yourself and disturbing for your relationships. But where to draw the line?

Philosophically speaking, there is no clear cut boundary. Pragmatically, however, there is. When your life becomes disrupted, or you begin to feel very unhappy, and you can no longer function in everyday life, you are crossing the line. At that time, it is important that you ask yourself: 'Is it possible that I suffer from a mental illness?' It helps to know what is going on with you. If I had been aware of the symptoms of psychotic depression, and had I recognized them, I would have felt less ashamed and bewildered and I would have possibly asked for help earlier.

2. Allow others to help you

When you have crossed that line, you find yourself in a very difficult situation. You have lost yourself in such a way that you can no longer pull yourself out of the swamp. Therefore, allow experts to help you. Even though you feel they do not understand you, or that you are beyond help, take the step anyway and ask for help. Let go of shame, guilt or pride. Even if you are afraid of losing face in the eyes of others, even if it is scary to talk about the morbid and weird thoughts and emotions you are having, do it anyway.

If you don't do this, you will stay locked inside your own hell, and a negative spiral may ensue which will make you become even more stuck in negative emotions, in obsessive thoughts or delusions. Whatever you are going through, it is *human*. There are other people who have experienced this as well. There are people who understand the problems that you have now. You can be helped: this begins by talking to someone about it.

One of the biggest obstacles to reaching psychotic people (manic or depressed) is that, as a result of their delusions, they have created a closed worldview. Within that worldview theirs is the only correct way of interpreting the events. For example, you see everything according to the belief that people despise you, or you are convinced that you have a special role to fulfill, that *you know it all* and that others are not as far advanced as you. You feel that your interpretation of the facts is so obvious that you are not open to counter-arguments of any kind. Someone who experiences psychosis is obsessively convinced that they are right, and they live in an ivory tower. If you catch yourself trying feverishly to interpret the facts according to a rigid scheme, dare to recognize that you are caught in this dynamic. It is a sign of great strength to do so. The satisfaction of being right does not outweigh the pain of isolation. Dare to admit that you are being obsessive and allow other people to enter into your world again.

3. Be open to the use of medication

Be open to the possibility that there are physical causes underlying your mental state. Depression, mania and psychosis are not just psychological phenomena; they are also accompanied by physical issues such as a chemical disorder or imbalance in the brain. Chronic sleep deprivation, severe traumatic stress, drug use or extremely violent emotions can affect the functioning of your brain in such a way that they cause psychosis, mania or depression. Even though you feel that your situation is totally unique and that you are different from all of humanity, please be open to the possibility that the extreme emotions and thoughts you are experiencing are at least partly caused by a disorder in your brain.

Be open to the use of medication in consultation with a general practitioner, psychiatrist or other expert. Let go of dogmas and taboos surrounding the use of medications. People with primarily a spiritual view of the world can sometimes be very biased against mainstream medicine. Of course, it is a good thing that we no longer blindly believe and swallow whatever the doctor says or prescribes. You should always use your critical thinking and your intuition when you obtain the advice of a medical expert. Using your critical thinking, however, does not take away from the fact that an experienced psychiatrist can offer very helpful healing tools, especially on the physical level, which is intimately related to the psychological level.

Hardly anyone likes to take pills. Psychotropic drugs, such as antidepressants, can have unpleasant side effects. Sedatives can be addictive in the long term. However, when you are really stuck in a depression or torn apart by psychosis, it is absurd to refuse medications on those grounds. Also, the argument often advanced in spiritual circles, that antidepressants flatten your emotions and therefore stunt your spiritual growth, is misplaced. The point is that in an extreme mental crisis, you have lost all mastery over your emotions. There is no longer any basis from which to work on yourself constructively. Suppose someone hangs onto the edge of a steep cliff. They threaten to fall down into the abyss at any moment. Will you not throw a lifeline to someone like that 'because they need to learn to climb to the top by themselves?' Such thinking is ridiculous.

Medication is not a magic cure. It is often only part of the solution. And of course it is commendable, after you have returned from the hell of madness, to begin therapeutic work on certain issues in your life. In the middle of a deep depression or psychosis, however, there is only one priority: to regain a minimum of calm and well-being in your everyday life; to return to Earth and restore basic physical mechanisms such as adequate sleep and regular meals. When you suffer from a psychiatric disorder you often live inside your head to the extreme. Returning to and landing back in your body is the first step to recovery. Medication can be temporarily helpful here.

9. Excesses of Spirituality

In 1997, after acquiring my doctorate and saying goodbye to the University, I had developed an aversion to the excessive intellectual and rational approach that prevailed there. I plunged into alternative approaches and read a lot in the field of spirituality and esotericism. Through my training in aura reading and an intense regression therapy, I discovered a new world that had a lot to offer. As a student, first undergraduate and then postgraduate, obtaining my PhD, I had spent ten years working with an entirely rational approach, and shifting to a spiritual perspective with its focus on intuition and actual experience was like manna in the desert to me. For a long time, I resisted the intellectual, rational framework that had inspired me for years. I thought it was narrow-minded, arrogant and failing to address the essential issues.

Now, more than seventeen years later, I am very much at home with the spiritual perspective and I have built up a practice based on channeling, written several books and met many people at our workshops all over the world. I have become intimately familiar with the kind of thinking that is common in spiritual circles, and I have to say that my contempt for the rational approach has lessened considerably. I am now of the opinion that a critical, rational mind is a useful tool *particularly* if you feel drawn to spirituality. I often come across supposedly 'spiritual' theories and ideas that I find to be amazingly naive or bizarre. In addition, I have noticed that highly sensitive people who are carried away by these theories may, through a lack of down to earth common sense, eventually *cross the line* and slip into psychosis or mania.

In this chapter I offer a list of attitudes or ideas that are presented as highly spiritual, while they are in fact excesses, that is to say derailments of spirituality. My impression is that these derailments can contribute to mental imbalance, especially in sensitive, emotionally vulnerable people. Also, I think these excesses give spirituality a bad name, and they prevent the development of a mature, balanced, socially integrated form of spirituality.

Pride and arrogance

In spiritual circles one often feels different and misunderstood by other people who do not believe in a spiritual worldview. The feeling of being misunderstood often creates, by way of self defense, an attitude of arrogance:

'I'm *more advanced* than they are. *Because* of that, they do not understand me.' This haughty attitude evokes resistance in other people and a hostile reaction from them becomes even more likely. A vicious circle arises.

Such a no-win situation is not always because the spiritual person is deliberately haughty and arrogant. Often sensitive, spiritual people suffer intensely because of their being different, with nothing that connects them with colleagues or friends, and they feel lonely and isolated with their experiences in the area of spirituality. However, if you find yourself in that zone (lonely, insecure, searching) you can be prone to listen to spiritual teachers and theories telling you that you are in fact very special and very different from the average person. That generates quite a good feeling: you *do* belong somewhere; you even belong to the elite! What goes wrong when you really believe in these fantasies is that you move even further away from the world and ordinary people and that you lose the connection with the earthly (and that includes you and your emotions). In extreme cases this can lead to psychosis or other psychiatric disorders.

Truly authentic spiritual ideas always *connect* you with reality: with Earth, with your humanness and with other people. Real spirituality has both feet on the ground and does not divide, but reconciles. Think of Jeshua. Was his message aimed at conveying a new spiritual metaphysics, a new system of beliefs? No, his message was not a theory or world view at all. He wanted to convey *the values of the heart*. He spoke in a universal language, a simple language, the language of love, that could be understood by supporters of very different belief systems. He talked about equality, about understanding and compassion, about the light in all of us, about courage and sincerity. All people intuitively understand these things. That is why Jeshua still lives on in the hearts of so many; his teachings unify humanity and transcend the level of world views.

True spirituality is not obscure or elitist and, to me, is profoundly separate from any world view to which you adhere. For example, someone who is very skeptical about the existence of the soul or life after death can be a deeply spiritual human being. Their actions may bear witness to a deep compassion and warmth. I believe that authentic spirituality is based upon the universal values of the heart.

It is important to keep the above principles in mind when you adhere to a spiritual world view and you feel that you are thus in conflict with your environment. How can you deal with this perceived dichotomy in a mature way? First, you have to recognize that there are multiple worldviews, that this is a positive thing and that each person has the right to determine for themselves what they believe in and what their values are. Secondly, it is necessary that you find out for yourself just how deeply you want to enter into a relationship (personal or business) with someone who does not share your world view. Once you have determined how valuable the relationship is to you, you can decide whether you want to break it off or continue with it. If you feel you want to pursue it further, focus on what you *do* have in common and find joy in that. Trying to change or convert the other person does not work. You can have a deep, fulfilling relationship with someone who does not share your worldview.

I think that part of the resistance that spiritual people meet with in the outside world comes from the way they tend to present their spirituality to the outside world. By this I mean in particular the *dogmatism* with which spiritual ideas are often bluntly proclaimed, and secondly the *inaccessibility* of those ideas. Dogmatism repels. If someone wants to convince you of their ideas in a fanatic sort of way, that tends not to be appealing; on the contrary, it tends to turn people off. It is much more convincing when someone quietly tells his or her story and completely allows you the space to draw your own conclusions, whatever they may be. In addition, many spiritual theories are accompanied by incomprehensible jargon. If you are not an insider, terms such as 'ascension', 'the fifth dimension', 'twin souls' and 'DNA activation' are at best unclear and at worst off-putting. It can be confusing and alienating when people dish out such terms generously and without explanation. Truly valuable spiritual insights are based on common sense and can be formulated in plain language. Simplicity is a mark of the truth.

Naive belief in clairvoyants

What amazes me is that many adherents of a spiritual world view are extremely critical of science and mainstream medicine on the one hand, while on the other hand they have no difficulty swallowing all kinds of speculative assertions or radical statements from the 'alternative' approach. People often show me, in joy and wonder, objects such as gem stones, necklaces or geometric shapes that are supposed to have a special protective or healing effect. When you ask how this works, often they base their beliefs on some form of clairvoyance. Through communication with the spirit world, some healer or therapist has received the message that a particular object or healing modality has a 'special' effect. Also, the internet is buzzing with predictions of the future - despite the 2012 non-event - which are in some manner based on information that has been received by way of clairvoyance.

How reliable is that approach? Let me say that I do attach value to many alternative therapies and resources. I myself have experienced more than once, for instance, that gemstones have a subtle effect, and that healings can give you a nudge in the right direction. However, I have strong reservations about the plethora of methods and remedies that are available in the spiritual marketplace. In particular, I do not find recourse to clairvoyance a very reliable source of information. I am myself an author of channeled works that include messages that I have received from spiritual guides. So my skepticism may raise certain questions, such as, 'Aren't you doing this also?' Precisely because I do channel and receive information 'from above', however, I am very aware of how many pitfalls there are. I believe that clear and accurate channeling exists and that valuable, empowering information can be obtained through that intuitive process. At the same time, one needs to keep a critical and discerning mind and take into account the following three principles:

– Being clairvoyant does not automatically mean that you are spiritually evolved;

– Intuition (something which everyone naturally has) is more valuable spiritually than being clairvoyant or psychic; and

– All channeled or clairvoyant information is filtered by the personality and world view of the recipient

I will explain these statements separately.

Being clairvoyant does not automatically mean that you are spiritually evolved

In many spiritual circles, you are regarded highly when you are able to *see* things, such as auras, past lives and those who have passed over. It is suggested that you have this gift *as a result of* growth in consciousness and inner development, as if spiritual growth is necessarily accompanied by an increasing psychic ability. Clairvoyance is not automatically linked to a highly developed inner awareness, however. Someone may receive all kinds of extrasensory impressions and not handle it well; for example, they may become unbalanced because the information overwhelms or frightens them. It is also possible to use clairvoyance for your own selfish interests and manipulate others with it. You can, in other words, take any direction with it, some with negative consequences.

When I was still in college, I went to a fortune teller with a friend. We had to bring a picture of ourselves, and she would tell us what was going to happen in the future. The woman received us in her home where we sat down at the dinner table, and she began to rub our photographs, while she occasionally stirred a large pot of soup that stood simmering on the stove. She gave all kinds of rather moralistic advice about what life was about and what we, as young ladies, should be careful about, and between those considerations she occasionally supposedly '*saw*' something. She predicted some things about my later life partner, his character and the children I would have. There were very specific details in her predictions, and some of them actually turned out to be right later. That some of those predictions came true could be called remarkable; however, it says nothing at all about the spiritual development of the fortune teller. Our entire visit to that woman had in fact nothing to do with spirituality, more with curiosity on our part.

True spirituality is about honest self-reflection, facing your fears and taking responsibility for your emotions. A spiritual teacher or therapist can help you, but not by telling you something about the future or about anything external at all. A true teacher helps you gain deeper insight into yourself and encourages you to rely on your own strength and wisdom. They use their intuition to bring you closer to yourself. A spiritual teacher has a feeling for what might be constraining you or what you are trying to deny or avoid. They have intimate knowledge of what it is like to be human and they have an open, non-judgmental mind. *A spiritual teacher never tells you something you do not already know deep down.* A fortune teller on the other hand, often claims to know something that you cannot know; they may imply that through their special gifts, they have access to knowledge that you do not and cannot have. Real spirituality is never about *special gifts*. If we think of Jeshua again, what made him special were not his psychic abilities. Perhaps he did have such abilities, but what made him into an authentic *spiritual* teacher was the fact that he deeply inspired people to discover the light within themselves. It was his wisdom, his clarity of mind, and the radiance of his love that touched the hearts of people permanently.

Later, after I had attained my PHD and had left the University, I visited an aura reader. Her way of conveying information was completely different from that of the fortune teller. She focused on my soul and my personality, my weak spots, survival mechanisms and talents. Her story was intelligent, coherent and had psychological depth. The consultation was very challenging and at the same time, it felt very true. It was as if she held up a mirror for me, in which I clearly had to see and then confront my own stumbling blocks. This psychic reader had a powerful and at the same time sweet and caring energy. I sensed a spiritual awareness in her that attracted me. She became my spiritual teacher for two years, in which I attended her various training courses. This was a teacher who used her psychic abilities at the service of spirituality. What made her spiritual was not that she could see the colors of people's auras, but that she was wise and knowledgeable and able to communicate her wisdom and psychological insights with compassion and clarity.

Conclusion: If you are presented with information that is obtained through clairvoyance, it is important to assess it on the basis of the quality of the content. Is the information clear, innovative and inspiring? Does it radiate the values of the heart? Does it make sense both to your heart and your mind? Can it actually be applied in everyday life? These are important criteria to use in deciding whether you can rely on it or not. The fact alone that information is obtained by means of psychic abilities does not say anything about its inherent value.

Intuition (something which everyone has) is spiritually more valuable than being clairvoyant or psychic

Every human has their intuition available to them. For all major decisions that you take, you make use of your intuition, whether you realize it or not. Rational considerations are usually not determinative. In the end you do what *feels right* and ideally, this feeling is not just an impulse, a fleeting emotion. It is a kind of deep, inner knowing that cannot be reasoned through in a rational manner. We are used to distinguish between reason and feeling, but it is better to make a threefold distinction between reason, emotion and intuition. In our everyday language, the word feeling refers to both emotion and intuition. But these are actually two very different phenomena. If you have an intuition, it is a calm sort of knowing that persists, and is not bound to a fleeting mood or stimulus. An emotion, on the other hand, is a strong response to something happening outside of you and may be turbulent and short-lived rather than calm. In a channeling called 'Dealing with emotions', Jeshua has said that 'emotions are your children; intuitions are your teachers'. (See *The Jeshua Channelings* or www.jeshua.net). Intuition is the language of your soul; emotions are the language of your inner child.

Virtually everyone who has mastered a particular skill, or has specialized in a particular field, has developed intuitive skills in that area. Just think of an experienced hairdresser who senses what hairstyle will fit a client, a chef who has a brilliant flash of inspiration for a new recipe, an actor who improvises at just the right time, or a psychotherapist who immediately picks up and translates non-verbal signals. Intuition is natural and is common to all people.

Intuition is spiritually valuable. If you trust your intuition, you are in touch with your soul. Following your intuition brings you joy and inspiration. It is part of your spiritual path to rely on your intuition more and more, and to overcome the voices of fear. Intuition is not a special gift which is reserved to a select few. We are all meant to develop and nurture our intuition. That doesn't mean that we are all becoming clairvoyant or psychic. We can access intuitive information in a variety of ways: through a feeling, a quiet knowing, a sudden flash of inspiration, a song on the radio or a talk with a friend. Intuition is attuned to the here and now. When you receive information from a psychic, always consult your intuition. It will tell you clearly whether something is right for you or not. Intuition is the language of your own soul, and you are not dependent on a clairvoyant for receiving the messages of your soul.

All channeled information is filtered by the personality and world view of the channeler

In my previous books and on my website (www.jeshua.net) I have spoken extensively about this topic, so I will keep this section short. Channeling is a human affair and therefore prone to human mistakes. As a channel, you are influenced by your cultural background and personal history in ways you are not consciously aware of. Even when you have done a lot of inner work, have faced fears, released judgments and dare to trust your intuition, you remain fallible. There are always filters at work. This is not necessarily a negative result: it gives each channel his or her own angle and timbre. What is dangerous is if as a channel you deny that you have any filters. In that circumstance, you claim to be a 100% pure channel, which is virtually impossible to achieve.

When reading or listening to a channeling, it is therefore wise to rely on your own intuition to determine whether the information is useful to you or not. And if you are in doubt, simply use your human common sense. If the message is moralistic, ominous, vague or unrealistic, think twice. Your emotional body often gives clear signals: it reacts with a sense of relaxation, joy and inspiration or with resistance, anxiety and boredom.

The purpose of this chapter has been to name some of the excesses of spirituality, which in the worst cases can lead to mental disorders. I have experienced on several occasions that people can lose their grip on reality by grasping at pompous spiritual ideas which pull them away from their earthly roots and realism. True spirituality is simple and *connects you* to everyday life on Earth. It encourages you to embrace your humanity and to see the humanness in other people. Real spirituality is not at odds with rationality and common sense. My feeling is that everyone would benefit if there were a stronger bridge between the two, so that spirituality could become more integrated into mainstream society. Spirituality would primarily take the form of an open reflection on the central questions of life that every human being faces. No dogmas, no preconceived certainties, but instead room for wonder, mystery and a good sense of humor. That to me is the face of a mature, integrated spirituality.

Part II

Spiritual Messages on the Dark Night of the Soul

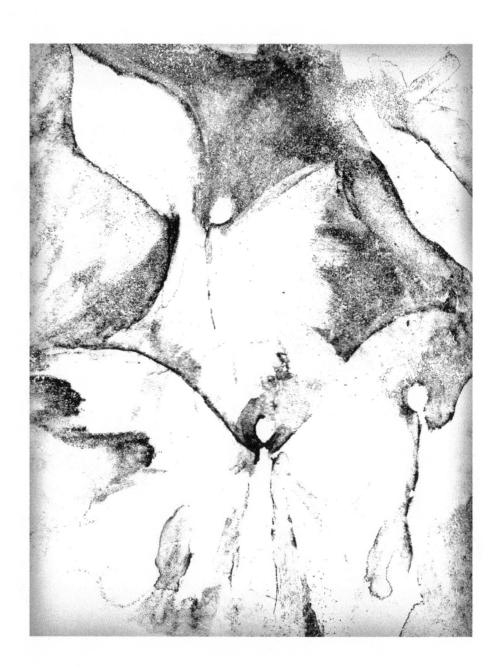

10. Mastery of the Dark Night of the Soul

I am Jeshua, your brother and friend. I am here to support you and to affirm the bond between us: *we are one on the level of the soul.* I approach you as an equal, as family. Do not see me as someone exalted above you. I am one *of* you and one *with* you.

You are here on Earth to discover who you are. You might think heaven is a better place to discover who you are because it has a pure vibration of love and harmony. Is it not true that in that atmosphere, it would be easier for you to feel who you are than on Earth, where loneliness, fear, and separation abound? But you are here now because there was a point in time when you deliberately chose to descend to this earthly dimension. From your soul, you said yes to this life. There was a determination and single-mindedness present in your soul before you came here. You realized there was something to discover here that you could not discover on the other side.

The heavenly spheres lack the emotional depth of Earth, which abounds with oppositions. Just think of how widely your earthly emotions can range in tone, from light to dark, from subtle to screaming. It is just these oppositions, precisely the duality, which bring great opportunities for experiencing, and that is what has attracted you to Earth. Only when you actually take the plunge into matter, inhabit a body of flesh and blood, and from there have every experience that life presents to you, can your soul awaken and grow to its deepest level. In an atmosphere with little opposition, for example, one of constant goodness and harmony, you would never discover your dark side, let alone transform it. Also, you could not have the experience of joy and expansion associated with inner awakening. Now you might say: 'Those experiences of joy and expansion do not outweigh the suffering that I have to undergo here.' But I am telling you that there will come a day when you realize it was all worth it and that you will be grateful for your life here on Earth.

I see your longing for an atmosphere of harmony and peace in which life is easy and smooth and where you feel intensely connected with all life around you. It is understandable that you have such a longing, because it is the energy of your Home that beckons and calls. The energy of Home tells you who you naturally are. That is why the desire, the homesickness, is not a bad thing to experience. What is most important to realize, however, is that you are on Earth to establish that energy of Home, *here*. You are not here to serve a prison sentence and to experience what it is like to be away from and missing Home. *You are here to channel the energy of Home into the world!* When that happens, you bring Home on to Earth. And when many individuals manifest the energy of Home, which is nothing other than the energy of their own divine essence, then they create heaven on Earth. Creating Home – heaven - on Earth is the ultimate goal of your incarnations here.

I understand why life here calls up resistance within you; life demands the utmost of you. On the one hand, it asks that you fully dive into the earthly experience and all the emotions associated with doing that. On the other hand, you are asked to hold on to the energy of Home and to realize that you are more than an earthly human being, and that in the end, you are an immortal part of God. What happens on almost every soul-path is that you drink in the earthly until you are overcome by it and threaten to drown in it. That is a painful experience that often goes hand in hand with a dark night of the soul, which is where you have become so far removed from your original, free, and divine nature that you get overwhelmed by negative thoughts and heavy emotions. Still, it is precisely during such a crisis that you can come to realize you are *not* those thoughts and emotions, that there is *something else*. When this awareness, this space around your emotions and thoughts arises, there will be a turning point where you rediscover the way Home. You will then experience the surrender that brings you Home, and you will discover that you can hold on to the energy of Home right *here* and *now* and emanate it around you.

You can be present on Earth from your soul only when you come to realize that you are *not* what you seem to be: a body of flesh and blood that will die at some point in time; a bundle of emotions that vacillates from high to low; a container filled with conflicting thoughts. Coming Home begins with the deep awareness that you are *more* than all those things. Simply stated, you will only experience your own *infinity* amidst the *finite.* This divine experience on the Earth plane is the reason for your being here and nothing less than that.

You are on your way to becoming masters of duality. And by mastery, I mean that you come to recognize all the energies that are here on Earth by having experienced them all: from extreme darkness to extreme light. At some point, you are going to know them so well that you no longer will drown in them or attach yourself to them – *you will allow them to be free to flow through you.* There then is a place within you of peace and unity, and the more you are present in that serene place, the more you can appreciate life and the less you resist difficult moments. Even in the midst of chaos and negativity, you can connect with that peaceful, quiet space within yourself, and you are then a master of duality.

This mastery is a resilient, quiet, open energy. It has nothing to do with power or control that is usually associated with the concept of mastery. The master does not want to put himself above anybody or anything. *Mastery is letting go, observing without judgment, being still.* If there is chaos and pressure, the master is in the calm eye of the hurricane. The energy of mastery is peaceful and grounded. There is a deep connection with the *here* and *now*, a being present *in this moment*, with no reaching out to the future or the past. When you become a master of duality, you become a rooted human with an anchor within yourself. You feel connected to the Earth while at the same time, you are open to the sky. To experience this balance while you are in the dimension of duality is your purpose on Earth, and you can only develop this mastery in a place where duality prevails.

The journey of your soul through many lives on Earth is rich in meaning and value, although I know it often does not feel that way. It is almost impossible to connect with that greater perspective when you are deeply immersed in negativity and inner struggle. So how do you deal with a dark night of the soul? How do you deal with a time in your life when your consciousness is shrouded by fear, doubt, and depression?

First of all: *have respect for the dark night of the soul.* From your human consciousness, your first reaction to adversity is usually the feeling of resistance, and you respond: 'This should not be; this cannot be right.' Or there is the feeling of fear, and you respond: 'I can't handle this; I can't bear this; I can't overcome this.' Such responses to resistance or fear hold negative judgments, and it is precisely these judgments that create the dark night of the soul. They close you off from seeing the situation as potentially purposeful, because they reject what is there. If you persist in this rejection, you will fall into a feeling of despair that can seem to paralyze you.

What happens during a dark night of the soul is that you do not know how to deal with a difficult situation in your life and you get stuck in fear or resistance, the opposite of openness and acceptance. Your refusal to be open and accept what happens causes you to become immobilized; a rigid part then arises inside of you that does not know how to flow along with what life is presenting to you. It is not *what* happens to you, but *your rejection of it*, which causes the dark night of the soul. If you were to remain open, then there would be a basic trust that whatever happens has meaning or purpose at some level, even though you do not yet understand what it is. Openness and trust enable you to experience a major setback in your life while *not* going into a dark night of the soul. Some people are capable of holding on to a certain amount of confidence even in the most disruptive and trying of situations, which testifies to a great inner strength. Then why is it that such strength is often missing in other people? Why can it be so hard to trust and to continue to surrender to what is happening in your life?

In your society, making judgments is learned early on. Emotions are divided into good and bad, positive and negative, and anger, fear, and sadness are to be avoided. The young child experiences its emotions very spontaneously, so its emotions alternate in a natural rhythm. When a child is told to restrain its emotions, adjustments are made artificially to this natural flow, and emotions are unnaturally divided into categories of 'good' and 'bad.' The child no longer dares to trust its 'bad' emotions, so, when the child is angry or passionate, it tries to suppress those emotions, because it knows that expressing the emotions will not lead to approval from the grownups. If it feels strong fear, it will try to hold itself together and crowd out the fear, which means that part of its own sensitivity will disappear behind a closed door. Thus, the child as it grows up becomes alienated from itself and comes to believe that there are forbidden areas in its psyche. The originality, spontaneity, and life force hidden inside negative emotions are forced into the background, and the meaningful messages that the emotions often contain are not perceived by the person.

Emotions tell you what is really going on inside you, and they contain valuable clues about what you need to heal. As an example, when intense anger spontaneously arises within you, this indicates that something is affecting you, and it is often the case that your intense response of anger is disproportionate to the event that gave rise to it. You might get upset about something about which another person would get only slightly annoyed. If so, the emotion shows you that there is a deeper anger at work that is *independent* of the outside trigger. The emotion thus gives you the key information that unresolved pain exists that is in need of healing. Once you understand this, you can do something about it. To observe your emotions and see them as an instrument for self-knowledge can be enlightening and inspiring, even when it concerns difficult emotions such as anger or grief. To honestly look at what is going on inside you, and to embrace it even when you fear you will drown in your emotions is a sign of maturity.

As I have said, however, what often happens in human society is that emotions are viewed as something shameful or even repulsive, and therefore they need to be controlled or suppressed. By doing this, you become unable to communicate and to feel comfortable with a very essential and powerful part of yourself. Deep emotions – what you really feel – are often masked by socially acceptable behavior. If a crisis erupts, all your certainties and defense mechanisms fall apart, and you are confronted with violent emotions, such as fear, fright, panic, grief, anger, resistance, or despair. Your learned response to these negative emotions is: 'This is bad; I have to stop this; this is not allowed.' Unfortunately, this reaction magnifies your suffering, because you deny yourself the possibility of working together *with the emotions.*

These strong feelings of anxiety, sadness, or fear are not 'bad'. They are *natural* human responses to what is happening in your life. If you could accept them as understandable expressions of yourself, that alone would bring inner healing and give back to you a sense of strength. If you acknowledge your true feelings to yourself when you feel hurt or let down, when you feel very sad or very afraid, then you are *there* for yourself. You do not flee, but instead, you remain present and reach out to the fearful feelings. In a symbolic way, you put an arm around yourself, and in this way you say to yourself: 'I understand very well how you feel, and why you are responding in this way.' This way of lovingly reaching out to your own emotions is calming and reassuring, and by doing this, you realize that you have a deep inner strength that accepts and can relate to your intense emotions, as does a parent to a child.

This may well *not* be what you learned as a child, although there are now more parents who are open to this approach. When you suppress emotions, or try to ignore them, you are abandoning yourself, and this creates the feeling that you are being helplessly dragged down into a negative vortex. What most of you have learned in your youth has not helped you to be able to live through a dark night of the soul. You can, however, bring change here. When you find yourself emotionally affected by something, then observe and see if you react to your emotions with fear, resistance, or judgment. Do you try to hide how much it affects you or explain it away? Realize that the emotion has something to tell you. Appreciate that the tendency to immediately disallow your emotions is something that has been *taught* to you, and that doing so goes against your original nature. Release the emotion to its fullest expression and notice what thoughts accompany it, how it makes you tense up in certain parts of your body, how it affects your energy. Allow it to roll out like a huge wave onto a beach, and follow its movement with a clear and compassionate eye. Instead of resisting it, allow the emotion to emerge in your consciousness and fully observe it. You then will immediately notice a shift within yourself, because you then become the observer. It is when you allow the emotion to fully present itself to you that something else awakens in you: *the perspective of your soul*. The soul looks at the emotion and surrounds it with understanding; the soul does not judge, but rather always *allows*.

When you experience the connection with your soul, your pain lessens. The emotion of fear, sadness, or despair is surrounded by a field of compassion. Your soul is able to understand why some challenge happens in your life; your soul can convey to you a sense of confidence, even if your mind still does not understand the meaning of what is happening. This basic sense of trust is sufficient; it is often too early to understand, with your mind, the bigger perspective, which is the background to the challenge you are facing.

A crisis usually comes your way because you do *not* understand something that is vital to your own well-being and your ability to connect with your soul. There are negative beliefs or feelings that you are not aware of, and they create a cloud between you and your soul (the sun). The crisis, as it were, puts a magnifying glass on this cloud, this blind spot. For example, perhaps you have never really been able to take good care of yourself and stand up for your own needs. A basic feeling of self-esteem is missing. Now you enter into a relationship with another person who claims to be your friend but in the end shamelessly cheats and betrays you. You become overwhelmed by a sense of powerlessness mixed with rage, bitterness, and sadness. You are in a crisis, and at this point, there are two possibilities. Roughly speaking, you can either become overwhelmed by your emotions or use the crisis to create the self-esteem that was lacking in the first place.

When you let emotions overpower you, and you adhere to the notion that 'this should not have happened', you see the cause of your suffering as coming from outside you: your so-called friend is the perpetrator and you are the victim. Although this may be true at some level, you will get bogged down and become bitter and disillusioned if you only live from that level. Your emotions are then no instrument for self-knowledge; they are simply negative presences that you would like to get rid of if you only knew how.

The other option, which requires courage and determination, is to choose to accept what happened and to acknowledge your sense of being violated and hurt. As you allow your emotions to flow through you and you look at them directly, you discover that you are *more* than and *distinct from* those emotions: *you are their observer*. And this observer is quiet and neutral, and not accusing the other person who triggered the emotions, but rather is merely interested in *you*. As the observer, you may notice that there were signals from the start that the other person was not fully honoring you and that you were afraid to express your opinions or wishes in their company. You may become aware that your own needs were less important to you than theirs. It is like a deep feeling of unworthiness already present within you has been exposed and brought to light by the behavior of the other person. The actions of that person were able to affect you so deeply because of a basic sense of unworthiness that lay dormant inside you. By looking at the situation in this way, you are able to turn the external event of being betrayed into a meaningful message to yourself: *recognize your own darkness, let go of your ideas of being unworthy, and love yourself.* Thus, the crisis can initiate a new way of relating to yourself. From now on, instead of making yourself small and insignificant, you are more self-aware in your friendships with other people, and you treat yourself with more respect and dignity. This will attract people into your life who reflect back to you the appreciation you have for yourself.

From the perspective of the soul, there is purpose and meaning behind the things that happen to you. You often cannot immediately understand the significance of a situation, nor do you have to do so. It is enough when you can allow your emotions simply to be, while you are present as their observer, their witness. As you go through the emotional turmoil with as much trust and awareness as you can generate, the situation will gradually reveal the perspective of the soul. This may take quite some time, but trust that it *will* happen. At the moment of the challenge itself, it is enough if you can remain open to the notion that there *is* a perspective of the soul, even though what is happening shakes your faith in that possibility. The key is that you do not oppose your emotions but reach out toward them. Thus you become their master instead of their slave. Not a forcing, controlling master, but one who listens with quiet compassion and who accepts and allows everything to be just as it is.

Here is another example: imagine you are engulfed by a deep wave of fear that washes over you. The fear may have a specific cause, or it can arise from nowhere. The fear settles into your body and confuses your mind. Mastery at such a moment means that you remain present to that fear. You notice where you feel it in your body and how your thoughts are racing and raging, and how it appears as if you are doing nothing to rectify the situation. But you do not resist, and you do not frantically search for a solution, you simply allow the fear to be there, and you are present with it. What then happens is that a space opens up within you, and in that space, there is no fear, because in that space you open to your soul. It does not mean that you will immediately receive a message that helps you understand why the fear is there or why you have now to go through this experience. What *is* important, however, is that you then will have connected with the energetic reality of your soul through silence and your openness. You will begin to feel courage and a sense of trust, and you will know deep down that all is well.

Sometimes you experience such an opening to the soul, but a little later that space again feels overcome by fear. You no longer can simply witness, and you temporarily lose yourself in resistance, worry, or panic. Please be reassured that dealing with fear is not something you learn all at once. It is a process by which you familiarize yourself over and over again with the ability to be still and to be a witnessing presence to the fear. The more you practice and offer yourself to the process, the more the channel to your soul will open. You will then assuredly begin to experience a calm reassurance from a source deep within yourself, and you will know that you are in touch with your soul.

Again, when you can manage to keep open your inner space more often, the fear becomes less threatening and, in time, you will view the fear as you would a child who needs your comfort and encouragement. You will then take the position of the parent, the master, and you will be in more constant connection with your soul.

Unresolved or pent up emotions are as lost children who want to come Home. If they are not allowed to be present in your awareness, they cannot be healed and transformed. The soul strives toward wholeness on every level, and this is only possible when everything that lives in darkness is allowed to come into the light.

One can speak of a true dark night of the soul when the open space in your consciousness, which is the bridge to your soul, has been completely occupied by fear, resistance, sadness, or depression for an extended period of time. Then the connection with the soul becomes lost. When there is still an opening to the soul, the most distressing events can be borne with some degree of surrender and confidence. But if the connection to the soul is lost, you feel as if you are descending into a fathomless depth, and you lose all trust and joy in life. In a true dark night of the soul, a human being is beyond reach of the light and the wisdom of their soul. Someone who experiences this, loses every anchor within themselves. The dark emotions experienced are beyond the guidance of the loving parent and the quiet observer. Therefore, these emotions become larger and larger until one becomes mired in extreme loneliness and hopelessness. Yet this is never the end of the story.

There is always the possibility for return: *your soul never abandons you.* Even if *you* lose connection with your soul, *she* is still connected with you. From the cosmic realm of love and wisdom in which the soul resides, she continually reaches out to you, for you are infinitely dear to her. You will eventually receive the rays of light she transmits to you; *it cannot be otherwise.* No matter how deep a human being becomes engulfed in negativity, a desire for light remains, because you cannot indefinitely deny your deepest nature. For everyone, there comes a moment when the suffering becomes too heavy, and that is the time when something in you again opens to the light. Then the resistance, the shame, the pride, the stubbornness, the anger, or the fear that has stopped you from receiving the light is released. The night always comes to an end; the return of the light is inevitable. Please remember this when you feel utterly discouraged or beyond help. There is a saying that the darkest hour is just before the dawn. Deep crisis has the potential of bringing profound and abiding love into your heart.

In conclusion, I would like to say something to people who see a loved one suffer and drift into a dark night of the soul. Often you can do very little. Only the person experiencing the dark night of the soul can decide for themselves to reopen their heart to life, to change, and to transformation. *Have respect for the dark night of the soul.* Thus I began my story, and with this I will end. During a dark night of the soul, you experience what it is like to be completely separated from the living light that you essentially are. This is a distressing experience, and yet it is an experience that brings you in touch with the darkness within *that wants to be seen and acknowledged, that ultimately has to be seen and acknowledged in order to be released.* The soul is highly motivated to becoming whole. Even if, for the loved ones of someone who experiences a dark night of the soul, it is almost unbearable to witness, there is in that person at the soul level the ability, the courage, and the strength to fully live through this blackness and to come out of it with greater awareness and love. There inevitably comes a moment of opening up and waking up.

Of course, as a close partner or friend, you want to know what *you* can do to help them. If a person goes through a Dark Night, they will be almost completely cut off from other human beings, and it will be very hard getting through to them. What you can do for them is to *trust their soul*; even if they display behavior that is very destructive or immature, remember there is a light shining inside them, a light that is eternal and divine. If you can hold onto that, you are actually helping them become aware also of that presence inside them, and even if they do not respond at all to anything you say or do, connecting at the soul level is beneficial.

For you, it is important to note that the process in which your loved ones find themselves *is meaningful and is finite.* You cannot know when the moment of return will take place, and it helps your peace of mind when you release the need to know when that moment will come. You cannot force this type of process, but on the other hand, there can be a sudden breakthrough when you least expect it. When you are dealing with a loved one who experiences a dark night of the soul, it is very important to seek peace and quiet within yourself to enable you to hold on to *your* trust. It is also necessary to keep your distance and to feel where your involvement ends – setting limits is essential. You cannot and should not go into the darkness with them. The dark night of the soul is an individual journey for the human being experiencing it. This is a lonely, isolating experience, even terrifying at times, but it is also an experience that can open you to the presence of love in a way that will transform you forever.

11. Meeting with Your Shadow Self

I am Jeshua. On Earth, I was the carrier of the Christ energy. I brought the Christ energy among you, and you who are reading this have been touched by it. You, along with others, are now a carrier of the Christ energy. But what is this energy about; what is new in what it brings? The Christ energy is one of equality and brotherhood. When that energy is awakened in your heart, you recognize all others as part of the whole, and you have a living awareness of unity and equality.

To be able to hold to this awareness is of great importance, because your awareness has then become expanded. You can recognize yourself in other people, even with all their distinct differences from you. You do not judge how the other person behaves, or what they say, or how they look, because you connect with the *essence* of the other person, to that which is connected to your own essence. By perceiving their essence as your own, you activate both. In this way, you make a soul connection, a connection from heart to heart. *That* is what Christ consciousness is about.

Christ consciousness is present on Earth. I was one of its carriers, but no one human being can carry the full Christ consciousness. This field of awareness is much greater than I am. It is a unifying consciousness that radiates light to all who are willing and able to receive it. It is a field of energy that arises from the open hearts of human beings. This field becomes greater and more powerful on Earth when the heart of any human being is awakened, when *your* heart is awakened. You strengthen this field when your awareness becomes more expanded and when you release your judgments and experience unity with others.

Letting go of judgment and becoming more aware of oneness does not often happen by itself for human beings. Most of the time, you are not even aware of how much you are paralyzed by your judgments and your sense of separateness. Your identity as a human being usually depends on how much you *stand out* from others. You are encouraged to feel empowered by the fact that you are 'special' and unique and that you are superior to another person. In order for the heart of a human to awaken, a crisis is often needed that causes a deep shift in these perceptions, and this crisis is called the dark night of the soul.

How open your heart can be to others is determined by how loving you are to yourself. You can only receive another openly and completely when your heart has been opened fully to yourself. Most people's hearts are closed to themselves. Parts of themselves are hidden under lock and key, and the prison bars are comprised of social conventions, rules about good and evil, and a deep feeling of unworthiness. That is the collective heritage of all people on Earth.

Whether you have had a happy childhood or an unhappy one, stubborn views are present in your human environment concerning the sinfulness of humans that affect every growing child. These ideas do not only reach the child through its environment, they also come from within themselves, from the legacy of past lives their soul previously spent on Earth. *The deep-seated sense of unworthiness, which lies dormant in you all, is the greatest counter-force to the awakening of the Christ consciousness on Earth.*

In a dark night of the soul, the chains of the old consciousness become visible to an individual, and it is precisely this visibility that can break those chains. When a crisis occurs in your life, you are confronted with violent, often painful emotions in yourself; fear, anger, despair, and sadness overwhelm you and throw you off balance.

Is there a spiritual stronghold in yourself from which those emotions can be welcomed? Is there a center inside you from which those emotions can be quietly perceived? Often that stronghold, that center, is lacking in people, and then one can speak of a real crisis. You fall into a pit, and you no longer feel any solid ground to support you. You feel powerless and at the mercy of deep, painful emotions, and there is nothing to break your free fall. Feelings of unworthiness resurface, and they are the main reason why the foundation is missing. These feelings will take you into the heart of darkness, the darkest of the night. You can barely accept outside help, because you cannot receive anything for yourself, since, after all, you feel you are unworthy of help.

To lay the foundations of *self worth* – that unconditional acceptance of who you are – is something that no one else can do for you. If you have to depend on another – a parent, a friend, a teacher, a guru – the foundation remains shaky and fragile; only you can lay the groundwork. I want to help you take this step and to hold your hand, but I cannot force you, only encourage you. Only you can experience your own dignity and embrace it. When you receive yourself in that way – *with dignity* – you connect with me, and with what I came to bring: the Christ energy.

Christ is an energy that is greater than I am and includes both of us. Christ finds himself on the periphery of your inner space, and He waits there for you. Where your space is limited in its perspective, where you become mired in judgments or fear, it is Christ who beckons you. He shows you that you can move those boundaries; that whatever you are keeping outside yourself is allowed to be what it is and *can be admitted*. The places to which you say no, where you can no longer bring yourself to say yes to life, Christ, who invites you, stands ready to help. I am His messenger, and I reach out my hand to you. Go across that boundary and take my hand.

Just imagine that you are running with me through a desert. It is bare, and you are moving on an immense plain with the Earth under your feet and the wide open sky above your head. Feel how the elements act upon you. Because you have been running for so long, you are tired and thirsty, but the environment around you is bare and empty, and offers you nothing refreshing or nutritious. You feel anxious and lost, and see no clear path before you.

Soon, night descends in the desert, and it becomes dark and cold. Find a sheltered spot to sit. You are tired, and you are cold. You feel wretched, and tears are about to flow, because you no longer know what to do. You feel despair, because you have lost your way.

Feel my presence, open yourself to me. There is someone with me who wants to show itself to you here in the heart of the desert – it is your shadow self. It is the part of you that has for so long carried your fear and your dark emotions. This shadow self seeks redemption; it wants to be seen and accepted by you; it wants to belong to you. The dark night of the soul leads you to your shadow self, to the part of you that has long been suppressed and that you have resisted. But to confront your shadow self feels threatening, which is why I am with you.

Imagine this: it is night, you are in the middle of the desert and you sense the presence of another being in the dark of whom you feel wary, yet rest assured, because I stand next to you. Ask this being to reveal itself to you. Maybe you first see the light of its eyes in the darkness. Focus on those eyes and remember that this being carries your pain and fear; that it is more afraid of you than you are of it. It has, in fact, been ostracized for a very long time and has felt compelled to live in the shadows.

Your shadow self is withdrawn, so its needs are not easily revealed. You must call it forward and welcome it, *and you can do this*. Open your heart and call to this being. Feel your compassion extend to a being who has for so long been burdened down by the pain of rejection and loneliness. Your shadow self feels itself to be an outcast who has been deprived of human companionship, of warmth, and of brotherhood for such a very long time.

I am with you and I light a campfire in the middle of the night. Let us sit around it, the three of us. Give me your hand and extend your other hand to your shadow self, so the three of us together form a circle, holding each other's hands. See if you can manage to allow your shadow self into this circle of light and warmth. If you welcome this part of yourself, it will come closer, because it longs to be appreciated and accepted by you. Your openness makes the coming together possible. When you allow this lost and rejected one to join with you, something special happens – *you come Home to yourself.*

Allow the energy of acceptance and appreciation to flow among the three of us. I am here to protect you and to reassure you, and I am the one who creates the bridge between you both. I am not someone or something outside you, *I am within you*. Let this energy circulate quietly among the three of us, so we merge with one another.

When you make peace with your shadow self, you become a healed human being with your two feet planted firmly on the ground and with an open heart to all that lives. A space has been opened in your heart that enables you to love yourself, and you can share that space with others. In this way, the Christ light appears and is experienced on Earth.

12. The Eye of the Hurricane

I am Mary Magdalene. I am here as your companion and fellow traveler; I am your sister. I salute you in these turbulent times, in which many things are turned inside out, and dark and hidden aspects are ushered into broad daylight. In the middle of this chaos and crisis, which you may experience in your own life as well, I invite you to be with me, in silence. Together we are in the eye of the hurricane: a place of absolute quiet and stillness in the midst of the raging storm.

As long as you are in the eye of the hurricane, you can take part in life without being swept along by the many winds that surround you. These gusts contain erratic emotional energies which may sweep you off your feet if you do not take good care of yourself, or if you are very open to the energies of other people, or if you are trying to help them too much.

Much is stirring in the realm of Earth. This is part of the transformation humanity as a whole is going through. You are experiencing this transition yourself on the inner level. You, who are reading this, are walking ahead of mass consciousness, and you already have one foot in a different and new world. That is why it is essential that you return to the silent space within, again and again. In this eye of the hurricane, you can *be* and *observe* without being dragged into the intense emotional energies awakened by this time of transition.

Inside the eye of the hurricane, there is a gateway to another level of consciousness. As you pass through that gate, you will find yourself in a flow of stillness, compassion, and wisdom, and you will seemingly withdraw from the hustle and bustle of everyday life. However, it only seems that you withdraw, because you are actually very present, but from another level of awareness. You look differently at situations; you do not judge them; you watch them with compassion, yet you always keep some distance. If you notice emotional turmoil in someone you care for, you do not jump in to take care of them and 'save' them. Your detachment arises from wisdom, not from indifference. You have amassed this wisdom throughout your many lives on Earth, and these times call for precisely that wisdom within you to come forth.

Remember moments in your past in which you let go of fear, negativity, and darkness. Feel the power of those moments, the freedom you gained, and acknowledge your own maturity and strength. Allow your breath to quietly descend into your belly, and connect to the ancient wisdom that dwells there. Accept that you are wise. Call on your wisdom when you are dealing with pain and sorrow or with situations that trigger old emotions which may overwhelm you if you do not realize *who you have now become*. Let these old emotions be, and stay in the eye of the hurricane. Observe the upheaval with the eyes of the crone, the wise old woman inside you.

I am appealing to the female aspect of wisdom here, as the female energy is perfectly suited to guide you through these times of crisis and transformation. Mature female energy is flexible and flowing, it does not hold on to rigid patterns and structures, nor does it take up arms against what is old and bogged down. The female face of wisdom radiates kindness and understanding, while at the same time embodies the radical power of true surrender: *letting go without looking back*. Complete surrender is what is asked of you in these times. Do not waste your energy battling the old, or saving the world or other people. Go within, and enter the gate to the new world with serenity and quiet knowing.

The crone, or wise woman, has gathered her strength within and is completely centered. She exudes peace and weathered wisdom, and she touches people with these qualities as she interacts with them. If you find her within, you will have found access to the New Earth. The wise woman inside you knows that spirituality is about taking good care of yourself just as much as taking care of others. She knows how to balance the flows of giving and receiving.

Dare to receive, to take yourself seriously, and to speak your truth without guilt or shame. No longer burden yourself with the many do's and don'ts you have been taught. These rules are old and many of them are fear-based. Seek out the people and the activities that resonate with you. The female energy in her higher appearance gently pushes you to surrender to the new and break free from the old.

The male energy also plays a vital role in the transition from old and fear based thinking to heart based awareness. This role has to do with *discernment*. The female energy is by its nature aimed at connecting and merging, whereas the male energy helps you *to be your own person,* respectful of your own boundaries. The ability to be yourself, and to be *different*, is crucial in these days. This is not about standing out in a competitive or aggressive way. It is about being self aware and open, and clear about who you are and how you feel. To embrace heart based awareness, you need to be able to say no to something or someone challenging you to regress into the energy of fear and struggle.

Imagine a wise old man, a sage. What do you see? Is it a priest, a wizard, an Indian, or perhaps Buddha? Go with what spontaneously presents itself to you. Notice how the sage exudes something unbending, unyielding, even if his eyes are kind and friendly. This man is true to himself, he dares to be a loner. He is a leader, not a follower, yet there is no aggression in his appearance, only calm. This is self awareness without ego.

Inside you, both sources of wisdom are available, the crone *and* the sage. Whether you are physically a man or a woman, you have access to both, because your soul has lived lives both as a man and a woman. Feel the richness of your past. From this wealth of wisdom you are able to enter the New Earth, so release your burdens. I invite you to travel with me in your imagination to this new reality. You can sense the energy of the New Earth in your body right now. Let your attention go down into your abdomen, to the open space in the area of your sacrum, which is a sacred space. Your breath touches this space each time you breathe in and out. Your attention may wander away ever so often up to your head, which is full of thoughts that sap your energy and seduce and fragment you and keep you away from the stillness deep down in your sacrum. *Be* the eye of the hurricane and let the storm of your thoughts and emotions rage, but stay in your center – stay in your belly.

You need not oppose or control your thoughts. If you try to do that, you will still be in your head, fighting thoughts with other thoughts. It is better to simply move your awareness elsewhere. Focusing your awareness on something is not the same as thinking about it. Awareness is an open space, and that to which you give your awareness will grow as a result. If you focus on silence and peace and savor it, the storm of your thoughts will die down. However, many people do not enjoy silence, because it feels like desolate emptiness to them. They are used to the flurry of thoughts in their heads, and this gives them a sense of safety, even if the thoughts are worrisome and not uplifting. It takes courage to be in silence, so go there with me. Only if you dare to risk feeling empty and at a loss can you be free of the hold that your repetitive thoughts have on you.

You are on the threshold of the New Earth, and being in the eye of the hurricane, silently and peacefully, is healing and liberating for you. You long for inner peace, and this longing is a sign of discernment. The world can no longer fulfill your needs, and you need to resist its clamor and agitation. As you go inward, and you follow the thread of silence and wisdom inside, you bring the New Earth closer, and not just for you, but for others as well. By going with the flow of peace and wisdom, you radiate the energy of the New Earth outwardly to others. This happens effortlessly; you need not work for it.

Many of you have become accustomed to caring for others in a way that depletes you. You give so much of yourself to your loved ones, your friends or people in need, that you end up feeling exhausted and disillusioned. You have tried to give too much, and often you have tried to lift people up to a level of consciousness for which they are not yet ready.

This way of giving is not part of the New Earth. This old way of expending your energy makes you lose your center, your inner peace and balance. The new way of giving is very different. You give simply by *being yourself.* You need not choose between being true to yourself and being true to other people. By entering the eye of the hurricane, you become an example of balance to others; you make the energy of peace and wisdom palpable and available through your eyes, words, and actions. Whether other people are receptive your vibration is up to them.

It may seem as if you step back and withdraw yourself from your loved ones, and indeed, you will no longer carry their emotional burdens; you will return to them the responsibility for their own life. And taking on their burdens was never an effective way of supporting them to begin with. Genuine help means you encourage them to get in touch with their own powerful light. You nudge them onward by stimulating them to believe in themselves and also by rejecting any inclination on their part to become emotionally dependent on you.

Your sense of obligation toward others is actually one of the major stumbling blocks to achieving inner peace and entering the New Earth. You have deceived yourselves into believing that you need to be there for other people, and when you step into the eye of the hurricane you feel guilty. The biggest obstacle to achieving that state of peace is not that you are so busy, or too much inside your head; it is that you are not *allowing* yourself to go there. Inside you is a deep sense of unworthiness that tells you not to break away from ingrained social norms and, rather, to be nice, sweet, and malleable. You have suppressed your radical nature, the part of you that accepts nothing less than truth and liberation – *that* is the problem.

From your birth in this lifetime onward, your soul has nudged you to be at peace with yourself and to express your innate wisdom in the world. At the time of your birth, you had already acquired a lot of experience and knowledge from other lives; you were mature and wise on the soul level. You are naturally inclined to seek the answers to life's questions on the inner level. As a mature soul, you are less fascinated by the world and what it has to offer. The tendency to give away too much of yourself, in spite of that, is caused by the fact that you have not been taught *to really value yourself as you are*. You still hesitate to fully show the world who you are. You are inclined to hide yourself and regard your true nature as something that should be kept secret.

You have experienced rejection during several lifetimes, and this harsh treatment has hurt you so deeply that you have decided to repress your true nature by not revealing yourself to others anymore. This has caused your sensitive, loving, and empathic side to become more dominant than your radical, innovative, and unwavering side – *you have become unbalanced and made yourself small*. Your empathic, sensitive side has been received with appreciation by the outside world, which is why you got lost in giving too much of yourself and neglecting your inner core.

It is now of great importance that lightworkers recognize this imbalance and start to embrace and honor their true nature. Surrender to your desire for Home. This Home is right here on Earth; it is not in some heaven or otherworldly dimension far away. You can get there by really coming Home to yourself, descending into the middle of your abdomen, your sanctum, and becoming very quiet. The eye of the hurricane is your Home, your anchor in this world. It is the place where you recharge your energy and remember your divine nature. By going there frequently, you will receive insights and inspiration about your life's path. The New Earth is a place where you can fully express who you are. By embracing your true nature now, you draw the New Earth closer and become a channel for it.

13. On Depression

I am your sister, Mary Magdalene. I am right beside you as your close friend. I am not elevated above you, but one whom you know from within. Feel for a moment our deep connection – we are one, part of the same family.

I, too, have known and explored the depths of being human on Earth, and in my life as a friend and beloved of Jeshua, I was touched by a bright light that took hold of me and has inspired me to this day. I have known the extremes of light and dark. Those extremes are poles that belong together; they are each other's driving force, so to speak. Even though light and dark seem to call up opposite feelings, there is a hidden connection between them: one cannot function without the other. Savoring the beauty and healing power of light is possible only for someone who has experienced its absence and who has intimate knowledge of the dark.

Never is light more palpable and rejuvenating than when you emerge from a dark, cold night. Nothing is more magical than the first rays of the sun, bathing the world in pure and fresh morning light. Contrast creates dynamics – movement, growth, change – and so yes, darkness has a role to play in our lives. As a human being though, you often experience darkness as the antithesis of light, as a trap or pit instead of a driving force for change and growth. Down in that pit it seems like you have lost all connection with light, and you feel hopeless and desperate.

You are all familiar with feeling cut off from light and being deprived of a sense of meaning and purpose in your life. When that feeling persists and you lose all sense of hope and direction, it can feel like you are dying. In fact, there is no such thing as physical death, because as soon as your body dies you live on in another body and you are very much alive both during and after the transition. But there is a kind of emotional death that occurs when you feel so stuck that it feels like choking, not physically, but emotionally. Your feelings do not flow naturally anymore, your mind is playing the same negative tunes over and over, and you feel deeply weary and alienated from yourself. This is when you have been hit by depression. You are disconnected from the living light that you are, and all inner movement ceases. You feel dead inside, and this sense of 'being without living' is one of the most painful states a human being can experience.

Travel along with me for a moment. Descend with me into that depressed state and investigate it with a curious and open mind. What happens if someone loses all hope, shrinks back, and feels powerless against all the feelings that well up from within? Usually this reaction is triggered by exterior events that are disruptive - events that a person is unable to place in their frame of reference, and which make everything in that person's life become uncertain. It can be big things, such as the death of someone close, becoming ill, losing one's job, or the breakup of a relationship. These are events that affect people deeply, and can bring them to the edge of the abyss.

However, the darkness can sometimes also reveal itself from within, without a clear cause on the outside. Old emotional burdens that you once stored in your soul's memory come to the surface. Painful experiences, possibly stemming from previous lives, spring up from your depths, and you have to deal with dark feelings, fears, and doubts. Deep experiences of lack, loneliness, and of being defeated can enter into your psyche without reason. They can make you lose your footing as much as any outward event that happens to you.

When someone gets caught in a depression, in a 'dark night of the soul', it always comes with the experience of being engulfed and unable to cope with all the emotions. The flow of painful, heavy emotions is experienced as being too great to bear. You are overpowered by them, or so it feels, and you shut down from a deep sense of powerlessness. At the moment you turn away and refuse to face the emotions, you become stuck. Those emotions want to flow; it is essential to emotions that they continue moving onward, like the surge of a big wave onto a beach. But you are afraid to allow that, so you refuse to go along with that movement and you pull back from these flooding emotions. You build a dam, a barrier, and you say: 'I cannot deal with this. I do not want this. I want to be done with it'. Your reaction, often out of a sense of sheer powerlessness, creates a depression, which is a state of numbness and of being closed off from life. Over time, that situation becomes unbearable, and you no longer want to live.

From an earthly perspective, you want to die because life is intolerable. Seen from the soul's perspective, you *are* dead (in the sense of completely stuck), and it is an experience so unbearable that you want to do everything you can to put an end to this situation. The desire for death is essentially a desire for change, a desire to live again. People who wish to commit suicide have a deep desire for life, not for death. It is precisely this feeling of being dead inside that drives them to extreme despair. It is their urge to live that leads them to terminate their physical life.

When you experience depression, there is in you a combination of deep resistance and at the same time extreme vulnerability. The depression is a way to defend yourself against the enormous power of the emotions that threaten to engulf you. You think they will destroy you, so in your powerlessness you build a shell around yourself; you wrap yourself in a cocoon of not wanting or being able to feel anything. You do not want to be here any longer, and like the proverbial ostrich with its head in the sand, you are suffocating, and yet that seems the only possible way out. After a time you no longer are able to get your head out of the sand, the depression. You have become so closed off from life and from any feelings that you are no longer able to turn things around and effect a change; the choice to say yes to your emotions seems to lie beyond your power. The depression has now reached a climax.

On the one hand, you cannot accept your emotions of fear, despair, sadness, and loneliness, or share them with others, while on the other hand, you know and feel that it is agonizingly painful to live *without* emotions; that it is a form of death, a total denial of your living core. After a time, you want to feel again. The pain of *not feeling* becomes greater than the pain of *feeling* your emotions. That is your salvation, and this is the turning point. The refusal to feel, and constantly saying: 'No, I can't, I don't want it, I want to be dead, I want to disappear', finally makes you so hollow and empty inside that you can no longer sustain it. What happens from the perspective of the soul is that life is now becoming stronger; it cannot be held back indefinitely. When the life force has been restrained strongly for a very long time, it creates an opposing force that eventually erupts. The strength of the tidal wave that wants to roll out onto the beach cannot be held back forever. At a certain moment, from within you, emerges a 'yes', even if you are not consciously aware of it. Nothing is static in life; the urge for life is unstoppable. When a climax has been reached, you create events in your life that provoke a change, that create a breakthrough.

Sometimes this happens in the form of a suicide attempt. If it fails, there may be an upward spiral, because the suffering of that person becomes very visible to the outside world. When someone discovers how much other people care about them, there may arise an opening to more light, and to the receiving of understanding and sympathy. However, it may also happen that someone does not open up and remains depressed. There is no fixed recipe for how a breakthrough occurs. However, life has a pushing and driving force that makes it impossible to linger endlessly in a static state of consciousness.

Even when the earthly life ends by actually taking your own life, you immediately have to face new choices on the other side, because you will still have to experience your feelings there. The gloom that you experienced while alive, with its accompanying feelings of pain and anxiety, is now able to come forward even more sharply, and in a less veiled way. Sometimes the astral realm where you end up after death confronts you directly with the emotions that you repressed, and through this they begin to flow again. For example, someone may feel desperate and horrified when they have passed over and discover that life has not really ended. Or they see the emotions of their family on Earth, their grief and sadness, and are very affected by it. By being so touched, a new movement can be set in motion in the soul who has passed over. It can lead to a breakthrough, making that soul open to receive help from guides who are always there, both on Earth and in heaven. Help is *always* available, provided you are open to it.

No matter which way you twist or turn, life is more powerful than any death wish. Life always reassumes its right to be, you cannot kill it; therefore, there is always hope. Hold on to that hope for yourself, but also for others whom you see suffering. Things *can* seem so hopeless at times, but there is always another outlook, even though you cannot imagine in your mind how that can be and how change is ever going to take place. Life is always stronger than death, the light stronger than the dark. The water eventually breaks through the dam, because water has the power to move: it pushes, *it is alive!* The power of the water is stronger than the resisting force that wants to hold it back.

Feel the driving force of life in yourself for a moment. Each of you sometimes finds yourself with persistent patterns that repeat themselves endlessly: doubts about yourself, feelings of inferiority, uncertainty, mistrust, anger, resistance. Now imagine that those parts are just there, and that life continues to flow around them at the same time. The water continues to flow, and although there remain boulders in the stream that seem so fixed and unmoving, they still are worn down by the movement and pushing of the water moving past them. It takes time, but do not forget who you are: *you are the living water!* The more you remind yourself of that, the more you can

126

reclaim the energy from those boulders and stones that lie in the stream. There is pain from the past that continues to be there. You do not have to downplay that, or make it irrelevant, but neither do you have to lug those boulders from the river. You only have to remind yourself that *you are the water!*

This can be difficult at times because, in part, you have become identified with those boulders that block your energy: 'I am someone who is not properly grounded; I have difficulty feeling at home on Earth; I carry sadness and traumas from the past', and that is all true. But imagine for a moment those ideas as rocks or stones in a large, wide river – a huge waterway – because that is who you are; that is your actual life force. It is your soul that flows and flows, always along its path: alive, bubbling, rushing and roaring, exploring and discovering. That flow has no judgment about those boulders that it encounters, *it engulfs them*. You do have a choice!

Of course, you occasionally get caught in such a blockage when you begin to identify with it for too long. You can detach from that obstruction, however, simply by experiencing yourself as the flowing water. Remember that you are a living, soul-consciousness, always moving and flowing and not confined to those boulders – *you are free*. The more you withdraw your sense of identity from those blockages, the rocks that lie there, the more easily the current can dislodge them and carry them downstream with the flow. They are liberated because you release your identity with them and identify instead with the dynamic, moving water. *The water is your soul, and it cannot be restrained.* Feel it flowing and moving and sparkling. Imagine that it is washing over you, and feel the bubbling strength, the light that glistens within it. Feel how your soul, in its deepest essence, is not threatened by the darkness that you experience, by those boulders that appear to be so solid and unyielding. Your soul is not at all troubled by them, because it knows they are an integral part of the landscape of life. Try, when you feel that you are imprisoned within such a boulder, to hear the water rushing by. Remember the water and the ease with which it flows, and remember that, in truth, you *are* that water.

You do not have to do everything yourself; life provides you with endless opportunities and possibilities. It might at times bring you into deep, dark valleys, but it also propels you up again into the light. Even when you have the feeling of no longer being able to struggle on, and you cannot see how things can possibly ever turn out well, life *still* propels you. The art of living is to preserve your trust, even when there seems to be nothing left to trust, and when everything of which you were certain has disappeared from your life.

At this time on Earth, many people are involved with the processing of ancient darkness; parts of the soul are coming into the light right now and want to be seen. And why is that so? *Because you are making a leap forward.* It really is a leap in the evolution of human consciousness as a whole. This leap cannot be made without embracing the darkest places in your consciousness, those that are filled with fear, distrust, or a very deep sadness about everything you have experienced on Earth. Do not be afraid of that darkness – *welcome it!* When you say yes to the darkness, it begins to release and flow, and that is the art of living this life. And when you feel: 'I can't really say yes to this', remember there is something in you that *still* says yes. That is what will save you and bring you farther along – *trust in life*.

I love you all, you are dear to me. Maybe you think: 'How can that be? You cannot personally know us all'. But you as a human do not know or realize how extensive the network of souls really is. When you have connected with another from the heart, that is a permanent connection. A bond once forged will not separate through time, because in our dimension *there is no time*. There is a living network connecting us as souls. We share a certain history, a certain desire, a flame that was once ignited in our consciousness. With this flame, the Earth becomes gradually lit. The awakened consciousness in all people brings us together and creates a new foundation from which that leap into consciousness is really going to take place. You do not need to ponder over this; stay with your own process, your own way – that is sufficient. Feel the powerful thrust of life, not only in you, but in so many others, through which a wave of new consciousness is flooding over the Earth.

14. The Inner Judge

I am Jeshua, I am in your midst and hold your hands. You are not alone in your life on Earth; you are surrounded by support, love, and encouragement from our side, from beyond the earthly dimension. The heavenly realm from which you emerged when you were born is still close to you. It is the realm in which your soul dwelt and felt at Home before it came to Earth. At times you get lost in the illusions, the fears, and the negativity on Earth, but remind yourself when that happens that Home is very near. Feel it around you *here* and *now*, through the presence of guides – dear friends on the other side, your brothers and sisters. They are involved with you and your path, in what you do in your life, *here* and *now*. If you could only feel their presence, how different would be your experience of life.

When a human being, as a soul, makes the decision to be born again on Earth and to live as a human being, a whole team of guides, helpers, and teachers are involved who travel along with that soul. *You are really much less alone than you think.* You do not need to know exactly who are here around you, but it is important to make an emotional connection, in order to put yourself at ease.

Know that this life on Earth is to a certain extent a game, a voyage that you make. Very close by is that other reality that is infinite and limitless, and where you are connected with friends and loved ones. Feel their presence with you now, as you read these words. Feel what they want to say to you. Their voices and their messages are so very different from the messages you often give yourself. You often are so severe and negative about yourself, about what you have or have not accomplished, about what you should or could have done, but did not do. So strong is this self-criticism that your radiance, your light suffers under it. With this kind of judgment, you demean yourself and block the free expression of your soul.

Compare that negative self-criticism that accompanies you throughout your days with how your guides and friends from the other side see you. Imagine them standing before you -- what radiates from them to you? It is awe and respect for who you are and what you undertake on Earth. It is also kindness and companionship; it is support and encouragement. These are the energies they want to envelop you with.

How would it be if you could really receive that energy in your life, if you could really see yourself through *their* eyes? Try to imagine that for a moment. See their radiant figures, their kindness; they stand in a circle around you. Enter into these loving friendly beings around you and imagine that you see yourself through their eyes. Or choose one from among them who stands out for you and enter into that person. Feel the open heart of that guide, that friend, and with how much compassion he or she looks at you. From a realm of unity and connection, that guide looks at you and at your path on Earth, and through those eyes, for a moment, see your own energy or aura. See if you can perceive how you carry a burden, how you are suffering under a burden of negative self-judgment: that you always have the feeling you are not quite sufficient as you are; that you have to be better or other than you are; that you have failed.

How does your guide see that? And can you become aware of the burden that you carry? It is obvious that for many of you it has become as familiar as a second skin that you no longer notice. You think it is right and normal to always criticize yourself, to comment on and to evaluate yourself, and to plan how you must be different than you are, how you will do things differently, and then how your life will be better. That voice removes you from the *here* and *now*, and therefore creates more fear than is necessary.

There are some things in life that *do* create fear for good reasons. Imagine you are running through a forest and you encounter a bear; then you have a *real* reason to be afraid! Or you cross the street, and suddenly a car comes toward you; then you also have a reason to be scared. Here you can speak of fears 'with a purpose', of a real fear that helps you to take the right action in that moment: to hide under a tree or take a step backward. But the fear that usually accompanies you in your everyday life is not a realistic or helpful fear. It stems from constantly judging and condemning yourself, eventually causing that fundamental feeling of unworthiness, of having to do better, and thus feeling agitated and under pressure. This fear is like a constant static sounding in the background that makes you restless and gives you the feeling of never being able to relax.

Fear then becomes something chronic that could affect your body in the end. Every day, you feel tense and your emotions follow the lead of your worried mind. This is how many people live, and it is far removed from your natural state. *You are meant to be free*, to live according to your nature as it is given to you, spontaneously, and not as the result of long and arduous work on yourself. And how do you get there? How do you break through that constant background noise of judgment and fear that drives you on? The first step is to recognize that the noise *is* there. How often do you deflate yourself with your thoughts by criticizing and evaluating yourself, and you do not even notice that you do this; it has become second nature.

You no longer know how it feels to actually send positive and nourishing thoughts to yourself. Doing that appears to you as artificial, as fake, as a contrivance. Is that not really sad, actually, that you are so familiar with negativity that you no longer recognize it? It is a grey veil that hangs over people, but they no longer perceive it as such. Your guides do, however. They see very clearly that you do not have to hide under that grey veil. That is why they try to remind you continually of the *real* you who is hidden under that veil and to encourage you to throw it off. It *is* acceptable to be different and you *are* allowed to break loose from the judgments and the fears that have been imposed on you for centuries. This entire pattern has been passed on from generation to generation, and that is why it has become so deeply ingrained.

Make no mistake about how such patterns arise. Who or what has forever pointed out to you that you are not good as you are? That you must obey, must adapt yourself, that you must strive to do your very best, that you have to work assiduously to earn approval? Who or what has forever told you that? It is the men in power who use these ideas to suppress people.

When human beings feel separate from the Source, they can try to bridge that gap by grasping for power. And power is exercised by making other people believe that they do not know what is right for themselves and that they need others - some authority - to show them the way. In this way, the person yearning for power can set themselves up as the leader, as the authority, as that someone upon whom others must depend – that is what power does. A ruler benefits when people deem themselves less worthy. That gives rulers the capability of extending and exercising power. Exercising power is actually the same as exercising control, and in many societies on Earth, people have been controlled in many ways for many centuries.

The need for power, and the urge to demean people to gain control over them, exist deep within the collective psyche of humans. All people take part in this collective psyche, this collective energy, and all people have in the course of their lifetimes played both roles, as a ruler of power and as their victim. Actually, humanity is still to a great extent chained to this power game. And many of you experience the remnants of this tradition as an inner voice that is negative, criticizing, judging, which is basically an expression of the way power has been exercised for many centuries in human societies. A sense of unworthiness has become second nature.

It is true that much has changed and that there are many more free societies on Earth than there were in the past. However, becoming free from power in your mind and heart requires a deep and thorough transformation in individuals. Only when this awakening of individuals takes place on a large scale is all of society influenced and the structures change. However, those structures first have to collapse to create room for new ones, and this process is now underway.

It is now time to break free from the past, but do not underestimate the paralyzing influence of the past and that of the tradition of which you are a part. You can liberate yourself only by fully realizing what influences there are and how they manifest in you as an individual: how you are still bound by the chains of power and powerlessness. A part of you suffers from the negative judgments that you have about yourself. You often chastise yourself with your thoughts as with a whip, but who is the one doing that? Inside you lives a ruler, a controller, who does the judging and demeaning. See if you can become aware of that figure and observe it. It does not really matter how you visualize him, but it can help to imagine him as a judge.

Look within yourself. You probably know the negative thought patterns you have when you evaluate others, but look especially at those that arise when you evaluate yourself. They can manifest in the form of perfectionism, dissatisfaction, impatience with yourself, anger, or self-doubt. Imagine that you allow the energy of those negative thought patterns to take the form of a judge. Maybe he is a man wearing a long robe and a white wig. It does not matter how you picture him, but look at the expression on his face. How does he look at you? How do you react to his energy, to what he expresses? What is his overall mood? And look especially at how he behaves toward you. In what way does his voice, his manner, make an impression on you?

Observe him impersonally while sensing the impact of his energy upon you. This is the energy of power, and it has been impressed upon you in the past. This energy causes the burden that you carry around: the self-denial, the dimming of your own light, your individuality, and originality.

Now imagine for a moment that you are still surrounded by your guides, your friends, your brothers and sisters from the other side. They see who you are; they see your original and natural light. And now, together with your guides, you confront the inner judge. 'Go stand away from me,' you say to him, and you direct him there. In that way, the judge is now outside your energy field. Sense how doing this affects you. Do you feel any heaviness drop away? Perhaps you sense this release directly in your body. In what way do you feel things become clearer within yourself? And what can you allow yourself to do or be now that he is gone? If you can easily feel or see energy or colors, you might perceive that something has changed in your aura, that it now has brighter colors and is more playful. But you may also simply feel more relaxed, when all those 'shoulds' and pressures drop away.

See if you can allow that figure of the judge to retreat even farther. Feel free and liberated. There is a lot more space around you if that voice falls away. The space becomes quieter and more open, and you become more grounded with both feet on the Earth. Your head becomes less crammed with demands; it seems as though you have been in a trance for years, for centuries. Feel how sad that is, that for so long you were convinced by others that you are a failure; that you are not good as you are; that you have to change yourself, to elevate yourself; that you are not allowed to follow your natural, spontaneous nature. Be aware of the depth of suppression that has been there. It is precisely that realization that helps to liberate you *from* the suppression. It is that journey of discovery that you undertake with yourself when the old, layer by layer, is slowly peeled off and you discover how beautiful you are, how pure and simple.

Take the time for that journey. It may happen that the figure of the judge, the critic, will at times return to your energy field. It is a stubborn figure, but now you know who he is. You can continue to instruct him to withdraw. You can remember who you are and demand mastery over your own energy field. You *are* the master, and not in the sense of being a ruler, but in the sense that you are a child of light who has the right to be and express who you are. You are good and loveable and worthy *just as you are*.

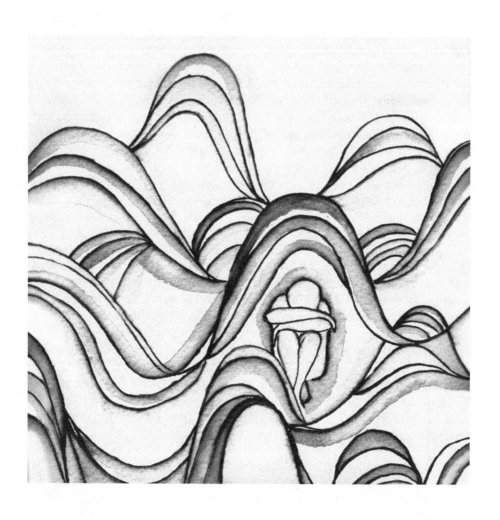

15. Two Types of Darkness

I am Jeshua, an old friend who loves to share this afternoon with you, simply being together in the energy of love and unity. This is something you desire so much, because quite often you feel adrift and lost in life on Earth. I am here to remind you of the truth that lives within you, in your soul. It is not observable with the naked eye, and you often lose touch with that truth when you are busy and involved in your many activities, duties, and responsibilities.

Please take a moment to become still and to let all those external pressures fall away. Sense the silence deep within you. The silence in your heart is not a void, but a *full presence* that can be only sensed if you take a step back from the hustle and bustle of your everyday life. We are here today to take that step back in order for you to remember who you are and to revitalize yourself with the fullness of silence in your heart. This enables you to begin to live again, but now with more ease and joy.

Life seems to be a battle at times, but that is not how it is meant to be. You are essentially here to experience yourself, to remember your strength and your beauty as radiant angels of light, and to share that light with others. By doing that you will feel at home on Earth. Life will become simple again, easy and joyful.

So go within, together with me, and remember the Source from which you came: the imperishable, eternal light that is ever moving and changing, taking new forms, and still always undivided and One. You are part of that stream, and in fact, *nothing bad can happen to you.* You are safe and whole even now, dwelling in your earthly body. You are safe even in this world, which seems to be dominated by struggle and conflict.

Today we talk about light and darkness, and about bringing light *into* darkness. And what is darkness? It is something that evokes resistance in you as a human being. No one wants to experience darkness; no one wants to suffer pain, sadness, or fear; yet it is part of our life. So why is that darkness there?

People have asked this question for centuries. Now, to start with, much depends on how you ask the question. Do you ask the question from an attitude of openness: 'Why is there darkness, why is this happening to me, what should I do with it?' Or do you pose the question from fear, anger, and resistance: 'Why on earth is that darkness present in my life, and how can I beat or avoid it?' Feel the despair and the resistance expressed in the latter question, and recognize those emotions within yourself, because it such a human reaction to resist what feels dark, unwholesome, or difficult.

The deepest challenge to you as a human being is to say yes to situations that you initially refuse to accept; to say yes to what you want to avoid at all costs. It requires great inner strength to say yes to what comes into your life in the form of darkness. If you cannot find that strength -- which is understandable -- and you say 'no,' you harden in opposition to that which happens, and the darkness becomes deeper and the despair increases.

There are actually two kinds of darkness in life. The first darkness is something external that happens to you on your path in life. It can be a divorce from someone you love, the loss of a loved one, a disease, or an accident. In short, it could be anything that deeply distresses you in the form of a crisis or a major setback. I will call this darkness *one*.

And then there is your *reaction* to darkness *one*, your emotional response. Every human being is inclined to initially resist fate, to rail against the darkness. But if you keep up your resistance and close down and keep saying no by passing judgment on what is happening in your life, then there is an additional layer of darkness, a second kind of darkness. I will call this darkness *two*; it surrounds darkness *one*.

Darkness *one* brings you into a level of intense, deep emotions. Something happens in your life that brings a lot of grief, fear, and pain, and as you experience those emotions, you are very much alive. Life flows through you like a thundering wave. Can you allow this to happen? Deep emotional blows strike you – they shock you – and then it becomes a question of whether you have the strength to trust that there is something in that experience that will take you somewhere that you would like to go. If you do find that inner strength, you begin to trust that life has meaning, even though you, as a human being, often do not understand the meaning.

To put it even more clearly, darkness *one* invites you to accept that your soul may have *chosen* to have this experience, perhaps to bring something hidden to the surface, to heal something you did not know needed healing. A pivotal moment of choice then arises when you are confronted with the options of either accepting and opening up or resisting and closing down.

It is most common still for humans to want to say no. I will not say it is wrong, but by doing so, you are putting an extra layer of darkness (which I have called darkness *two*) *onto* the darkness already present (darkness *one*). Darkness *two* comes from within; it is your reaction to darkness *one*. If you persist in saying no, the flow of your emotions will come to a stop, and you, too, will become immobile by saying, 'No, I do not want to experience this; I refuse; I cannot accept it'. If you persist, you will be filled with resentment, anger, and bitterness. These sentiments are not really emotions; they are *judgments* that freeze the natural flow of emotion inside you. Darkness *two* prevents life from flowing through you; you have put up walls and defenses. In the end, this may attract grave forms of darkness to you, such as deep despair, alienation, and depression. When you are in a deep depression, the flow of life has almost halted. You feel dead inside.

Life is always subject to change. Life inherently holds the possibility for growth and healing, for a new birth, if you trust it at a basic level. But if you persist in saying no, you shut out that possibility. You keep insisting that life is not as it should be, and as you judge life in this way, you disconnect yourself from life and can sink to the deepest darkness that a human being can experience. It is not darkness *one* (external situations) that brings people to the deepest level of darkness, it is the persistent refusal to accept the emotions arising from darkness *one*. This is darkness *two*: an inward hardening, a shutting off of your feeling nature.

How does a person bring light into this kind of darkness? If someone arrives in the first kind of darkness, and becomes very sad, anxious, and distressed, you can still reach them. They are still alive, they are in touch with the emotions running through their body and psyche, and they actively seek for the meaning behind what is happening to them. This person is still whole and healthy from a psychological standpoint, even if they face very grave situations. A person dealing with darkness *one* is in need of comfort and compassion, and they are able to receive and appreciate a loving gesture from another – they are still very much alive.

But someone who persists in their refusal to accept, who keeps saying no, such a person is shut off from receiving love. They close down, not only against their inner light, but also against the light from outside that wants to come to them through others. That is loneliness, and isolation, that is being lost – *that is hell on Earth*. And I tell you that each of you knows this hell from within. Maybe you are not fully aware of it, but for most people, a process of closing down started long ago during their childhood.

You know how a child stands spontaneous and uninhibited in the world, and how their emotions flow easily. These emotions often pass quickly through their being, because no barriers have been erected, no gates have been closed. Generally, life freely flows through a child. There are exceptions, of course, because some children carry burdens from early childhood or past lives, but you get the point I am making. Being a child is to be in a state of relative openness. A child is alive and spontaneous because it cannot be otherwise; it has not yet learned to rein in itself the way adults do.

But as you grow older, you start to experience emotions with which you do not know how to deal. People are trained by society to shy away from difficult emotions. Thus, the adults around you often do not help you understand those emotions and they avoid speaking about them. Most of you become confused as a child. You start to believe you are strange and different. Maybe as a child you were still full of inspiration, enthusiasm, love, and dreams, and then those dreams bump against the harshness of reality. You begin to put up barriers against your feeling nature in reaction to the fears and prejudices that exist in your family environment, or later at school and in the people you meet. Inner doors close, and this often happens subconsciously, but some of you may remember it as an old grief.

See if you are able to find the child within yourself, the symbol of your spontaneity; a child who is outgoing, uninhibited, alive, and someone who says yes to what presents itself as experience. Can you see that someone who says yes to joy, pleasure, and enjoyment, as well as to grief, fear, and anger? Imagine that this child within wants to come to you. It is still there; space and time are illusions. In the inner reality nothing is ever lost. Your original life stream is preserved, and still wants to join with you.

Imagine for a moment that a smiling child is coming to you with an attitude of openness. In your imagination, hear it say: 'Do you remember who I am?' Look at that child, and ask what you can do for it. There is a heart-wish the child wants to see fulfilled, something you may have pushed away for a long time. Let the child speak for a moment. The child stands for the yes in you, the part of you that wants to live, so let it speak.

A child still possesses trust. As adults, you have absorbed ideas that are full of fear and mistrust, and that feeds saying no to life and contributes to darkness *two* in you. Try now to sense or visualize this second kind of darkness; the part of you that is opposed to life, which no longer wants to experience pain, and which actually wants to escape this life. Can you feel that element of hardening and contraction within yourself? Can you feel it physically, or perhaps see a color associated with it?

There is a part in you that is very tired and no longer wants to live, because it has seen and experienced too much pain and struggle. Feel the weight of that part. Can you say yes to it? Do not try to change it immediately; try to understand how that has come about. No one deliberately closes off themselves because of an unwillingness to live. It is an act of desperation; it is the not knowing that there is another way to live that leaves you with that reflex of shutting off, of shrinking back, of saying no.

I do not ask you to only say yes to darkness *one* in your life: the difficult events, illness, pain, suffering, or whatever. I ask you to also say yes to darkness *two*, to that within you that has closed off itself from life as a *result* of painful events; to that which no longer wants to experience life and rejects it. And to reach that part in yourself, you have to be very gentle, because insistence and coercion do not work there.

That is the essence of light; the light that can flow into the darkness. This light can reach every corner because it carries no judgment. It does not say, 'Oh, this is bad, we must break down this defense or that blockage, because life *must* flow again'. It never says that. The light simply says: 'I understand'. The light says: 'It has been so very difficult for you, I can see that. I can see how you have tightened up, how you have closed down yourself, and how that contraction has eventually made you tired and empty.' Light is gentle and fluid. It can penetrate into the deepest pain and suffering, and the most hardened human soul.

I ask you to again open yourself to that light. If you cannot find that willingness within yourself, if you do not feel the openness to let go of the 'no', then allow that to be as well, because the light is always there. It is with you even in moments of despair so deep that you feel that there is no more light within you. It is there during those times, and in those situations, where you have totally lost touch with it and never again expect to see it.

The fact is, the light is not *yours*, it belongs to *all that is*. The entire universe, and all creation, *is* light; everything is imbued with light. Know it is there and put your trust in the light and in life. As soon as you allow even a small opening for trust and surrender to enter into your life, you are opening the door a crack. Know that even during the darkest night, your soul is always connected to you and offering you light and consolation. Although that door is open only a tiny crack, the light will find that opening. You do not have to do anything except allow it to happen. *The light is with you, life is with you.* Ultimately, your 'no' to life cannot maintain itself.

I ask you to surrender to the light, where light means saying yes, and not only to the difficulties in your life, but also to your problem with *saying* yes, the resistance you put up against deep emotions that make you feel naked and vulnerable. Become like a child again. Live! *Say yes to everything.* Envelop yourself with compassion and understanding. In doing this, you bring flow and movement into your life. *You can do it!* I see your strength. In each of you is a flame of consciousness, a bright flame of light. I am here to remind you of it.

16. Making Your Own Choices

I am Jeshua and I greet you all from the heart. Feel my heart, for I am connected to you; breathe me in. There is brotherhood between us, there is like-mindedness between you and me and a larger group of soul friends, of lightworkers. Some you know, others you do not, at least not in the earthly sense, but there is an affinity, a greater union of which you are a part. Feel that union inside yourself.

You all are trying to find a balance between your earthly being and your soul being. On the one hand, you are an earthly human, born in a body with a predisposition toward a certain personality, and you are raised in the cultures and traditions of Earth. On the other hand, there is the larger reality of your soul, your cosmic heritage. Your soul is much older than this single life and has built up a lot of experience in various incarnations. On top of that, as a soul, you are part of a larger spiritual family which, in addition to your earthly family, dwells partially on Earth and partially in other worlds.

The merging of your soul with your earthly self is often confusing for you. How do you integrate both? Many of you feel the reality of your soul. You feel something flowing through you that is 'not of this Earth', something that cannot be attributed to your upbringing, genes, or cultural background. There is something unique and unfathomable that makes you 'you'. Sensitive people can catch glimpses of their soul, because they are intuitively connected with an inner world beyond space and time, and they often want to be fully of that other world. They feel that their Home, their Source, is there, and they are correct. However, because you are living as a human being, *here* and *now*, it is necessary to give the connection with your soul an embodiment – 'hands and feet'. You should not sever the connection between your soul and Earth, rather just the opposite: put yourself more firmly *into* that connection, and do it with enthusiasm and passion. Then you have truly integrated your earthly self and your soul self.

The reason this is often difficult for you is that many of you lightworkers give precedence to your soul over your earthly personality. You assume your soul knows best what to do. However, although you as an earthly human should let yourself be *inspired* by your soul, *you* are, and you *should* be, the one who determines the choices and makes the decisions. *You* are the one who ultimately creates your life, and let me explain.

You often wonder: 'What should I now do? How should I handle this situation? What does this mean for me?' You are inclined to look for the answer outside yourselves, and by that, I mean, outside your earthly personality. If you are not yet that far along on the path of inner development, you look for a person outside yourself to give you the answer; someone you look up to, someone who you think has the necessary expertise in the matter. So your question to the other person tends to be: 'Can you tell me what to do?' When you do that, you make yourself small – as far as insight and knowledge goes – by placing the other person above yourself. However, when you become more spiritually mature, you take responsibility for yourself *and* your choices. You can still consult another person, someone you esteem highly, whom you respect, and you can evaluate this person's advice from all sides, but you yourself must decide what you do with that advice. That is the way of a mature soul, a mature human being.

Now, you all know that you should not lean on another person for your choices, but you still do that a lot in your relationships with your spiritual guides and your soul. For example, you wonder: 'What should I do in this situation? What is the best choice for me?' From your desire for security, you turn to a spiritual source for advice: to your guides, teachers, or angels on the other side, or to your own higher self. Or you consult a spiritual medium to provide you with 'higher' information, or you try by yourself to get in touch with your soul, your higher self, or your guides. But look a little more closely at what that means. You are, in fact, taking the same action as when you turn to another person to ask their advice: you are searching outside yourself for answers.

Of course, you can say: 'Yes, but those spiritual sources really know better than I do; they have a better overview or perspective; my guides are further developed than I am; my soul moves in a higher dimension, so it is good to turn to it to get advice.' But again, you are depreciating your 'little' earthly personality when you do that. You often consider your earthly personality not to be the wisest and highest part of yourself and that you have to turn to some 'authority' who better understands the situation and what you should do with your life. *This is a mistake*, and that is my message today.

First of all, the soul is not perfect – it is also developing. It is a dynamic reality which is continually enriched by experiences. Certainly the soul has a perspective that transcends the perspective of a human being and often has a greater vision. The soul also understands more deeply and has more of an overview of the whole puzzle, while you on Earth have a few puzzle pieces in your hands and do not see the bigger picture. But the important point is that, yes, it is good to feel your soul, to connect with it, to consult it, and to get information from that multi-dimensional, developing, dynamic source. But eventually it is you, the earthly self, who carries your earthly name – that unique self that you are right *now* – who must make the choice! There is a moment of choice in everything you do, which is, and always will be, completely yours. Neither your soul, nor a guide, nor the wisest teacher on Earth – *not even God* – can do this for you. In fact, a real spiritual teacher does not ever want to take over for you.

The necessity to make your own choices actually addresses your own unique power: *that you create your earthly life in your own way.* And in addition to that, you can still appeal to all kinds of sources of knowledge and wisdom, earthly as well as cosmic. But the challenge for you is to relate these external sources to your inner truth and to feel what is right for you and what is not. There is no such thing as absolute knowledge – everything is relative. What is true in your life reveals itself in the relationship between *you and the world,* and that relationship is unique and different for every person. No matter how much information you receive from outside yourself, what is important is for you to evaluate this information and to relate it to *your* situation – your everyday reality and your earthly being – to see if it is applicable.

Feel your earthly personality, with all its facets: its fear, pain, hope, joy, and all those emotions that so deeply and tangibly form earthly, human life. These emotions are often confusing, even overwhelming, and you are looking for something to hold on to above or outside yourself. But I would like to stress that the answer and the foundation lie within you, and not in your soul or in your higher self, but *within you.* You actually *are* your higher self and your soul, but you are a part and not the total. You are an aspect of your total Self; you are the aspect that has incarnated *here* and *now*, and who is gathering experiences, and that is why you know best what is good for you.

Descend into your body, which is so closely connected to your earthly self. Let your consciousness descend into your body in a comfortable, relaxed way. Imagine that your consciousness is a light, and that light is who you are and who makes the choices. It chooses to be completely *here* and *now* and to descend into your chest, your abdomen, your upper legs and knees, and all the way down to your lower legs and feet. Feel the light completely penetrate your body, and feel your body's power and vitality. Feel how your body is much more than a combination of physical cells: *it is a living, wise, inspired being*. And who are *you*? You are the one who has connected with this body for this lifetime. You are beautiful and vast, and you have connected to this being who now carries your name. Feel the courage and the bravery it took to do that.

You came here as a beam of light from your soul, and you incarnated in this body and personality, which are completely new. You are part of your soul, but you also add something essential to your soul, something new and unique, and that is *you*. You are a self-reliant whole; you are not dependent on forces larger than yourself. You are a creation unto itself – better said: a *creator* unto itself. Feel the value and the power and the beauty of being that creator. My deepest wish is that you will recognize your own value and will no longer speak about a higher or lower self, but that you will recognize your earthly self as *the anchor of your existence, here* and *now*. From that self, you can consult other earthly sources, guides, teachers, therapists, advisors, doctors, or your own soul by way of meditation or inner contemplation, and take in all that information, but then you will make your *own* considered choices.

And how do you do that? That is probably your next question. Try it. Imagine that you now have a question in your life that makes you feel desperate, of which you think: 'I really don't know what to do'. Now completely descend into your earthly self, say your own name, feel the light of consciousness in your abdomen, in your root chakra. Then again ask yourself the question and feel an answer come up from deep within: from your foundation, your core. *You just know it*. You have the inner knowledge and resources that are necessary to answer your life's questions.

It is in you; you are the fount, the source and collection point of knowledge, experience, light. And from everything you have built up in this life, you make choices, based on your power of discernment. *Own that power, that freedom*. That is what makes you 'big' and allows your self-awareness to grow, so start trusting your own discernment and choices, your sense of what is best for you. It is not about knowing things for certain; it is about daring to trust who you are and what you feel deep inside. You are here, not to make 'perfect' choices, but to experience your own creative power by learning and growing from the choices you do make.

That is why I now want to symbolically give a torch of light to you to express that you do not have to look to me for the light. It is in *you,* and I want to make you aware of that; I want to give it back to you. In the past, you have searched outside yourselves too often. See if you can accept the torch that I offer to you, and internalize it as something that is *yours.* Look to where that torch goes in your body, to where it has its natural resting place. There resides your deepest knowing about what is your path. *You make the choices, and you learn from the choices you make*, and that is exactly how it should be in this human life.

Do not underestimate the true power of 'you', the embodied earthly you. It is the most intimate source of wisdom you will ever have. You are the creator of your life.

17. From Heart to Belly

I am Earth speaking to you. I am your mother, and I carry you in my lap your whole life long. You are cherished by me, even if you are not aware of it and are too busy and caught up in your day-to-day affairs. I hold you and invite you to connect with me, as I wish to stir your memory and remind you of something old and precious, which in this modern world seems to have been forgotten. It is about the natural safety of being on Earth.

To remember the natural safety of being, you can look at nature around you. Watch the seasons, how they come and go all on their own; see the plants and animals go about their daily life; listen to the rustle of the wind or the murmuring of water. In this way, you are briefly reminded that the most important things in life happen on their own, as a result of nature running its course. Nature is all around you and it is *in* you as well, for you also have a nature and it is part of nature as a whole.

You have become so oriented to living from your head, especially in the West, that you have forgotten you are a natural being, like the plants and animals. Look at how the animals naturally surrender to life; they almost cannot do otherwise. They do know emotions, such as fear and resistance, but they cannot oppose themselves to life the way humans do. Human beings, by excessive thinking, create a cage for their own nature and, in time, that causes problems. Life cannot be organized and controlled by human thinking. The primal forces of nature are vaster than that, and sooner or later you will find out. There will be a moment in which you have to surrender to nature.

You often reach such a moment through a crisis, a situation in which you become trapped and that asks of you to release control, because you no longer have a grip on things, either inside or around you. Releasing control hurts and can be a struggle, yet it will bring you Home. You think you are lost and drowning in chaos, but you are actually coming closer to the natural safety of Being itself. Life holds and loves you. And even though crises often seem cruel and unjust, they, in truth, always carry within them, nature's, or if you want, God's, invitation that says: 'Come Home, come back to me'. There is a guiding hand within the crisis, which seeks to support you and show you the way.

All who read this are on the inner journey to wholeness and completion of the self. You are seeking to bring down and express your soul in a human body of flesh and blood. On this path, the soul gets embodied - or descends into the body - in different stages. When you have only just started on the inner path, you will probably become acquainted with it through your head. For instance, you may become attracted to certain books or people who may shed a different light on ideas and values you always took for granted. You may be shaken by their new thoughts, and yet strangely attracted to them. It will fascinate you to read and learn more about them. You will let go of some of the more rigid structures of your thinking and open up to something new. Reading and speaking to like-minded people can be helpful incentives in this process. This is how the journey within begins for many; you devour spiritual books like they are cookies, because deep within you something wants to awaken and change, and this translates first into the need for a new way of thinking.

After some time, you start to long for more. You start to think: 'Well, I understand what they're talking about in those books, but how do I apply all of this to my own life? How does this knowledge come alive, and how do I truly integrate it into my feelings and actions on Earth?' This question may haunt you and drive you to despair, but you cannot force life to provide instant answers.

At a certain moment, however, something will happen in your life that will help you make the breakthrough from head to heart, and often it is a crisis of some sort. Changes might occur in the area of work, relationships, health, or there might be the loss of a loved one. Whatever it is, at a certain moment, feelings will arise inside you which are so intense that they cannot be ignored. You have to allow them in and let the transformation take place. That is when your soul incarnates deeper into your heart.

Your soul first descended into your head, inspiring you to take in new ideas through books, talks, etc. Then the soul knocks at your door at a deeper level, the level of feeling. You will get acquainted with layers of your emotions you never knew existed before. Crises spur these on; they will make old emotions from childhood come to the surface, perhaps even memories from before this lifetime. You will explore these layers of emotions and this is how the center of your heart opens up. Your soul incarnates deeper, filling the heart chakra with its energy.

The transformation that takes place at that stage may give rise to several complications. You start to look at the world with different eyes and your relationships with other people also change. Deep within, the awareness of Oneness awakens, which means that you realize that all of us, human, animal, plant, nature, are held together by a divine force, and that we are bound to each other, each a mirror to the other. This awareness can be overpowering and for many of you the breakthrough from head to heart causes an increased sensitivity inside you. This heightened sensitivity may create imbalances, because boundaries with others get blurred and you might take in a lot of other people's emotional outpouring, not knowing how to release it, causing your moods to go from very high to very low. The breakthrough from head to heart, however, though powerful and essential, is not the last stage in the incarnation of the soul. The soul wants to descend even deeper, into the belly.

When the soul has descended to the level of your heart, you have partly awakened. You are aware of your feelings, you dare to look at your emotions, you are prepared to go within and face your inner wounds. But you also feel weakened by your high sensitivity and the instability that arises because of that. Because your heart is so full of feelings, you lose your grounding at times, and this can be difficult and happens to many of you. When the heart center is opened radically, your sensitivity may become too much for you and you may want to withdraw from the world. You may not express yourself creatively any more, because it is all too much and too overpowering, and this can make you feel anxious and depressed.

The answer to this problem is not in going back into your head; the answer is in your belly. You are ready for the next step in the incarnation process of the soul: *the transition from heart to belly.* The soul wants to flow even deeper into your body. In the middle of your belly is a space or point of silence. Go there with your awareness now, as I speak. In that space, there is no language, no thinking, no concepts. You may hear the rustling of leaves in the wind or the sound of the beating of waves, and those sounds can help you become aware of the silence that is within this center.

At this level, your spiritual knowing and feeling become instinctual, or as it is sometimes called, your second nature. There is no need to think or even feel for it. A deep knowingness is present from which you act, and life pours through you easily. Your soul has then become your true nature; it has descended to the level of instinctual awareness. *This gives you the balance you need!* You can remain centered and calm amidst a demanding and turbulent environment. Your feeling center (your heart) wants to connect with your belly in order to be truly grounded and for you to feel safe and secure on Earth.

Let us now visit that place in your belly. Trust that it is there, and tell your soul it is welcome there. Allow your soul to flow from your head, inspiring your thinking, to your heart, radiating love and kindness, to your belly, giving you trust, self esteem, and a profound inner knowing that you are who you are and that you are good and sufficient as you are. Feel your belly opening up to you. Sense how the golden light of your soul flows down to your root chakra and connects with me, Earth. Go deep within and be the center of silence, and know that from there, your high sensitivity will be balanced with peace and calmness. In this balanced state, you will know how to put boundaries around your feelings; you will know when to open up and when to keep your distance, by staying close to yourself; and you will determine when to say yes and when to say no, when to connect and when to let go – and the key is in your belly.

To help you connect with this center, I suggest you imagine an animal that represents the inner power residing in your belly, and take the first animal that comes to mind. Remember, animals are very spontaneous creatures; they live from their instincts, their natural reflexes. This animal reflects your instinctual inner knowingness. It is already there waiting for you. You do not need to create it, you only need to see and recognize it. Invite this animal to come near you; say 'hello' and look into its eyes.

Now ask the animal whether it has a message for you, something that will help you to descend deeper into your belly, and let the animal speak. This animal embodies the wisdom of the instinctual, and because you have a head and a heart, you can receive, feel, and articulate this wisdom. That is the beauty of the cooperation between head, heart, and belly. Not one of them is better or higher than the other. Rather, it is their balanced cooperation that makes you whole and complete.

Your head can give you much pleasure; it can be useful and fun. It gives you the opportunity to communicate with others, as it provides a common language. Your heart provides the possibility to experience joy and the whole range of emotions of which human life is comprised – *it is a beautiful gift.* Your belly gives you your foundation, your I-ness, if that is a proper word. It allows you to be really *you*, firm and rooted, drawing your own boundaries and using your discernment. From this foundation, the interaction with your heart and your head becomes a joyful play.

If these three layers of your being are aligned with each other, you feel whole, and life on Earth is worth living. It can be full of inspiration, love, and happiness. You can surrender yourself to what moves and inspires you, while at the same time not losing your foundation, your inner point of silence. You can remain close to yourself, yet at the same time freely give and receive what life offers.

I salute you all. My love and compassion are close to you always. I am playing this game together with you and I am a part of it. You are beautiful and rich as human beings, so have faith in the beauty and power of the instruments available to you: the instruments of *thinking*, *feeling*, and *being*.

18. Balancing Your Ego

I am the voice of the Earth. I am your foundation, and I carry you by way of the body in which you dwell and live. The cells in your body are connected with me and carry in them my strength and vitality. Your body continually informs you about who you are and what is going on within you. Your body is the bearer of your sensations and feelings, and it is by way of your feelings that your soul speaks to you. It is not easy for you to hear the voice of your soul speak through your feelings, because you are accustomed to approaching life from your mind, but this approach goes against nature. Life, in you and in me, is born from passion and creative power, and the mind can have no understanding of the dynamics of life without connecting itself with the heart and the belly.

Only when the light of your soul descends fully into your body, down to your abdomen, can the soul express itself in your life, your work, and your relationships. The abdomen holds three energy centers which are of crucial importance: the solar plexus chakra (stomach), the navel chakra (*hara* center) and the root chakra (tailbone). These centers, located along the spine, are like a bridge between Heaven and Earth. They connect your soul's energy with your humanness, and if they function properly, they translate or channel your deepest inspiration into material reality. When the lower three chakras are balanced and open, you are attuned to the rhythm of your soul and, in this way, living from your soul becomes 'second nature'. Spirituality is no longer something you study and approach from the head; you now have an intuitive knowing that needs no words or concepts. When the light of your soul descends that deeply into your being, an inner transformation takes place: you begin to radiate from the inside outward.

This time on Earth provides the possibility for you to fully embody your light. This is a time of awakening and making key choices. When you choose to receive the unique light of your soul on Earth, you are allowing your soul's energy to descend from the head, to the heart, to the belly. On this descending path, the area of your abdomen (belly) is of great importance, because your deepest emotions dwell there. It is there that your passions and desires, as well as your fear, anger, and doubt are alive. Only by fully connecting with your very human emotions and shining the light of your soul into the darkest corners is your soul able to descend completely.

Many of you have a lot of wisdom in your head and a lot of good intentions in your heart, and you are looking for a practical way to manifest these inspirations in everyday life. You struggle with the blocks and the resistance that come up, both from without and within. The battlefield is often located in the area of the lower three chakras, because that is where you interact with reality as a human being.

I love you for trying to find your own way, and it is my sincere wish to assist you. In this, and the next two messages, I will describe the inner journey of the descent into your abdomen, discussing the solar plexus, the navel chakra, and the root chakra successively, with their corresponding themes: balancing your ego (this chapter), embracing the inner child (chapter 19) and feeling safe inside your body (chapter 20).

The solar plexus, which is an energy center close to your stomach, is the physical locus of your earthly self: the personality that belongs to you, which is also known as the ego. The ego is an inseparable part of you as a human being. A balanced ego keeps you connected with your heart and helps you, through thought and action, to bring the whispers and urgings of your soul into material form. In that way, the ego is the bridge between the Earth and the soul.

In many religious and spiritual traditions, the ego is seen as something negative. These traditions teach that the primal longings located in the belly are to be distrusted, and the aim of these traditions is to eliminate or to transcend the ego. I tell you that your passions are *not* a hindrance. They are an essential starting point for letting your soul descend on to Earth. The fire in your belly, in connecting with your soul, is meant to become an inspiring torch of light for the world. This fire includes your emotions, your passion, and your desires. The purpose of inner growth is not that this fire be extinguished, but that it receive direction from the heart.

While religion is traditionally against the ego, the ego is powerfully encouraged by your society: ambition, success, and outer recognition count heavily. This emphasis on outward achievements can make it difficult for you to find your own unique way. Before you are aware of it, your thinking and acting become motivated by exterior norms that are often based on fear. A pursuit of success might stem from a deep fear of 'not being good enough as you are' and the recognition of others appears to take away this doubt, but the result is that you become dependent on exterior forces beyond your control. If you become fixated on outer values, your ego becomes the dominant force within you and you lose your connection with the larger whole. In this way, a 'big ego' comes into being; one that struggles to maintain the edifice of success and respect, while your very foundation is being eaten away by fear and uncertainty.

The fire of the ego can be either weak or strong. In your world, you are encouraged both to make yourself small, as well to make yourself 'big'. Religion preaches that you are sinful and insignificant, while society demands that you be attractive, productive, and successful. Most people have a mix of both tendencies in their ego. The one tendency is toward vanity and making themselves bigger, while the other tendency is toward docility and making themselves smaller. Seen from the vantage of the soul, neither tendency is healing. Whether you have a strong or a weak ego, you feel fearful and abandoned deep within, because your ego is not connected with your heart. In both cases, the ego flounders in a void. It does not take root in a fertile soil that provides nurturing and security.

The feeling of being lost that you have when your ego stands by itself can only be dispelled through connection with your soul. No religious or worldly power can provide the security and connection needed to live in joy and confidence. Only the soul is capable of inspiring the ego from within so as to lift the ego out of its loneliness. This can happen only when the ego is willing to give up its separateness and surrender to something greater than itself. When you connect with the voice of your heart -- the voice of your feelings – you open the gate between your ego and your soul.

Listening to the voice of your heart

In order to recognize the voice of your soul, try to be as aware as possible of your everyday emotions, especially the recurring ones, and open yourself to the possibility that there is a vital message contained in them. If you listen to your emotions and consider them to be messengers, you start to relate to yourself very differently from the way you have been taught. You now have the tendency to condemn your emotions and push them aside, so there is much that you deny yourself. Your emotions often tell you about an inner desire that wants to be seen and heard; a desire for a deeper, fuller, and more creative life in which you have meaningful connections with others. On the one hand, you hear the call of your soul, but on the other hand, you push that call away, because it is asking you to break away from acquired certainties, habits, and expectations. Your soul wants you to stand up and to live from your own truth, yet this urging can terrify you. You are afraid to let go of certainties; afraid to deviate from the norm and to come into conflict with the world around you. Because of these inner doubts, many of you hesitate on the brink of a real breakthrough into your actual destiny.

However, life does not stand still – it propels you forward. Life always asks of you to choose the voice of your heart, over and over again. What finally helps you over the threshold appears most often in the form of a crisis. Disease, burn-out, job loss, death of a loved one, or a relationship breakup, set adrift all your certainties. In such a situation, life seems to become rudderless. Your ego, your earthly personality, finds itself face to face with forces it cannot control. This puts before you a choice: do you resist or do you surrender? At such moments, life provides an opportunity for you to really open up. In a crisis, an inner breakthrough can take place. However, this requires of you that you let go of preconceived expectations about your life by giving up what you thought were secure certainties.

A crisis brings loss into your life, yet at the same time space is created for something new. In a crisis, you are compelled to connect with your deepest feelings and to be consciously present in this flow. A crisis calls for great inner strength, because what is happening is often not agreeable to the ego. It will resist, panic, and not want to linger in the emotions of fear and anger. During a crisis, your resistance to change usually intensifies, while at the same time you are deeply challenged to let go of the resistance and to jump in and to risk going deep. When you dare to go with the flow of your feelings, without condemning them, new horizons will open up and new ways will unfold.

By saying 'Yes' to what happens in your life, and surrendering to your feelings, you create a channel between your heart and your solar plexus – the voice of your soul becomes audible. You open up to the deep and powerful feelings that well up and you treat them with respect. In this way, you become aligned with your true and unique being, and you focus less on outside rules and standards and distractions. In attuning to your own unique energy, you will start to make life decisions based on your feelings rather than on your thoughts. By feelings, I do not mean emotional impulses that flutter about with every change in direction of the wind. I am referring to the joy and inspiration that are present when you make decisions from the heart.

The heart as guide

To choose from your heart means to decide from a quiet knowing, without being able to explain why intellectually. It is important to realize that the function of the ego is not to *make* choices; it is to *carry out* your choices in the everyday world. The ego might seem to be more rational than the heart, because it calls on so-called facts and common knowledge and standards but, in fact, the ego operates from fear and does not want to deviate from the known and predictable. When you base your life decisions on the ego, you are not really *living*, you are *being lived*. This will gnaw at you and bring inner turmoil.

To make decisions from the heart might seem scary, and the choices you make are sometimes difficult to explain to others – and even to yourself. Yet this is the only way, once you have chosen to embody the unique light of your soul on Earth. Once you have taken this step, you will switch over to a different way of living. From the flow of rationality, you enter into the flow of synchronicity. Synchronicity refers to surprising and positive events that take place in your life without effort on your part: encounters that truly 'hook up', and opportunities that appear from nowhere. Whatever you need in order to pursue your heart's desire enters your life spontaneously: it seems the universe is on your side.

Synchronicity cannot be explained in a rational way, and it cannot be controlled by the ego. The flow of synchronicity is essentially nothing other than 'the rhythm of the soul'. When you are attuned to the rhythm of your soul, miracles happen. When you listen to your intuition and you do not push and shove against life, people and opportunities spontaneously cross your path that help you radiate the light of your soul on Earth. You do less and allow things to just happen. The ego is no longer 'the captain of the ship'; it has given over the 'wheel' to the heart. Your solar plexus or third chakra is now at the service of your heart and, in this way, creates the bridge between soul and Earth.

From the perspective of the soul, coincidence does not exist. The good that you attract when you live from the heart is a reflection of your inspiration, joy, and surrender. The question is not so much how to create these good things, but more whether you are open to receive these gifts. Is your ego flexible enough to bend and is your mind sufficiently empty? Can you live without expectations? Can you be thankful for what you have, even though there is still a lot missing according to your personality's standards? To allow yourself to be moved by your soul, surrender is required – a leap into the vast unknown.

You are accustomed to trying to force and control life, which often produces problems in the area of the solar plexus. Many people, for example, have stomach complaints which are the result of stress and tension. The energy center of the third chakra can become overly stimulated by your need to control life, and in this way, you disconnect from the flow of trust and surrender that are necessary to feel the rhythm of your soul. In the process of the soul's descent to the belly, the solar plexus is often blocked by an excessively active will that tries to control life from a restrictive tunnel vision. Often a profound crisis is needed for you to break free from this tunnel vision. This is not to say that you *have* to wait for a crisis in your life before you begin to listen to the voice of your heart and the rhythm of your soul. If you are aware of your own tension and unrest, then there is already a space opening for change in your life. How can you increase this space? How can you create a balanced ego that is neither too weak and docile, nor too big and controlling? I would like to offer three guidelines.

Dare to be different and unique

Realize that your path is unique. Your soul wants you to express what is unique to you, what makes you different, while the ego usually lets itself be guided by what is required or expected from without, by society or by family. Choosing your own way means that you let go of these motives and allow yourself to be guided by a truer source of leadership: *the voice of your soul.* How do you know when you are connected with your soul? Connection with your soul gives you a sense of joy and inspiration. The voice of your soul tells you to believe in your dreams and desires and, at the same time, the guidance of your soul will be practical and down to earth. In your everyday life, there will be opportunities coming your way to realize your goals and express your gifts, and to do that step by step. Through this process, you will be challenged time and again: do you succumb to the fear of standing out and being rejected, or do you dare to choose from your heart and be unique?

Dare to surrender

Dare to surrender to the wisdom of your heart and realize that surrender is a *creative force*. You sometimes think that creating means you must focus intently on a particular purpose for as long as it takes; however, a true creator sets a goal and then *lets go*. The true creator realizes that it is not their ego or their mind that is able to do the creating. It is the bigger power of your soul that really makes things happen. And with your mind, you often cannot fathom what your soul has in store for you. If you try to create by focusing on mental images, you limit life in what it is able to give to you. In your mental imaging, you may still be thinking from a tunnel vision, because you are not aware of how restrictive the ideas are that you carry within yourself.

Truly creating is opening to the possibilities of the *unknown* and not fixating on a predetermined purpose. *Dare not to know!* To surrender to the heart is to be open to something new and fresh that you cannot yet entertain with your mind, and this surrender is not a passive letting go. It means relying on the power of your heart-felt desires and dreams and placing your human hand in the hand of your soul and relying on its guidance. In that state of alert receptivity, you allow life to unfold, and you only need to do the things that keep you in touch with a feeling of joy and peace.

Honor the natural rhythm of your soul

When you align yourself with the voice of your heart and do what gives you joy and inspiration, you will live according to the rhythm of your soul. This rhythm is not always to your liking and it might even be in conflict with what the outside world expects from you. The soul is not interested in direct results. It is much more interested in the *way* you experience things, and it will value a painful experience if it brings you greater awareness or deepens your strength and wisdom. Often, making your dreams and inspirations come true on Earth means you must first confront the parts of yourself that block the dream and the inspiration - the parts that are full of fear or resistance or anger. As they come up, it might seem that you move away from your goal rather than toward it, but the soul sees it differently. It values inner transformation more than external results, and it does not care about the passage of time as you do; your soul has *a lot more patience*.

For your human awareness, it might seem that things fall apart after you have chosen to listen to your heart, and there might be moments in which you lose all hope and confidence. It is indeed not rare that dreams and visions come true only after you have given up on them – the way of the soul is one of paradox and seeming detours. However, know that when the seed of a heart-felt desire is sown, it will eventually come to fruition. The process of getting there becomes lighter and more joyful when you understand and appreciate the rhythm and timing of your soul. Have respect for the slow and arduous parts as well as the magical synchronicities that happen spontaneously and out of nowhere.

19. Embracing Your Inner Child

I am the Earth. I embrace you, gently and firmly, as a mother. I carry and protect you. Feel my presence in the ground beneath your feet. Let the cells of your body take on my life force and energy by opening yourself to me.

I will now talk about the center of your emotions, the navel chakra, which is located in the belly. We have in the previous chapter discussed the descent of the soul to the level of the solar plexus, the third chakra, which is in the area of your stomach. Farther down the body is the second or navel chakra, which sits in the middle of your belly slightly below your actual navel, and this chakra is related to emotion, sexuality, and intimacy. It contains your ability to experience deeply and intensely. This area can be a source of true joy and pleasure and connectedness with other people, but it can also be overshadowed by feelings of inferiority, fear, and loneliness.

As you open up to the voice of your soul, you may discover that there lives within you a sense of emotional insecurity, which might stem from experiences of rejection in the past. As a child, you are very sensitive to the approval of your parents. Actually, as a young child you consider your parents to be gods: they are your creators who have brought you to Earth. They are the persons in the first years of your life on whom you, as a child, are entirely dependent for your physical survival and emotional well-being. How you experience that relationship will have a major influence on your self-image as an adult.

The fears you are experiencing in the present are fears that are partly inherited from your parents, often at a subconscious level. Your basic beliefs about life are largely formed by them. These beliefs, and their accompanying emotional habits and reactive patterns, were transmitted through their words, actions, and reactions. You absorbed their energy into every pore of your body during your early childhood.

Letting go of your childhood

When you mature, and you consciously go within and look for your soul's voice, you choose essentially to be born anew – to experience a second birth. This new birth happens when you become aware of the fears and unconscious beliefs that your parents transmitted to you, as well as your ability to confront them and to let them go. By allowing the light of your consciousness to shine on this heritage, you detach yourself from it and take responsibility for your own life. You take your inner child under your *own* guidance and protection, and you become your *own* mother and father. You raise yourself ('grow-up') a second time, as it were, with new, empowering beliefs that lovingly replace the old insecurities and fears. You create a new sense of security for yourself, which means you receive yourself unconditionally and with love.

Your belly is the area where you can emotionally experience the greatest empowerment of who you are as a human being. It is the center from which you intimately connect with others and from which you respond spontaneously and instinctively. In many of you, it is here where basic negative beliefs about yourself are stored, beliefs that contain fear and judgment. For example: 'I'm not good enough; I need to control myself; I need to work hard; I have thoughts and feelings that are wrong; I'm not worthy of love; I should not distinguish myself from others; etc.'

The central component in all these beliefs is the idea that *you are not sufficient as you are and that you should do something in order to receive approval from the world.* This idea can easily captivate a child, because you – like nearly all children – experience that your parents are not capable of giving you unconditional love. And as a child, you soon come to believe that you know the cause of this failure – it is a deficiency in *you, as you are.* The next step is that you believe you ought to be other than you are – better, more attractive, more successful – and that by changing your behavior you will gain your parents' unconditional acceptance and love. You will try all sorts of ways to earn this love, and it is because you nevertheless continue to experience the lack of this love that a basic feeling of unworthiness and insecurity takes root in your belly.

The tragedy in all of it is that the promise of unconditional love from your parents could never be fulfilled to begin with. The truth is that you as a child *did not fail*, but that most parents, because of their own negative beliefs derived from their own childhoods, cannot love themselves as they are and so they cannot express their love to you in a way that makes you feel fully accepted by them. In most cases, they themselves have never experienced unconditional love.

How can you break this pattern of inherited lovelessness? How do you recognize where you are still trapped in the fears and uncertainties of your parents? In this chapter, I invite you to examine how the energies of your mother and father have influenced you so you can see clearly in which areas you lack a sense of security and safety and how you can give it to yourself.

Letting go of your mother

The first intimate relationship in your life is the one with your mother. In the womb, you are physically and emotionally fully connected with her – you are hardly aware of where you end and she begins. Her emotions and moods are the setting in which the seed that you are comes to live and evolves. Her belly is your temporary home, and it forms the gateway to life on Earth. Your mother is, in those early life stages, a symbol of the female. Although every human being carries both the female and the male energy, at the moment you become a mother, you are an expression of the female energy of creation. You represent, for the child in your belly, the receiving, connecting, and nurturing aspects of the female energy. In this expression of the female by the mother, the beliefs that the mother has about herself and her femaleness will leave its stamp on her motherhood and the relationship with her child.

In the society and cultural tradition in which you grew up, the female energy has often been undervalued. For a long time, the male energy has been deemed superior. The struggle between the male and the female energy has left deep scars in the lives of both men and women. Both sexes have suffered as a result of the oppression of the female energy. Women were not allowed to experience their strength, and men were not allowed to connect with their feelings. This has been disruptive to the balance between the female and male energies that both reside within all men and women. The ingrained beliefs that live in your culture about femininity and masculinity are naturally passed on by parents to every new child who is born. This chain can only be broken when women and men begin to experience for themselves that these beliefs are constricting and they consciously decide to explore the energies of male and female anew.

What images of the female and femininity have you inherited from your mother? The female stands as the archetypal energy for empathizing, receiving, and connecting with another. The female energy is fluid, flowing, and inclined to transcend boundaries; it represents in its highest forms the qualities of the heart: unconditional love, compassion, and caring. Could your mother accept and embrace her femaleness as something beautiful and precious? Imagine how, as a small child, you rested in her belly. What do you feel first? What sense surrounds you there? Is there joy and connectedness? Or do you feel fear and worry? What energy stands out as the most important one that you absorbed from your mother? See how that energy affected you and whether it threw you off balance. Notice what you need in the womb and then allow what you most missed to spontaneously emerge *now* and give it to yourself. Time is flexible and you can heal the past from the present. Send healing energy to that child from the *now*, and feel it being received. That child you see before your mind's eye still lives. It is energetically present in *your* belly and waiting for *your* love. You can give it everything that it may have lacked then. In doing so, you heal the wounds in your second chakra and you let go of the energies that you once absorbed from your mother.

Letting go of your father

How was the relationship with your father when you were a child? Just as have women, men have inherited a distorted image about the male energy, as well as an image about the female energy. Men are often encouraged to repress their emotions. Acting 'like a man' often implies that you maintain control, show no emotion, hide your vulnerability, and act decisively. This image of maleness and masculinity, synonymous with emotionless, has harmed the soul of men, just as degrading the female energy has psychologically wounded women.

How did your father experience his male energy and the demands that were put upon him as a man? Did he repress his sensitivity? Could he emotionally connect with you? Allow an image to come up of the both of you together. Imagine that you as a small child stand beside him and he holds your hand. What do you feel first? What does he radiate to you? Do you feel good and safe with your father? Is he emotionally present for you? Look at what you missed then and give the child who you were what it needs. Kneel down before the child and observe it. Let the child know through the look in your eyes that you are there for him or her and that it is safe and secure with you.

In its highest form, the male energy represents *conscious ego power derived from inspiration*. The healed male energy is honored when serving and protecting the female energy. Discernment, wisdom, a broad vision, courage, and self-awareness are the qualities of a balanced male energy. The one-sided emphasis on thinking and on dominating nature, both inwardly (your emotions), as well as outwardly (your environment), is replaced by a harmonious interplay between feeling and acting, and between inspiration and manifestation.

Become your own man or woman

In each person there is an interplay between the male and the female energies. No person is purely female or male, because your soul is not male or female. However, if you incarnated in a female body, then you are naturally more strongly connected to the qualities associated with the female energy. When you are born in a male body, the qualities of the male energy are closer to you. During the process of your second birth – the path of descent that your soul undertakes in cooperation with your earthly personality – you will sooner or later encounter the question of how things stand in relation to this balance within you between male and female energies.

Only when both aspects are allowed to be present in your being and support each other will there be true emotional security in your belly. In practice, this means that you as a man may again feel at home with your emotions, your vulnerability, and your sensitivity, and as a woman, it means that you discover your inner strength and dare to consciously inhabit your space. In general, on the path of the descent of the soul, women are asked to take back their power, while men are asked to embrace their gentleness and to connect again with their feelings.

Many women have been taught as girls that they can earn approval only by giving – giving understanding, care, and service. For the 'searching-for-love' child, giving becomes a means to being accepted and appreciated. When, however, giving is driven by the longing inside for unconditional love and emotional security, you soon begin to live an unbalanced life. You feel you *need* to give in order to feel good, because your self-esteem depends on it. This leads to giving without bounds and a loss of self in relationships. It leads to emotional dependency, whereby you chronically undervalue yourself. For many women, it is important that they find their strength and independence and dare to live for themselves. They benefit from the male energy of standing up for themselves and setting their boundaries relative to their connection with others.

With men, the reverse is often the case. Showing your power is not taboo for boys. They are taught that to stand out, perform well, and excel are valued qualities. The 'ego-force' is emphasized, and the connection with others is de-emphasized: performance is the motto. Through this image of what is ideal, 'guys' get the idea that it is good to suppress their feelings, which are linked to vulnerability and weakness. You get recognition through performance and by masking your vulnerability. However, through the crowding out of your feelings, you lose the connection with your soul. When outward performance is not supported by inner inspiration, you increasingly become alienated from yourself and eventually you live *only* for outward recognition and appreciation. This creates a great emotional insecurity within the person. For men, connecting with their feelings and expressing their emotions is of great importance. In order to create a guiding light of emotional security within himself, it is healing for a man to create emotionally meaningful connections with others and in this way to allow himself to be guided by the female energy of the heart.

Restoring the balance between the male and female aspects within yourself is an individual path that you travel. In this message, I have given some general guidelines. However, it is also quite possible that, as a woman, you are experiencing problems with daring to enter emotional relationships, while as a man you may experience problems with standing up for yourself and with setting boundaries. A woman who naturally has a highly developed male energy may experience resistance in surrendering to gentleness and intimacy. A man who is naturally sensitive and feels at home with the female energy can especially experience difficulty with standing up for himself and manifesting his ego-force. Often there is a mixture of both aspects present in people.

Making yourself whole

In whatever way this balance in you takes form, the fact that you have taken up this quest for wholeness testifies to your inner strength. By seeking this balance between the male and female within yourself, you stop searching for the ideal mother or father in others; for example, in a parent, a beloved, a close friend, or a teacher. Deep in every human being there is the longing for the perfect mother and father: the mother as a source of inexhaustible love, nurturing, and understanding and the father as an unconditional source of wisdom and protection. The desire for the perfect mother and the perfect father is essentially nothing else than the desire for balance between the male and female energies within yourself.

When you begin the journey of inner awareness and growth, you will need to let go of the idea that someone else can be your perfect mother or your perfect father. Neither your earthly mother and father nor a beloved partner can meet this expectation. Still, as an earthly being, you often project this desire onto the most intimate relationships that you have. The search for the ideal mother or father, who fully understands, accepts, appreciates, and loves you, is a primordial desire of the child in you that has been deprived of this love and is still experiencing the pain of that deprivation. It is your task as an adult to embrace this needy child within yourself with your own female energy of gentle nurturing and your own male energy of protection and wisdom. No woman can embody the archetypal mother energy for you, and no man can give you the energy of the archetypal father.

By letting go of this expectation, you liberate your relationships from a demanding pressure and heavy burden, because no other person can release your deepest inner pain. Unrealistic and high expectations about others are released and make space for openness and flexibility in your relationships. You alone take upon yourself the responsibility for the needs of your inner child. You are then able to leave to the other person what he or she is: a human being with his or her own unique history and mixture of fearful and loving energies.

Become your own mother and father by embracing the child within and giving it back the truth. And the truth is that *you are good as you are*: that you are brave, loving, and innocent in everything you think and feel. The more you support yourself in this way, the lighter, more joyful, and more creative the child within will become. This knowledge will transform your relationships with others, and you will no longer look to others for your emotional security. You are secure and safe, in and with yourself. You then can be open to an emotionally intimate connection with another person. Being independent and secure as you are, you have much to share with another, as well as being open to receive. The love and friendship you receive from the other will confirm what you already know: *I am good as I am*.

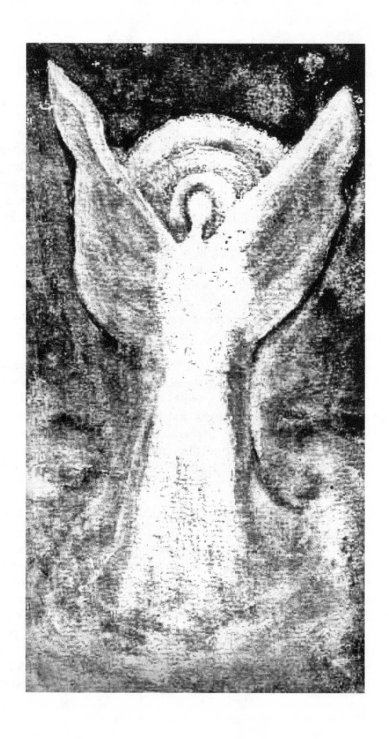

20. Feeling Safe and Secure in Your Body

On the path of the descent of your soul, you come ever closer to me, the Earth. *The aim of your soul's journey is that you will eventually completely connect with me.* Your soul wants to embody itself on Earth at the level of the head, the heart, and the belly. The root chakra, the energy center at the bottom of your spine, symbolically contains your 'roots' to Earth. It reflects your basic beliefs about life in a body on Earth and the ability to express yourself freely, securely, and safely in the material realm.

In many people, fear lives in the root chakra - the fear of being completely present in the body and in the feelings. You are inclined to think that being fully present creates vulnerability and, therefore, weakness, but that is not so. Because of painful memories from the past of rejection and of being hurt – both emotionally and physically – you have partially retreated from your body, especially from your belly, which is the area where you can experience severe emotional pain. Many people are not fully present in this part of their body, and this is caused by emotional trauma you experienced in the course of this life or in previous lives spent on Earth.

It is possible that you experienced a lack of emotional security in the family in which you grew up. As described in the previous chapter, as a young child you can already come to believe that you need to be other than what you are in order to *earn* the love you are seeking. This makes it difficult, at the level of the solar plexus (the third chakra), to rely on the voice of your heart and to let go of outer standards imposed on you from the world around you. In addition, unprocessed traumas – painful soul memories – from previous lives can be playing themselves out in your life, making it possible that you have not incarnated on Earth in a heartfelt way. These painful soul memories can result in 'incarnation pain', which made it difficult for you to establish a good grounding at birth and to feel at home in your body. For many people, the unprocessed traumas from previous lives trigger and reinforce the emotional wounds from this present lifetime.

When you do not know how to heal the pain in the root chakra, or you are barely aware of it, you will try to escape reality. Addictive substances such as alcohol, drugs, or candy temporarily may give you the feeling that all is well. For others, it may be that certain distractions, such as TV, shopping, or excessive hard work are necessary to give you relief for a while from the unrest that lives deep within you. However, by this kind of 'flight' behavior, you eventually lose your grounding as you disconnect from your emotions and your body in the *here* and *now*.

To be properly grounded means that you experience a flow of giving and a flow of receiving that both connect you with the Earth. The giving flow entails that you express yourself on Earth by manifesting your unique soul energy in your daily activities with joy and fulfillment. The receiving flow means that you enjoy what life has to offer and that you say 'Yes' to being fully present on Earth – *here* and *now*. Not being grounded means that the inspiration in your heart does not or just barely manifests on Earth, that you feel unable to creatively express yourself, which results in your experiencing a lack of fulfillment in many areas of your life. This sense of lack from not being grounded can make you feel like an outsider who does not belong on Earth. You may wonder, 'What am I doing here and what is the sense of it all?' Feelings of alienation, loneliness, and sadness can emerge. If the giving flow falters, there also results the inability to fully receive. Part of you does not want to be here and doubts itself or feels unworthy. , These feelings make it difficult to allow abundance to flow into your life and to truly receive.

Seeing the pain in yourself

The key to healing the root chakra, and thus creating a stable grounding, is to face the pain within yourself with loving acceptance and awareness. This is certainly not easy to do, as it takes courage to look with fully open eyes at your deepest emotions of fear and despair. Refusing to see and experience that emotional charge, however, eventually brings greater problems. You can be stuck for years in a relationship or work environment that fails to nurture and inspire you, or you can become addicted or depressed. But whatever happens, fleeing reality eventually causes more pain than confronting it does. In facing the pain, you confirm who you are: a being that is greater than the pain and who has the strength to face the pain and overcome it, and this is a healing experience.

Facing the pain is something you can do consciously; for example, through self-reflection or certain forms of therapy. However, you can be certain that life itself will also continually present you with situations that require of you to go within and to ask yourself what deeply inspires you and what motivates you. Life itself is directed toward growth and healing, and in nature, everything is directed toward self-development: an acorn instinctively wants to become an oak tree and a tadpole a frog. Your inner nature similarly wants to evolve and flourish, and life wants to support you in doing that. For a human being, this process is one of engaging consciously on the path of development and daring to entrust yourself to the inner power of your own nature. This human desire is as strong a motivating force as the instinctive impulse of the tadpole that wants to become a frog or the acorn that wants to become an oak tree. Your soul knows who you really want to be on Earth. In the same way that a tadpole instinctively carries within the blueprint of an ideal future as a full-grown frog, so there also exists in your heart intuitive knowledge about the full development and expression of your potential as a human being. And just as the tadpole encounters obstacles and problems in its development, so you also experience inner and outer resistance in the development of your unique nature on Earth.

Humans are the only creatures on Earth that are challenged to *consciously change inner obstacles into creative forces*. The human being is capable of transforming emotional burdens with conscious awareness. In human consciousness, this intentional transformation leads to self-knowledge, understanding, and compassion. Animals are also capable of self- healing on an emotional level, and they instinctively make use of the healing power of nature. However, they cannot deliberately choose to turn toward or to turn away from their emotional pain in the way humans can.

Animals have unconscious healing forces, whereas humans can *develop* conscious healing power when they dare to say 'Yes' to their inner pain. By saying 'Yes', I do not mean that you just tolerate the pain; I mean that you stop resisting the pain and allow the emotional burden to fully manifest itself in your body and your feelings so you can accept it with full awareness.

An example may clarify this. Suppose that from an early age you had the feeling that you did not belong. Maybe you were sensitive and introverted, and you found it difficult to express yourself in communication with others, or maybe there was little understanding in your family environment. Whatever the cause, this feeling of not belonging was so painful that you tried to push it from your consciousness. It could be that you shut yourself off from your emotions and from your surroundings. Maybe you had a hobby or a fantasy world into which you could easily flee and become absorbed. And when you became an adult, you found work that you performed well and into which you could become totally engrossed. Your performance resulted in approval from others, so working hard became addictive and an easy way to not have to feel anything until you began to demand too much from your body and your mind, and you were confronted with burnout.

When such a thing happens, you are faced with a choice: 'Will I heal only the surface symptoms of the burnout or do I go deeply within and ask why I *need* to work so hard?' This is a time when you can choose to turn toward the deep pain of the child within you that feels emotionally abandoned. Saying 'Yes' to this pain means you allow the child within you to express what it is still feeling. You can, with your imagination, encourage this child to make known to you what it is experiencing. Perhaps you see the fear, sadness, or loneliness well up; these are precisely the feelings that you were trying to mask by hard work. In saying 'Yes' to the pain, you say 'Yes' to the child within yourself, and you ask it to be completely present in your life. In time, you will notice that this child not only carries within it negative emotions, but also quite *positive* emotions, such as cheerfulness, hope, and a sense of adventure. The child holds your blueprint: the seed to growing into a fully mature oak tree.

The blueprint of your soul is never lost. Time and time again it offers new opportunities to expand yourself. Sometimes encountering a crisis or a dead-end is necessary to get you to the point where you really decide to be true to yourself and to choose *for* your own true nature. There is *no wrong way* to come Home to who you are, and it is also *never too late* to align with the blueprint of your soul. The soul is eternal and transcends living and dying in a mortal body. Rest assured that there *is* time and that there will always be new opportunities. Nevertheless, it is important to make a choice for yourself, so that you prevent the emotional pain from deepening and causing you to suffer needlessly. Turning away or fleeing from the accumulated pain in the root chakra holds you back from a fulfilling life on Earth. *It is my desire to see you thrive and radiate here!* Just as a fully mature oak tree enriches itself and its environment, so will the manifestation of your soul energy enrich the Earth with valuable inspiration. My wish is to see you come to full maturity, and I know that this wish corresponds to the blueprint of your soul. *You and I have a common goal.*

How do you restore the balance and harmony in your root chakra? How do you learn to trust the Earth again and to connect with the emotions and feelings that live within you? How do you create stable grounding in which the flow of giving and receiving abounds?

1. Acknowledge the value and power of emotions

Do not repress your emotions. Your emotions connect you with the inner child and the spontaneous, uncensored emotional life within you. This emotional life is the source from which comes power and is the seat of your passion, your zeal, and your unique being. A young child considers itself to be the center of the world. It does not as yet experience reality through imposed standards and ideas. Only later does a mental filter appear in its perception of the world. Initially, the child does not doubt what it feels. If there is anything that is unsettling, it allows emotions such as anger, fear, and sadness to flow through its body as a natural power, without restraint or judgment. The child as yet can do nothing other than this.

As an adult, you can see this process occur in a child, and you realize that you have lost this innate spontaneity. How does this happen? In your adult world, people aim at controlling the natural flow of emotions by managing and tempering them. Many of you are afraid of the power of emotions. This power is associated with chaos, impulsiveness, and irrationality. By wanting to restrain the flow of emotions as a result of your fear, you make negative judgments about your emotions. You drive a wedge between you and your feelings. For example, you feel anger arise within yourself and immediately you say inwardly: 'This is not good'. Or you feel fear and you immediately condemn it by thinking that fear is something that must be repressed. A conflict and split arises within you. Through the mistrust of your emotions, you turn against a natural force that you need in order to live a life inspired by your soul.

Your emotions connect you with life itself. The natural force that manifests itself in emotions is not irrational, chaotic, or destructive. *Emotions are aimed precisely at restoring harmony.* An emotion that you accept consciously allows you to better understand yourself. In this way, an emotion such as anger or fear, embraced with awareness, helps you to understand in what ways you are sensitive and vulnerable. The conscious handling of emotions can deepen and strengthen your connection with yourself. In this way, you bring more harmony into your life. Only when you deny your emotions systematically and repress them do they become explosive and uncontrollable over time. You cannot indefinitely deny that which lives deep within you. Repressed emotions will eventually manifest as a disruptive occurrence in your life. By contrast, in their natural and original state, emotions are similar to a rain storm. Over time the storm stops by itself and the sun begins to shine again. It is a natural phenomenon that has a beginning and an end. An emotion is like a wave that is best allowed to roll quietly onto the beach. If you want to dam it or obstruct it halfway, you create counter-currents that will eventually batter you.

The key to this process is that you begin to work together with your emotions. Connecting with your emotions means that you do not resist them, but that you surround them with attention that is free of judgment. If you are angry or sad, observe this within yourself and feel how this mood affects your body and your thoughts. Through observation, you take a step back, and you realize that you are *not* your emotion. The emotion is like a child who wants to be heard and seen, and you are the guide of this child. You reassure it and let it know that it is safe to make itself known to you. You can do this in a concrete way whenever you feel emotional about something, and you do this by encouraging the emotions to make themselves known through the child. Let this child come toward you in your imagination and allow it to express itself freely and spontaneously. Give the child your attention and compassion, and tell it that you understand its feelings and that you receive and appreciate the message it longs to give to you.

What do you do with this message? The choice is yours. Suppose you feel hurt and rejected by someone. You have consciously admitted to this emotional pain and have faced it. Now you ask yourself how you can best support the child within you. It may be that the pain is already largely resolved by your devotion to the child. Along with that, you can also feel the need to speak to the other person about what you have experienced. If there is an opening with that person, the encounter may deepen the relationship between you. However, it could also be that you feel there can be no opening with the other person and that you decide to seek less contact with that person and to focus on other relationships that nurture and inspire you. Connecting with your emotions means that you take their messages seriously and in consultation with the child within you, feel and weigh what feels best for you as a course of action. The key is that you cooperate with your emotions rather than fight them or suppress them.

2. Experience the natural beauty in and around you

The first chakra, called the root chakra, represents your connection with the Earth. It can help you to connect with me in a gentle and safe way by finding a place in nature that you like and where you feel comfortable. Every human being is sensitive to the beauty of nature: the trees, plants, and flowers; the animals, birds, and clouds; the course of the seasons. The simple rhythm and harmony of nature inspires awe, and you can be moved by the beauty and innocence of life in nature. Go regularly to a natural setting that evokes these feelings in you. If you cannot go outside, then look at the plants on your balcony or the flowers in a vase on your table. When you enjoy the beauty that you perceive, take note of what this beauty consists. This is not a 'perfect' beauty. What you see does not meet society's predetermined norms and standards. It is a wild beauty that is not concerned with approval from others, and it is a beauty that evokes a sense of peace and harmony within you. You feel the surrender of the plants and trees as they silently submit to the seasons. You feel the innocence of the animals that gently and quietly follow the pace of their lives. A wisdom speaks through nature that brings you into connection with your own nature, your own inner knowing.

What I would like to ask of you is to recognize yourself in nature. Amidst the harmony and simplicity that you find there, you may feel left out as a human being: an outcast from paradise. You, however, are no outsider – *you are part of nature*. The beauty, balance, and rhythm you observe in nature flow also through your being. Because of your excessively active thinking, it can be difficult to connect with this flow of tranquility and simplicity. But allow the beauty of nature to completely penetrate you. As you open up, you come Home to the non-thinking, silently knowing presence within yourself.

Your body is the bridge between you and nature. Through your body, you are connected with me. Look for a moment at your body in the same way that you look at the wildness of nature, and admire your body. You are accustomed to seeing your body in a judgmental way: is it attractive, strong, and healthy enough? These are *outer* standards, but can you also feel your body from within? Can you experience the primordial power and the wisdom of your body? Can you feel how your body wants to be nurtured and free to experience life in its own way, regardless of exterior standards that have been imposed upon you? The prevailing standards of beauty and health create a yoke under which you suffer in trying to live up to them. Your society designs images of beauty and health that are inauthentic and contrived, and as cold and clinical as the minds that conceived them. These images find no basis in reality; they are not bearers of truth. Look at the living beings in nature; even the leaves on the trees are all different and unique. No single being in nature strives to resemble another. The obligation of each living creature is to be itself, because when everything is itself, there then is harmony in the whole.

That is also the beauty that you experience in the natural wilderness – you experience the harmony of all things being part of the whole. Everything and everyone has its own place and contributes by being itself in coherence with the whole, and you, too, are part of that whole. You have a unique contribution to make simply by being who you are. How do you know who you are? You experience this by fully letting go of outer norms and standards. What is your deepest desire? What are the dreams of your heart? Can you make space in your daily life for what you really desire? Do you dare identify and then break away from what is inauthentic and contrived in your life? Follow your own nature and you will find your place within the whole. Trust that your own wild nature produces the same harmonious beauty as nature's wilderness. You are accustomed to adjusting to the demands and expectations of society, but what the Earth and humanity really need now are leaders, not followers. We need people who dare to connect with their deepest nature, with the most original, lively, warm parts of themselves, and with what makes them grounded and inspired human beings.

3. Connect with your body

Focus your attention for a moment entirely on your body. Imagine that you are a part of nature, such as a strong, big tree is a part of nature. Inside you flow energies and fluids that know exactly where they have to be. Your heart is beating, your blood is flowing, and all organs, tissues, and cells in your body strive naturally toward health and vitality. Feel that you are included in the healing and renewing force that is essential to nature. Your body has a self-healing capability, and you can connect with that capability simply by listening to its messages. Your body may tell you that you need rest, relaxation, and enjoyment, or attention and being held by another. Your body not only tells you about the physical aspects of yourself, but also about your emotional well-being. Listening to the signals from your body is nourishing for your soul. Your body is a finely tuned instrument that should be considered as a messenger of your soul. The body is not something lower that must be transcended; it is a gift that can bring you into deeper connection with your essence. Feel it now from within, and feel the Earth force that is alive in it. Feel the presence of your soul, which has entered into a dance with your body.

Imagine there is a warm life force in your root chakra, your tailbone, which you may perceive or visualize as a glowing red globe. From this inner fire, allow a healing energy to flow throughout your entire body – through your hips, your spine, your belly. Let this energy flow up to your shoulders, your arms, your hands, while at the same time feel it flowing down your legs into your feet – feel this from within. Become conscious of the life in all parts of you. Now ask your body: 'How do you feel? Is there anything I can do for you? Do you need something from me?' Ask and wait quietly and patiently. It is possible that your body does not immediately respond, so perhaps you need to get used to talking with your body – and this is entirely possible. The body responds to your attention – it basks in it! You are its inspiration and the sun in its universe. You can influence your body in a positive way by enveloping it with your consciousness, and by saying 'Yes' to the dance that you have undertaken with it.

Your soul manifests itself in and through your body. Connect with your root chakra to see if there is doubt or fear there that inhibits you from being completely present in your body and on the Earth. Embrace the doubt or fear with love and compassion. Do not condemn it; allow it to be, but stay present with the pain. By remaining present with the pain, you dissolve it. Contrary to what you often think, you do not have to 'work on yourself'. The aim is to remain present whenever pain and fear reveal themselves in your emotional life and to not run away from them. By being there for yourself – in complete openness and acceptance – the pain is transformed into strength. By embracing your fear and pain, you transform them and thereby you feel safe and secure on Earth. This safety and security only you can give to yourself. Real safety and security do not exist because the world welcomes and affirms you, but because *you* do that for yourself.

As you heal the root chakra, you create a channel for your soul to come down on to Earth. The more this happens, the more joy, abundance, and fulfillment you will feel. This is your destiny as human beings and not a distant dream, but a real possibility. Just as the acorn naturally grows into an oak tree, and the tadpole into a frog, so are you intended to radiate as a human angel on Earth

.

21. The Cycle of Your Seasons

I am the voice of Earth that speaks to you from the ground beneath your feet. I speak to you from the heart of Winter, which is a season of the year that brings much to you even though you do not always believe this. In Winter, there is a withdrawal of the life force into the core, and the season of Winter revolves around that core of light inside you: the fire -- the power of the spirit -- that burns deep within you. In Winter, the outer falls away; the branches are bare, and life withdraws into the trunk and into the roots; then there is silence and tranquility in nature. But this silence, this emptiness and barrenness, is not without life and not without soul. Feel it when you walk through the forest or in the fields; life is there, invisible, but tangible. Life withdraws into the core where it gathers force to sprout again in Spring.

This gathering of forces, in order to bring them forth anew, takes place in a cycle that repeats itself, again and again: Winter, Spring, Summer, Autumn, and Winter again. Such a cycle also occurs in your lives. There are times when your soul's energy on Earth entirely manifests itself; moments when the light from your heart connects with this reality and you completely express who you are. Think of such a moment from the past. Ask yourself, 'Which moment from the past brought forth a complete fulfillment of who I was? In what, and where, and with whom did I allow myself to be fully seen? Where did my energy flow well and completely?' Feel this for a moment in yourself.

Within a full cycle, this is a time of reaching out, of radiating, of Summer. Then, the next phase of the cycle is the energy withdrawing, in order to reflect on and rearrange itself. And then the cycle revolves again to a subsequent level of reaching out even farther, so as to express the soul even more fully on Earth. So you find yourself in a constant rhythm of reaching outward and coming inward; a return to the core in order to reach out, yet again, and to be yourself joyfully and to share yourself with the world.

Now, feel that core in yourself into which you withdraw. There is a place in your belly, just below your navel – your hara -- where you can feel your humanness, *here* and *now*, deep within the core of your incarnated being. I ask you to sink into this spot and from there to feel the primal strength that lives within you. Your heart belongs to your angel-being – your higher self – while your abdomen is the place of the 'beating heart' of your humanness.

Your objective in this life is to connect to that place in your abdomen, for only there do you incarnate on Earth and become fully human. Only from there does your light truly make a deep connection with earthly reality.

Connect with the flow of energy in your abdomen by allowing your breath to sink into that place, and feel the life that is there. Feel how this energy flow is connected to your creative power, with the vitality of the body itself, and also with your sexuality. Sink deeply into the center of your abdomen, and let go of the outer world for a moment. Feel how forces are gathering there that enable you to begin a new chapter in your life on Earth and that give you precisely the powers and talents you now need to manifest yourself more fully on Earth. Speak to that power, and allow yourself to be embraced by that immense power in your abdomen, which is your humanness. Feel how, in that place, you are deeply connected to me with *my* core – the center of the Earth.

Now take a fear from your everyday life that you frequently encounter. Where and of what are you afraid? Name it for yourself. Is it the fear of being rejected, or of being judged, or of being alone? Feel then how that fear gravitates to you, especially around your shoulders and head, because fear attaches itself strongly to thinking. Fears are fed and grow larger through thinking, because your thoughts are often panicky and lack confidence. Feel for a moment how the fear is not really related to something in the outside world, but rather stems from within your own mind and comes out of your own being. Now imagine that fear as a cloud of dark energy within you, and with your hands, guide that energy cloud to that silent, still point in your abdomen, into the power that flows quietly and confidently there within you. See how your abdomen receives and greets your fear in a very impersonal, neutral way.

Feel the elemental forces of nature in your abdomen. You are bigger than this fear, so console it. Let the fear see how strong you *really* are, and how you are part of Eternal Life. You are now embodied here on Earth as flesh and blood. Your body is a sacred Home that you animate with your own light, but your essence is eternal, regardless of whatever form it takes. Feel the serenity of your unparalleled strength, and then see and know that the fear remains on the periphery, not in your core. Let the fear circle around you, while you pull back into your core, into the deepest inner knowing that belongs to you: 'I am good; I am accepted here; I am beautiful as I am'.

I am Earth, and I recognize and greet you as the angel you are. Trust in my powers, and trust in the instincts of your body. Now in this Winter season, take the time to withdraw and to create as much emptiness within as you can. Remain in that silent space and feel what it is you want from your core – what wants to manifest on Earth -- and know you have the strength to rise above your fears. When you become aware of your fears, it is a sign that you are ready to transcend and transform them. If your fears become perceptible, consciousness is ready to receive them with compassion – the time is ripe.

Have no fear of your 'fears', and when fear arrives, call on your deepest power, your core. The fear makes it possible for your core to be felt, so be sympathetic toward the fear. You live in a world of duality – *near the darkest part the brightest light is always present.* They call out to each other and together form a dance. In your earthly life there is always the cycle of going inward and then reaching outward, and again going inward and then outward. And every time you go inward, you burrow a bit deeper into the dark, so that even more of your light can flow outward.

Deep within you the light and dark are dancing together. Honor this dance, for it is how the life energy functions on Earth. It naturally alternates between light and shadow, so honor the shadow as part of life. Just as a tree loses its splendid foliage in order to turn completely inward, so you also do something similar in the seasons of your life. By turning inward, you connect for a time with your pain, loss, and mourning. But it is also a beautiful movement in that the connection helps you to come closer to yourself, to enter more deeply into the core of who you are.

Accept this process. Do not abhor your darker parts, because they nudge you forward. They cause your light to incarnate even more fully. Welcome the parts of you that have carried the darkness within you and are bringing it into your awareness. If you have compassion for them, and accept them as part of your path, they will become your best friends through a deep sense of intimacy and connection. You are allowed to be human. You are an incarnated angel who experiences the extremes of light and dark so as to create 'gold' by accepting both. By transforming your own shadow, you create the 'gold' of compassion, wisdom, and a deep sense of Oneness with all life. That is the reason you are here on Earth, and that is why I love you intensely and welcome you from the heart. Whenever and wherever possible, I will support you with my strength. Feel this strength present in the ground beneath your feet, in the air you breathe, and in your body.

22. The Healing Power of Nature

Enjoy the Spring, when life unfolds in a new round of growth and blossoming. Allow yourself to be delighted by the colors, the sounds, and the fragrances, and the splendid emergence of new life. You are part of nature and you are also included in the cycle of the seasons. In you the new Spring comes to life, too.

Many of you have difficulty being on Earth. You often experience this world as a dark and dreary place where violence and oppression toward people and nature are commonplace. Experiencing this can make you feel gloomy and sad. Many of you even entered this incarnation with resistance, with a sense of: 'Do I really have to go down there and again be in that realm of pain, fear, and density?' There lives in you nostalgia for another reality where harmony, gentleness, and joy prevail. In your heart, you remember the vibration, the energy of this otherworldly reality, and when you are in the freedom of nature, this memory in your soul comes to life. In the freedom of nature, you reawaken to the beauty, the balance, and the connection that you carry in your heart. It is what you so long for, and nature can bring you Home to who you really are. The silence, the rhythm, the peace you experience there reflect deeply who you are. In nature, you can experience a regaining of your balance, yet at the same time, this experience evokes homesickness and sadness. There lives in you a deep desire for a reality that is free of the heavy, negative energies on Earth. The question is how to deal with this sadness and this desire.

It is important for you to realize that these feelings are not wrong. Homesickness is the call of your soul reminding you of who you are in your essence. Your soul *wanted* to incarnate on Earth. From a very deep place within you, you have chosen to be here, even though there are parts of you that resist and lose courage occasionally. By connecting with your soul, you remember not only who you are, but you also remember that you are here for a reason and with a purpose. The homesickness you feel refers not only to a lack, a deficiency, but also to a positive purpose – *that you are here to manifest the vibration of harmony and unity.*

How do you do this? How do you bring this purpose and energy into everyday life? *The key lies in reminding yourself of who you are in everything you do.* The more you can hear the voice of your soul in your daily pursuits, the more you align with your life's purpose. I would like to tell you how nature can help you to remember your true self. In particular, I will focus on the healing power of plants and trees.

All trees, plants, and flowers that live on me are rooted in the energetic flow of unity that supports life. In other words, the plant kingdom is very close to Spirit, to the Source, or whatever you call this divine energy flow. Consciousness in plants and trees is barely, or not at all, individualized, in contrast to the situation with humans and, to some extent, animals. Through the plant kingdom flow universal energies that are connected to the angelic realm. Trees and plants have no such thing as an ego, an individual 'I' that stands and acts in the world. The consciousness of the plant kingdom has an unbroken connection with the whole. Trees and plants are direct manifestations of the realm of the angels.

Angels are a part of vibrant energy fields that radiate unity and love. While the divine manifests itself in humans as an individual soul, in the angelic realm the divine takes the form of trans-personal, universal energy fields. There are different energy fields in the angelic realm, all of which emit a specific quality, such as love, or courage, or clarity. The plant kingdom on Earth developed its material forms by utilizing the energy of angels that are oriented toward unity and harmony. You experience their vibration quite naturally when you are in nature and become calm and centered. By being open to nature, you receive the healing power of the angelic realm – yet there is more. Whenever you align yourself with this angelic energy, you realize that in your essence, your core, you are *one* with this energy; in other words, that *you are an angel*.

Your origin as angel

You have not always been human. Before you incarnated on Earth as a human being and began your long cycle of lives, you were an angel. You found yourself in less dense surroundings – a more ethereal setting than you now experience as a human. You had yet no earthly body and you were not constrained by the laws of time and space. You could go and be where you chose, whenever you chose. The creative power of your thoughts enabled you to immediately manifest what you desired. There was still no individual awareness in you as you now experience it. You felt strongly linked with the group of angels, that vibrant energy field to which you belonged. You experienced yourself as part of a larger organism.

Imagine that you are an angel and that you are not yet bound to the human body. Maybe you see yourself as a sphere of light, or more traditionally as a beautiful being with wings. It does not matter how you visualize this angel, it is above all about feeling the lightness and freedom that correspond to this awareness. From this plane of existence, you chose to become involved in the creative adventure on Earth. Know that angels themselves are also in development, because nothing in the universe is static. You were creative, enterprising angels who felt attracted to planet Earth and saw that here, a multitude of life forms could emerge with opportunities for growth of consciousness. You wanted to test your own power to create and to support the Earth in her development and to inspire her.

Imagine that you, as an angel, implanted thought forms as 'seeds' into the consciousness of plants on Earth, causing all sorts of new forms to arise: new plant species, a refinement of existing species, beautiful flowers – a true diversity of life forms. Imagine how the image of a beautiful flower arose spontaneously in your mind and how you fondly offered this image to a plant that you felt was receptive. Out of your etheric body flowed the power of your imagination into nature – the plants and the minerals. These beings received the etheric seed-thoughts that gradually began to manifest within their physical forms. In this way, you helped to develop life on Earth.

Maybe this all sounds too magical and far-fetched and too much like a fairytale to your modern ears. Nevertheless, I ask you to let it play in your imagination and to feel whether something in it deeply resonates with you. Feel the love in your heart for life on Earth and how deeply you are bonded with me. You have been a co-creator with me of the life forms here. I myself am an angelic being who worked with you in ancient times – in joy and gaiety. I was already embodied in matter as a planet, and I was the receptive soil that received your creative energy.

My angel quality is harmony. The energy field that I emit as an angel helps to make possible the peaceful coexistence of different life forms. I want everything that lives on me to feel and be connected; I want to reveal the unity that exists throughout all diversity. When human beings recognize how they are interconnected with other humans and with everything else that lives on Earth, harmony and peaceful coexistence will be possible. This is my dream, my vision.

As an angel, you have contributed to the fulfillment of my dream. From a desire for unity and inspiration, you connected with life on Earth, but later, when you incarnated as humans, you forgot this. You came to know the reality of the body and the cycle of birth and death. You began to experience the duality of light and dark, love and fear. As you descended more deeply into matter, you began to lose some of your connection to the angelic realm and with the angel that you are. This has happened for a reason; this was not a mistake or an error; there is a purpose behind your journey of incarnation. One of the aims is that you allow your angel light to descend deeply into matter so that it becomes visible and manifest in my physical reality.

Feeling at Home on Earth

I know it sometimes seems impossible for you to hold on to your light in this physical reality. There are times when you wonder whether you belong here or if you are welcome here. You experience fear, doubt, and uncertainty when you try to manifest and express who you truly are. These feelings stem from memories of being rejected, either in this life or in previous lives. The pain that you experienced in previous incarnations has not left you. Some of you have sworn 'never again to give of yourself' when on Earth. You have decided to swallow your passion and your dreams and desires in order to never again be so vulnerable. I understand how this could have happened; however, this hardening comes with a price. By not wanting to give of yourself again, you disconnect from your soul and you reduce your consciousness to the level of the person by whom you were rejected. By pulling back you admit defeat, and mistrust and cynicism triumph over openness and optimism. In your heart there is sadness, because your soul continues to desire to fulfill its destiny: *to become a fully incarnated angel on Earth*.

In order to feel at Home on Earth and to open your heart again to life here, it helps to connect with the angel energy in nature. When you are in nature and you perceive the harmony around you, you feel your original connection with me. Your bond with me is older than your being human, and this bond does not have to be undermined by the fear and rejection you have experienced in human society. There is a great difference between the energy of Earth and

192

the energy of human society. You can experience this difference, especially in silent, quiet places in nature. Here you can experience that the spiritual Home for which you are looking is not located somewhere else, in other-worldly or heavenly planes. Home is not far away – *it is here, just below your feet*. My original energy of harmony and unity is familiar to you.

I embody the energy of Home for you. Feel again who you are – recognize your own beauty, grace, and divine inspiration. You do not have to remember this literally, from your human memory, but feel the truth in your being. The gentleness, beauty, and harmony that you experience in nature is the energy of Home, the energy of your origin -- *the energy of your soul*. That is why it touches you so deeply when you see how nature is being violated by people, and that is why it fills you with awe to be in nature with the plants, the animals, and in the open air, the woods, or by the sea.

Try not to judge what people are doing to nature – focus on *your* life. Do what makes your heart sing, and in this way, you naturally vibrate the quality of harmony on Earth. Your light shines the strongest when you feel at Home here on Earth. When you remember who you are, the old pain that you carry within will no longer block you; your heart opens and you become *inspired*. Your openness to life then directly transforms that old pain into a bridge to the heart of another. When you dare to live in openness from your soul, your true beauty is visible to yourself and to others.

Meet me, angel to angel. You are an angel and I, too, am one. I know you and you know me. I am still the receptive ground on which your soul can play and dance. *You are welcome!* As an angel, you came to me with your energy of renewal and adventure, and you descended into my physical reality. On this path of descent, you sometimes get confused, but do not let that discourage you -- *I can still see who you are*. Trust and live again according to your deepest desires and your boldest dreams.

Articles by Gerrit Gielen

Black Holes Inside Us

by Gerrit Gielen

Many people continually bombard themselves with negative thoughts: 'I cannot do this, this is not for me, I am weak, I must hide because who I am is bad, the world is not a safe place, this will probably go wrong'. Etcetera, etcetera.

How did this happen? Why do we do this? The reason for this self-destructive behavior is that all of us have at some point, whether in this life or a past life, been traumatized. Traumas are negative experiences that are so intense that our personality cannot handle them; a part of our awareness 'freezes' and remains stuck in time.

Take, for example, someone who in a past life experienced how their country was occupied during a war. People were picked up from the streets and suddenly disappeared. There was the continuous threat of violence and you could not feel safe anywhere. The past life personality suffered intensely from the overwhelming fear and could not come to terms with the situation for the rest of their life. A part of this person was traumatized and has become stuck in time, stuck in the reality of war, and keeps sending messages to the present day personality as if it is still war: 'Life is dangerous, there is much violence out there, you cannot trust people, you are powerless.' The current personality does not realize that these persistent thoughts are related to a very different reality; he simply believes the messages and becomes used to viewing life through the eyes of the traumatized past life personality. Unfamiliar people are regarded with suspicion; there is a sense of doom and a fear of violence always in the background, and the belief that it is best to lock yourself in your house, because if you go out you may never return.

Trauma acts like a black hole

The traumatized part of us is the biggest source of the fears from which we suffer. Note that fear always tells us that there is something *out there* which is dangerous, hostile, and harmful. Fear makes you focus on the outside world as the source of your problems, and not on the trauma itself. When

197

someone who is terrified of dogs is in the same room with a dog, their entire awareness will be focused on the dog, to the exclusion of everything else. But most of the time, the dog is not the problem; the real issue is their fear of dogs. If you keep on focusing on what is outside you, your perception becomes distorted. You focus on what you are afraid of and thus you tend to see it everywhere; your fear exaggerates the actual danger and you waste a lot of energy avoiding it.

This reactive pattern creates a vicious circle: the fear narrows down your perception of reality in such a way that reality seems to confirm and justify your fears even more. When you read the paper, your attention is automatically drawn to news about dogs attacking people or spreading infectious diseases. When you walk on the street, dogs seem to look at you in a threatening way, ready to jump at you. This circle keeps the traumatized part of you imprisoned, and that part of you cannot be released until the circle is broken. A traumatized part of the personality, caught in a vicious circle, can be viewed as a *black hole* inside us. It sucks up energy, it sucks up light, and it reverts us back into the past, to moments in time where our awareness became frozen and stuck.

I myself have an inborn fear of travelling. When we went on a trip to France this summer, I continually felt that the car would break down, and I saw signs of that everywhere. Just before we left, the belt of my trousers broke, an ominous sign, I thought. On the road, I noted stranded cars everywhere. When we were taking a break at a parking spot, I thought I saw traces of oil behind our car. On the car's dashboard, a message light appeared that told us we should go to the garage to change the gear box oil (this later turned out to be a mistake in the dashboard's computer). At another time, I noticed some tools in the back of the car, which to me felt like a sign that the car needed fixing. Etcetera, etcetera.

During the trip I decided to go within, into my black hole. I saw there a man lying at the side of a road, and I could only see his back. As I approached him, I was shocked; I saw his face and his eyes were stabbed out. He was far away from home, and the people there had not trusted him and had done this to him. He died, thinking of home, and wishing he had never left it.

In the past, I hardly ever travelled, nor did I drive a car. I thought I had very good reasons for this behavior, but I was unaware of the black hole inside me. Now, I travel often and the many trips we make bring me a lot of joy. All over the world, we have wonderful meetings with like-minded people and we enjoy visiting beautiful places in nature.

Arguing with people who are in a black hole, i.e. who have a narrow and fear-based perception of a particular issue, is hardly possible. When you try, they will immediately point to countless 'facts' and reasons to back up their worldview. They refuse to open up to the possibility that their fear - and not the outside world - is actually the problem. They are convinced their fear is caused by actual threats in the outside world and is therefore reasonable and justified. If you do not agree with them, it is you who is being naïve: you refuse to see the obvious facts which are right under your nose. The bigger the fear, the more rigid and firm the beliefs. Many websites on the Internet, which are full of ominous predictions and conspiracy theories, originate from black holes on the inner level.

Black holes may become so powerful that they suck up and take over the whole personality; in such cases paranoia (extreme suspicion) will arise. Everything people say or do is interpreted in a negative way, which makes normal communication impossible. Threats and conspiracies are perceived to be all around. Friends and family members, who try to break the spell of your obsessions, are considered to be under the influence of evil forces themselves. The paranoid persona has become completely isolated and imprisoned within their own mind.

To some extent we all suffer from paranoia. Almost all of us have some inner black hole regarding a particular issue which distorts our perception and our relationship with other people.

What can you do?

1. Realize that there is a black hole inside you

The first and most important step is to recognize that a part of you has been traumatized and is sending messages to you which are not right. Whenever you notice that your thoughts are particularly negative, or whenever you feel disproportionally afraid of something and you expect the worst, be prepared to go within, into the black hole, and face the traumatized part.

Ask yourself the following questions: 'Could it be that there is a black hole inside me? Could it be that there is a traumatized part of me which distorts my entire view of reality, a part that shuts me off from all the good and positive things that happen around me? Is my outlook on reality and my attitude toward people based on fear or on love?'

2. Enter the black hole

Step into the black hole, not to suffer, but to bring light and love into this part of you. Make an image of the traumatized part. Imagine, for example, that it is a lost child, and realize that it needs a lot of love and caring. Connect with this child, look into its eyes, and feel what it needs to gradually release the fear.

Every time you find yourself harboring negative thoughts, gloomy feelings, or irrational fears about life, about people or society, encourage yourself to go within. Search for the black hole inside you: the prison of the traumatized part. Be present as a loving angel; bring comfort, reassurance, and light.

3. Tell yourself the truth

The gospel of John says: 'The truth shall set you free.' Words that are true carry enormous power. Truth originates from love, not from fear. Feel the love available in the universe; feel the love of mother Earth for humanity; feel the love inside you and approach the traumatized part of you from this love. From that source, formulate a few short sentences and frequently repeat them aloud.

For example:

- Life is good to me.

- The Earth loves humanity and helps us.

- Humanity is awakening and becoming more aware of its unity; this unity is starting to manifest itself everywhere.

Speaking this kind of true message is a very powerful instrument when you wish to relinquish fear-based thoughts.

Nowadays, there is a lot of literature on 'positive thinking'. People stand in front of the mirror and start to repeat positive messages to themselves:

affirmations. This only makes sense if these messages are true, and they are true when they are based on love.

Someone may repeat to themselves: 'I am rich, I am rich', hoping that reality will conform to their intention. But is this affirmation based on love, or on the fear of lack, the fear that the universe will not take care of them? If the latter is the case, the affirmation will not work.

Before you start endlessly repeating affirmations, go back to the source. Connect with the love inside your heart, and see what messages come up from this well. Start with loving yourself and embracing the traumatized part of you. *Affirmations based on fear do not work.*

If the affirmation is right, it is not really essential that you repeat it often. Have you ever experienced that someone said something to you that deeply rang true? Was it necessary that this message be repeated all the time? It probably was not. If a sentence that really feels true to you is spoken out loud with the right intensity, you do not have to say it over and over. One time a day is sufficient.

However, the first and most important step in this three-step process is to honestly face the black hole inside us. As soon as you realize that fear is distorting your perception, you can start to embrace that fear with love, and from that love find affirmations which are true and effective.

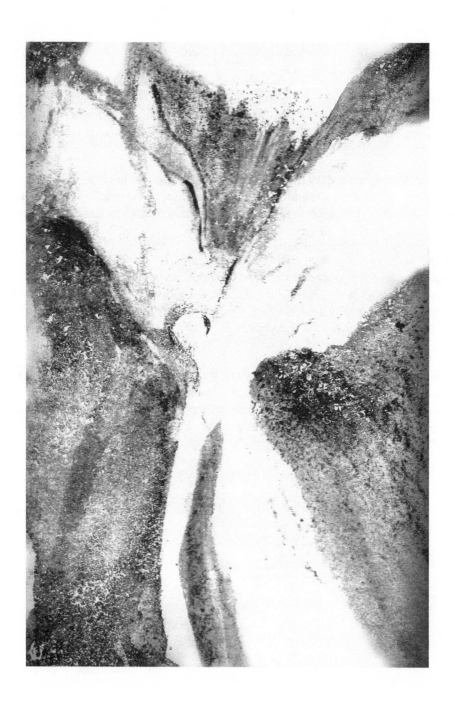

Meeting our Past Selves Outside of Time

by Gerrit Gielen

In this essay, Gerrit explores the consequences of a non-linear notion of time for the field of regression therapy. He argues that getting in touch with other lives is not so much about remembering something that is over and done with. Rather, it is a creative interaction with living presences who are still growing and evolving just like you do. The past is basically as open and undetermined as the future. This throws a fresh light on the meaning of regression therapy and offers wonderful possibilities for healing.

From the fields of science, philosophy and mysticism comes the argument that the linear progression of time as we experience it does not actually exist. This is most evidently expressed in Einstein's Theory of Relativity, which clearly shows that the 'now' is not a unique moment. A moment that is experienced by one person as 'now', may be in the future for another person, and in the past for someone else, depending on their respective positions in space and their motion. Events that occur at the same time for one observer could occur at different times for another. But if the 'now' is not a singular or unique event, then our traditional conception of time collapses, and the division of time into present, past, and future falls apart. This means that the past is not fixed. *Everything* takes place in the 'now' – including our 'past' lives.

What does this mean for reincarnation therapy and the task of a regression therapist? To answer this question, let me first address the meaning of memories. If we remember something, we are reaching, psychologically, to another point in time. We connect our own 'now' with another 'now', which, to us, lies in the past. However, if the past, present, and future are in fact part of one extended 'now', then the past is not something that is definitely over and finished. Remembering is not a passive process, but an *interaction with a living energy,* i.e. an interaction with the part of us that is experiencing that particular past moment as their 'now'-reality. Also, as we reach out to that past self through remembering, the interaction goes both ways. If we connect with a time in the past, we touch this other 'now' with our energy, we influence it, and we also receive energy and information in return.

If linear time is an illusion, remembering is communicating

Remembering is, in fact, a communication process. To remember is to communicate with the past. This also applies to memories of past lives. Here, too, an energetic exchange takes place between the present you and the past you. At some level, every regression therapist knows this. A good therapist will never ask a client to try to remember something. He will always make the suggestion to move toward it during regression. For example, he may say 'Go to the true origin of the problem.' The therapist knows that the latter approach works much better the former. Why? Because this instruction corresponds more closely to what is actually happening. There is something to go *toward*: another 'now' in which the traumatic event was first experienced.

What happens when you connect your 'now', your present, with another 'now' and when you start to communicate with the part of you that lives in another 'now'? The result of such a communication process is the creation of a new and *'shared now'*. As soon as you begin a dialogue with someone else (in this case your 'former' self), you are sharing the 'now', the same present. And from this 'shared present' new possibilities arise: specifically, it means that you can send healing and understanding to your past self, thus influencing the past in a real way. As the past is not over in absolute terms, you can change it from the future.

What does the above concept mean for reincarnation therapy? In my experience, there are three important consequences:

I. Healing the past instead of reliving it

According to the traditional view, what we can do with painful experiences in the past in regression therapy is to relive them and thereby take off the sharp edges of the experience. Take, for example, someone who has a fear of heights. He sees a therapist and discovers that he appears to have fallen to his death in a previous life. This event is lived through a number of times and the fear of heights seems to have disappeared.

The traditional view is that the deadly fall in a previous life has created a fear that has not been sufficiently processed, in one way or another, with the result that it manifests in this life as a fear of heights. To be made aware and relive the cause of the fear seems to provide the solution.

I, however, believe that what actually happens is the following: somewhere in space-time, someone is falling, and is feeling fear. The fear is so intense that a cry for help is sent through space-time that is caught by an incarnation with a related psychic structure, or by an incarnation of the same soul, who then experiences the cry for help as a fear of heights. When this person enters into regression, they connect their own consciousness with that of the falling person and in that way the latter person's fear of heights is eased.

The crux to letting go of the fear is, in my view, not the reliving of the fear, but adding a clear, loving consciousness to the fear. This lucid consciousness is you, in the present. As you reach out to the past with clarity of mind and the intention to heal, you actually touch the past self who is suffering like a spiritual guide does or a 'guardian angel' if you will. Because you, as guide or angel, take compassion on the anxious person, the other you in that other 'now', that other you can let go of their phobia and find peace. In that past, they will have a sense of peace and surrender. In this case, the person falling to their death may die in a state of surrender, and the resulting trauma of this death will be less intense. By recreating the past in this way, your present is affected: you, in turn, are also set free of your fear of heights.

Be with your past self as their guide or 'guardian angel'

Reliving a trauma from a past life, a technique that is often used in regression therapy, only makes sense in a limited way. In the worst case, it can bring up a lot of unnecessary anxiety and tension. I feel that it is much better for the client to enter regression therapy as a helper, as a guide and friend to their past selves who are in pain. You then do not identify with the problem, but much more with the solution: you are not the victim, but the healer. You do not need to relive the darkness, but bring your light into the darkness.

Specifically, before entering a past life, I invite my clients to see themselves as a being of Light, an angel who can travel through time and space. When they sense the truth of this, I ask them to reach out to the traumatized person that they encounter in a past life, and be of assistance by sending love, encouragement and understanding to that person.

I once had a client who had considered suicide during a very difficult period in his life in which he suffered from depression. At one point, he heard a voice that encouraged him and told him that he did not have to take his own life. It was a voice of trust and reassurance. I advised him to travel to that difficult time in the past from the present as an angel. By the end of the exercise, he realized that it was he himself who had been that voice; from the future he had helped himself through that difficult period.

II. Approaching unexplained anxiety as a call for help

Many people suffer from inexplicable fear that is ever present in the background. It may be mixed with other feelings, such as sadness, grief or anger. It is often a feeling that has been present since childhood, for no apparent reason.

Behind that fear is always a cry for help. It is a call from another 'now', another life, or sometimes from one's childhood. In my view, the aim of regression therapy is to discover what that fear is, and to help that other person just as you would help a good friend in need. You go to that person, speak to them with encouraging words, and surround them with support, love, and understanding.

Instead of regarding the persistent fear as a sign that something is strangely and irrevocably wrong with you, you regard it as belonging not to this 'now' but to another 'now', another 'you' who is reaching out for help. You - the client - are the one who can resolve the fear by bringing understanding and sympathy to it and by seeing the fear as a call for help from someone else. This 'someone else' is you in another 'now' moment. As soon as you find that person, and you observe them with neutral and compassionate awareness, their fear will become understandable to you and it will be easier to accept it and to gradually let go of it. The anxiety is relieved by seeing it as someone else's problem, because in that way you dissociate from the energy of fear. From the objective perspective of the 'now', in which there is often no cause for fear, you realize that you yourself are greater than the fear and that you are able to embrace it with a more expanded awareness.

The fear thus becomes a doorway that leads you into another life, that connects you with another 'now'. By allowing yourself to move gradually toward that fear in regression therapy, you will discover its source and you can start to heal it. Often, to create the necessary shift and to disassociate from the fear, it is enough to simply ask the question: 'To whom does the fear that I feel belong?' By addressing it as a call for help from another point in

206

time-space, you create a bridge to the fear. This bridge does two things which are beneficial: it creates *distance* between you and the fear and it brings *healing* to the fear.

III. Creating a new past

Another possibility arising from this new perspective on time-space is the possibility of *recreating the past*. If the past is not fixed and over, and if to remember it is to exchange energy with it, then our traditional view of causality goes by the board. Traditionally, things cannot be caused by events in the future, only by events in the past. But what about the man in distress - in the example above - who hears a voice from the future telling him to have faith and who decides to live on because of that? Here, the future seems to have a very real impact on the past.

How can the idea of creating a new past have a bearing on regression therapy? I often invite the client to rewrite the past in the following way. After they have become aware of trauma that occurred in another life, I suggest they connect with the past life personality *before* the trauma occurs. Almost always there is a critical moment in time, at which the personality could have chosen a different path, one of which would have lead into a more beneficial future, in which the trauma would not occur. While in regression therapy, you can still choose the road not taken; you can pick the alternate pathway or 'timeline' and activate it.

Imagine a sensitive, prophetic woman who has been burned at the stake as a witch in a previous life. There were times during that lifetime in which she sensed the need to better protect herself, or run away perhaps, or to break off ties with certain people. In regression therapy, she attempts to connect with such a crucial moment, a time when she could have made choices that would have prevented the burning. If that works, and the client gets emotionally connected with an alternate timeline that could have developed, the trauma is partially or completely erased from the past of the client.

To achieve this, the following steps are required:

- The client makes an emotional connection with the traumatic past life. The point of entry is usually the time of the trauma itself.

- Subsequent to that, she travels back in time to a moment before the trauma when the decisive choice is still possible.

- The client then begins to communicate with the person she was in that previous life. She explains to that person why she can and should make the positive choice. She encourages her and provides her with insights from the larger perspective that she now has. This will create a new shared 'now' with possibilities for healing for both parties.

- The past life personality feels inspired to take a different and new course of action and the traumatic events no longer take place.

As you send healing to the past life, it in return sends healing back to you. By creating a new past, the present is altered as well. According to this view, the past is not fixed: the past, like the future, is an ocean of possibilities. From the present, our current 'now', we can choose again and again which pathway to pursue, which timeline to activate, whether it is in the past or in the future. Our lives take place in a time-space continuum which constantly moves and changes; we are constantly interacting with our other lives and they with us. The part that does the interacting is our consciousness, our conscious awareness. This part is our essence and it is independent of time and space. It travels *through* the time-space web but it is not *in* time. It is the part of us that is eternal and unchanging. Because consciousness itself is independent of time and space, it is a source of Light and healing for all that exists *in* time. The more conscious we become, the more we enter a timeless realm, from which we radiate light to all of our lifetimes.

In conclusion

I realize that introducing this new and dazzling perspective on time and causality in the area of regression therapy raises a lot of questions which cannot be answered within the context of this short essay. I do feel however that a non-linear notion of time, which is much more flexible and open than our traditional notion, offers great promises for this area and does far greater justice to the mysterious nature of our soul. The soul is like a sun with numerous beams, each representing a lifetime expressing a part of our Self. The beams all radiate their light simultaneously and as they do they are connected at their roots and interact with each other through the center of the sun.

Many years ago, I was sitting on the shore of a lake on a hot summer day, staring at how the water reflected the sunlight. I thought about life as a human being on Earth. The irregular patterns of the light patches on the water, together with the heat, had a hypnotizing effect on me. The image of an eternally shining sun which split itself up into countless dancing patches of light seemed to provide a metaphor of what life is about.

The light patches are the many human lives we live that each in their own imperfect way reflect a higher source. Together they perform the perpetual dance of life; together they create a perfect whole. In reality, there is no time; everything exists in one big present. When one patch grows larger because of the movement of the water, another one immediately shrinks in size.

We all have many lives on Earth and they are interconnected in dynamic and deeply meaningful ways. All these lives are geared toward the same goal. Together they reflect a higher source; together they are whole.

I belief the same goes for humanity at large. On a deep inner level, a level outside time, we are all connected to the same source of Light. It is our mission to express this source of Light as best as we can *in* time.

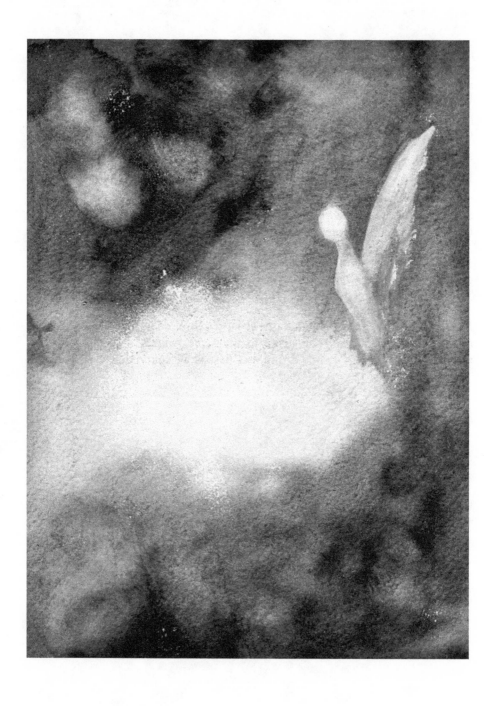

Appendix - Past Life Regressions

In part I of this book, I referred to the regression therapy that I did in the year 2000, which affected me deeply and initiated a rebirth on the inner level. This appendix contains what I recorded in my journal at the time.

This account is a fairly spontaneous representation of what I experienced during the regression therapy. It contains twelve short chapters, which correspond to the twelve lives that I have witnessed. These lives are not described in chronological order, but in the order in which I observed them.

1. The Humble Monk

2. The Spiritually Advanced Nymph

3. The Sexually Abused Woman

4. The Fanatical Scribe

5. The Imperious Queen

6. The Concentration Camp Victim

7. The Roman Prince

8. The Priest Scholar in Atlantis

9. The Prostitute in Colombia

10. The Medicine Woman in a Snow Landscape

11. The Fiery Campaigner for Justice

12. The Follower of Christ

1. The Humble Monk

I see a simple, narrow little boat that sails through a channel between the reeds and moors toward a wooden jetty. I am sitting in the boat, a monk of about forty - forty five years of age, dressed in a brown, jute habit. I am of solid build, have a monk's haircut, a bald spot on my head and a pale complexion. I have a robust look, somewhat boorish, muscular and stocky. I am of medium height, and have deep-set, light brown eyes. Not really handsome, but what I do have is a special tenderness and thoughtfulness in the way that I act and move about; this is striking when compared with my robust, earthy appearance. I'm sitting in the boat staring at my hands and feeling a bit abandoned, and also somewhat discouraged. But I have no strong emotions, more of a silent, somewhat sad resignation.

At the end of the jetty there is an area with pebbles and trees; the weather is clear and the sun is shining; the terrain is located near some kind of lake with mountains behind it. In the distance, on a bay in the water, there is a white city. I am no longer allowed to go there. I have been banned from there, but why?

I see the semi-dark, brownish interior of a church, not a church of great splendor and opulence, but a simple space with some wooden benches, with a plain altar at the front. Now I see a high-ranking church official standing there in an immaculate white robe with glittering jewelry, large rose-purple and green stones, and a high white-golden mitre. He stands before the altar and I stand at its side. He gives some instructions, and he clearly has no knowledge of how things work with us in practice. I do not agree with him and I protest. It is not about something theoretical or theological, but rather about practical, everyday matters - how those need to be done. The priest focuses on principles, and I see things from a practical viewpoint, from the way things are.

I come from simple stock and have had little education. I am an intuitive person, have a mystical kind of contact with nature, the land and the birds, and also with the humble folk that live there. I am unable to reason or argue very well with the priests. I do have something fierce and hot-blooded in me, something that revolts against this injustice. But I do not have the gift of words, and the emotion of anger actually does not really fit me, because I am by nature peaceful, quiet and intuitive. But what the priests want is so blatantly unreasonable that it arouses a mixture of bewilderment and indignation in me.

My opposition is not well received. I am told that I do not understand because I am from modest stock, and I cannot grasp the higher principles of the religious leadership. I do not rebel directly against the priests, but I refuse to cooperate with their regulations and, therefore, I become ostracized from that ecclesial community. I then go into the ordinary village community to live among the people and work in the countryside, in the fields. I do not mind so much because I connect with the elements, and I feel at home in nature. I am physically muscular and strong. I live by myself in a kind of hut at some distance from the village community. But I can get along well with the inhabitants; they are friendly and humble and I feel at home there, in contrast to my not feeling at home with the authorities of the Church.

I do feel a bit lonely. I do not have my own family. I have been a monk for so long. Moreover, I am somewhat socially awkward; I do not know very well how I would relate to a woman. Also, I know that I have something special, and that is reflected in my mystical connections with living beings in nature. I feel that I have a very thick skin, and deep down inside me there is a well with very clear water. The water can't really flow out; only sometimes that special 'something' comes out through my eyes, sort of like a warm glow that can give people comfort or encouragement. Sometimes I allow it to be seen.

The people know that I have this 'something', that I can give that warmth unexpectedly. They accept that from me without really asking for it. I can be very tender. But I don't know how to combine this trait with a relationship with a woman. I am also somewhat bashful. I do long for such a relationship, and for the warmth of physical contact. There is a woman in the village that especially draws my attention. I find her quite beautiful, and when I look at her I am weak in my stomach; she is folksy and a bit weathered through hard work, but she has something special in her energy, something melancholy in her brown eyes and her smile. Her melancholy reminds me of the mystical atmosphere that I sense around the animals, trees and fields. She and I connect with each other through our eyes. I know that there is a kind of recognition between us, and that she also feels something for me. But I really don't know how to go about initiating a relationship with her, and anyway I suppose she sees me as a monk, with whom you can talk but not really someone with whom you can become intimate. I am afraid to get close to her. That makes me sad, but I accept my continuing solitude. I am not a fighter for that kind of thing.

I experienced my greatest moments of ecstasy in that life at the prayer meetings in that humble church with a group of monks. Every day at five o'clock in the morning we used to come together, and we sang and prayed. Also, there were times when I was the only one sitting on the wooden benches in that church space, while the daylight filtered through the windows, and I felt so connected to the divine world. The silence and simplicity made me deeply aware of the other, non-physical world. After I was expelled from the Church community, what I missed the most were those morning services with my brother monks, or sitting alone in that church. Sometimes I went back with my little boat to that place, and I looked from a distance - from the jetty - to the small church that used to be my home; my separation from it made me sad and melancholy.

I died in the village community when I was somewhere between sixty and sixty-three years of age. I think I died of a lonely, sad heart. The villagers came to me quite faithfully during my illness. She, too, that one woman, she also came to my sick bed a few times. That of course did me a lot of good, but it also pained me because I could not explain my love to her. I had missed experiencing that love with her during my life. Perhaps she missed it too. We did make a connection with our eyes. I died in the morning as I lay on my bed alone. I heard the birds outside and felt the soft rustle of the wind. I had no more pain and left my tired body. The body was still strong and could have lived much longer, but my heart was sad and lonely. Very lightly and quietly I rose from that body and left my beloved little church, the land, the beautiful natural world and my silent love. I think this life took place in the early Middle Ages.

I rose from my body and was received and welcomed by some of my monk-brothers who had passed before me - to the other side. I felt reassured by their familiar faces and friendship. I continued on in a world of white beauty, love and wisdom. I remained in this realm for a while to recover from my grief, and this is where the desire to reform the Church was born, a longing to bring justice to the Church, so that true faith would prevail there and bring joy and relief among the (ordinary) people. I had a strong feeling that it was the mission of the Church to care for the weak and vulnerable, to offer consolation and a spirit of community. My wish was for these values to become central in the Church. I was sincere in my desire but also naive. I actually had no knowledge of evil. I had the idea that the Church's leaders simply did not see the truth, and that I would be able to show them, like a child that reminds its parents of the beauty of the sky, or the rapture of a budding flower. I was not sufficiently aware how power corrupts, and in that way I also had no idea of the defenses surrounding the Church authorities. My innocence made me into a pure human being, but it was also my pitfall because I underestimated the stubbornness and difficulty of the whole power game on Earth.

If I look back further on this life, I see that it was unfortunate that this monk hesitated to approach the woman from the village. Had he done this, then the second half of his life would have been very different. The woman would have responded to his love, because she had gone through a lot of hardship (the marriage with her deceased husband had been hard) and she sensed the monk to be a soul mate. I get the feeling that they would have been able to give each other much love, and that the monk would have learned about sexuality in a positive way. I even see that they could have had a baby together, even though the woman was older. The monk would then have had experienced, through that ordinary life, the fulfillment and joy that he now experienced only in the Church. And if that had been the case, his attention toward the end of this life would not have been so exclusively focused on reforming the Church. He would have seen that love and genuine care do not necessarily have to be spread through the Church; and he would also have been less naive, as he would have benefited from this woman's weathered, common sense wisdom.

However, the promise contained in the second half of the monk's life was not fulfilled, and I feel that had a lot to do with the way in which the monk was brought up. As a small boy, he was different from other children. Although he was a solid, muscular boy, he had a certain sensitivity and gentleness in the way he went about doing things. Because of that, he could not get along so well with the other children. He often preferred to stay close to his mother. He felt safe with her feminine energy, although his mother responded in a rather ambivalent way. On the one hand, she tolerated his constant presence with her, but on the other, she was disturbed by it and felt it was not normal. Something like: 'Come on boy, get out into the world.' That attitude of hers resulted in the boy's feeling that it was wrong for him to rely on his mother (the feminine energy). This feeling added to his trepidation regarding the woman in the village. The fact that the boy was different had also been the reason why his parents 'gave him to the church'; something that he had not resisted.

2. The Spiritually Advanced Nymph

If I go back in time to the point that generated the humble monk's mystic inspiration, I find myself in a kind of gym with an orange-red floor. I stand there wearing an ethereal, blue dress in a stance of meditative dance: on one leg, leaning forward with one arm stretched gracefully ahead. I am a young woman, Japanese, of slim build with black hair of medium length tied in a pony-tail. I belong to a spiritual order, which is located on a high mountain plateau far away from the 'ordinary world.' I can see myself walking outside, along beautifully trimmed Japanese trees, and I know I have a lot of contact with nature. Then I see the face of my teacher: he is a man of about 50 years, with a distinctly Japanese face, with golden brown eyes that have a kind, peaceful radiance. From him I learn much about the spiritual, the inner life.

During that life, I develop a vast and deep concentration on my inner self. This produces in me the ability for a refined perception of nature and of people. Because spiritual development in this order (in Kyoto?) is combined with physical dance meditation, the body's sexual energy is sublimated and despite celibacy, no sexual-physical frustration builds up. I feel very safe and protected in this order, separated from the coarser world outside. I believe it is the third century BC. I barely get in touch with ordinary people and life outside the order, nor do I feel inclined to do so. My top priority is my own mental development and I make remarkable progress in this area.

However, inherent in this exclusive focus on myself is also a kind of narcissism and contempt for ordinary people. I do not understand what their lives revolve around, nor do I feel it is important to me. I am focused on my own growth, which is what I have been taught by the order in which I live, and I do not doubt my order's authority. I consider their views as the truth; their worldview is for me just a given. Later, I teach students myself, and I am firmly convinced of the truth of my own ideas. I have developed a kind of spiritual arrogance, but I am not really aware of it; I possess wisdom, but I have little warmth and compassion. My sympathies lie with studious pupils - I pay a lot of attention to them and have patience with them. I also admire advanced masters. I have no sexual relationships, no children or partner. I do not miss those relationships at all because I feel comfortable within the order; the members of the order are my family.

My dying in that life is as my life had been; I die - at around age 50 - very knowledgeable about the dying process, but with hardly any human connections or emotional attachments. There is something cold and clinical about that whole lifetime. I do not know the extremes of despair and joy, of romantic love and desolation, of fear or deep mourning, and because of that lack, the development of my heart (love, compassion) remains stunted compared to the development of my mind (third eye).

3. The Sexually Abused Woman

In the life that I see next, I am confronted with coarse, ordinary reality in no uncertain way. The first image I see is that of a woman, about twenty five years of age, who sits half-hidden in the corner of a dirty, dark barn or stable. I am slim and wiry, have a fair complexion, short brown hair and brown eyes. I feel fear in my stomach. A muddy figure appears in the doorway.

When I look through the mud, I see the face of a man of about forty-two years, brown eyes with a phony expression, yellowish teeth, and he stinks. He has evil on his mind, and I cannot get through to him because he is mentally, emotionally, and spiritually underdeveloped and very self-centered. I can't talk to him as one person to another. He is a kind of overseer; he comes from common folk but has managed to work himself up the ladder by his cunning to a more or less powerful position in the community of that village. He is full of aggression and frustration. I am in service to him and his family as some kind of housekeeper. I live there as well (in the barn). He loves to use me as a slave, because he sadistically notices that I despise him somehow. I am spiritually more developed than he is, but that higher development does not come from this life; it stems from a life or lives before this one. I now live in a feudal era in which the position of women is one of total submission to men. I cannot escape from that man's household. I come from a family that paid little attention to me. My spiritual development and a kind of arrogance that accompanies it are innate and are interpreted by the overseer as pride, and that taunts him.

He rapes me regularly. I feel debased and disgusted by the sexual abuse, and I resent the man deeply. I try shutting myself down, completely disengaging, but I cannot avoid the feeling of humiliation from entering my consciousness. In the beginning I am still green and vulnerable, and the rapes cause pain, sadness and confusion. Later - over the years - I become cold, hard and withered. I develop a deep hatred of the man and try to take revenge by manipulating him psychologically. His ego is his weak spot, and I manipulate him in the area of his social position. In this way, I manage to influence his actions as overseer, and I also acquire some power within the family.

Emotionally I am very lonely. Because he is the only man that I know, over the years I begin to have some hope for a shred of affection from him. Sometimes I even sit in that barn waiting for him. Whenever he arrives to give full rein to his sexual lusts with me, I always hope that, during the sex, he will show me some affection as a person. After all, we have lived under the same roof for so long now. But he does not do that. He has sexual intercourse with me in the straw, then gets up and just walks away without even a look back. I remain lying there, and I am intensely humiliated and disappointed. Each time, I hope for some love, because I am so terribly lonely inside. I do not find the physical sexual experience itself so terrible anymore now, and I even experience a secret delight - a very ambivalent kind of pleasure, namely a form of enjoyment that is strongly intertwined with submission and power. It is no longer during, but only after each sexual experience that I feel horribly humiliated, dirty and alone. I am in fact a hunted animal that is alone and grasps for some love, or at least to be seen as a human being. I do not conceive a child. The man's wife dies at a certain point in time, but I remain a servant. After the man's death, I live in the house and feel even lonelier. Perhaps I am still in service with his now adult children.

At the time of my death, I am alone in that cottage (it contains an eating area behind a small sitting area) and I have a heart attack or something causing me excessive respiratory distress. I can no longer draw any air into my lungs. I can see myself against the wall in the sitting area trembling and collapsing slowly. I am in my early sixties. I am lonely and hardened. There is no one to whom I need to say goodbye, and no one will miss me. I see that my eyes bulge out and I die. When I come out of my body, there are angels who catch me, but I am not receptive to their gentle love and comfort. I have become withered and my heart has turned to stone, and a deep gray depression hangs around me. I have grown cold, and there is no longer any light or warmth in my being. However, there is hardened anger. And at the end of this life, a dangerous residue remains present in me: the only thing that in fact gave me a semblance of happiness in that life was sex mixed with power. I emerged from that life with a distorted and painful image of sexuality.

4. The Fanatical Scribe

I am a man of about forty-five years of age. It is the sixteenth or seventeenth century A.D. I walk around in a white robe with a golden cord around my waist. I look a bit like Harrison Ford (!), well built, muscular, dark blonde hair and dark brown eyes that can have a fanatical and angry stare. I am a scholar and clergyman, but I am also out in the world a lot where I spend time talking and arguing in quite high circles. I am passionate about my religious-social ideas, and intellectually I am well developed due to a good education (Monastery, Jesuit?). I have an innately keen mind. I live in Belgium, initially, but due to my outspoken views and fiery temperament, I create turmoil in my region. Because of that turmoil, something happens to my mother. I get embroiled again with the higher members of the clergy. I see a spacious room before me in which I enter into a debate with the authority figures. I try to convince them with all my fire and passion, but I do not realize that they are less concerned with the truth and more with maintaining their own positions of power. In that sense, despite all my sharp reasoning, I am rather naive. The authorities show me the door, and I am exiled to Spain. This rejection and exile makes me feel bitter and resentful.

In Spain, I live (somewhere in the Southwest) in a remote area, in a spacious white building complex with a large square courtyard. An image pops up of me sitting in my room and looking outside. I see a young Spanish woman in the courtyard playing with her child, a little boy, in the afternoon sun. Both have soft brown skin tones and dark eyes. What affects me the most is their innocence, the childlike intimacy that they radiate in their carefree daily activities. I feel a level of basic peace and surrender in them that I myself am incapable of experiencing. Because of my high-minded idealism, I have always ignored the ordinary, simple things. I can't actually really enjoy simple pleasures in this life, because my moral mission lies heavy on my shoulders. I feel called to combat evil and injustice and I am consumed by this inner fire. Because of that, I rarely relax, and I am hardly open to emotional contacts with other people, such as women. I have little patience for their 'weakness', their feelings and whims. It is not so much that I am hostile towards women, but rather that I do not even notice them. I am extremely focused on the spiritual and the intellectual during this life.

My life in Spain ends, and during the last phase of my life I am embittered and also very solitary because, apart from the occasional contact with former acquaintances, I see no one - except the Spanish people around me. However, I do not experience my loneliness very emotionally like the abused woman did. Mostly, I feel misunderstood by my peers and having been rejected and exiled still enrages me. Because of my passion and indignation, I have become devoid of emotion. I do not desire human contact as much as I desire the satisfaction that comes from people realizing that I am right.

In this lifetime, I am hot-tempered and highly principled, but I do not desire power for the sake of power. I am focused on truth rather than power, and I focus on this with great zest. At the end of my life, I am still enraged and bitter, but I start to realize that the image of the mother and child playing in the courtyard conveyed something essential to me. The innocence and natural intimacy this vision radiated is the key to what is missing in my life, a key that I have consistently overlooked. Despite my keen intellect, I lack the natural grace and wisdom that the woman and the child have. I feel disheartened as I grow old, and I start to doubt the value of my intellectual quest. Could it be that real truth can only be found on another level, having to do with living life with all its emotions and relating deeply to other humans? I know I will not find the answer in the remainder of this life. I die with a mixture of anger and doubt in my mind.

5. The Imperious Queen

This lifetime took place during the late Middle Ages. I again had a fiery temperament, but this time I had no illusions about the Church. Disillusioned, my passion was aimed at more worldly affairs, and I did not bother with high-flying ideals. I was a kind of queen to a French court, and I had real power. I see myself walk through dark, damp corridors in my palace, and I also see a large room where an audience is seated. People are gathered around a podium on which I sit, and I wear a silk, regal robe, laced at waist, stomach and chest, such as was the fashion at the time. I wear a white wig with curls, and my face and chest are powdered in white. It seems that I do not go outdoors very much. I have a finely chiseled face, small, dark brown eyes (somewhat vitriolic, beady eyes), a small nose and narrow, red dyed lips. I have thick, flax blonde, straight hair, but I usually wear a wig in public.

I'm domineering and also impatient. People are afraid of me, but they also laugh at me behind my back. I am lonely; there is no man in my life. I suspect that my husband was a lot older than I and has already died. I am about forty years old. I am in charge, and I am determined to keep pulling all the strings. Therefore I demand to be kept up to date on everything. In that regard, I am quite paranoid. But it is not easy to manage such a large domain, because you never have a complete view of what is going on in all the relevant places. As a queen, you cannot be everywhere, and you have to put your trust in certain confidantes. I have a few, but I never really do trust them. These high-ranking men are only interested in increasing their own power.

I also have several lovers, and this is what makes me most vulnerable, because in these contacts I cannot entirely suppress my need for love and affection. From my – often younger – lovers I expect sexual pleasure, flattery and obedience. In exchange, they have an opportunity to achieve a better social position. However, I am quite erratic about fulfilling my promises to them; sometimes I simply do not fulfill them only to demonstrate that I am still independent, and that I am the one who undisputedly is in charge. I am also afraid to give political power to my lovers; they might turn against me. I always operate behind a mask, and I show little or no compassion toward the people around me, or to the workers on the estate. My politics are callous, but I tell myself that I am just and fair.

I feel that I come to my end in this life in an unnatural way: by intrigues that I have not foreseen in time to prevent them. One day, I am overtaken by a group of men who invade my palace. I'm being dragged from my throne. I feel powerless rage coupled with horror. My paranoid fears have come true. The men take me outside, everyone pulls at me, and my attackers and others are beyond themselves with rage. There is no one to help me. I am led to a scaffold and beheaded. I see a standing, light-wooden rectangle on a light wooden block with a grey, large knife at the top that drops on my neck. I feel an intense fear, but it all happens very quickly. I see my head lie there. Blood flows out of it. For a while, it looks as if I am still in my body while my head is off already. I wonder where I am now, in my torso or in my head. I feel how my torso is paralyzed. Then I ascend upward, and from that scene I see my body cut in half lying there surrounded by a crazed crowd.

I ascend upward, feeling nothing initially. Then I feel anger toward those who have betrayed me. Questions rattle through my mind about how this could have happened and how could I have prevented it. I am overcome by these thoughts, and therefore I do not notice the guides who are close to me and who try to explain to me that this earthly life has come to an end, and that it is time to let go and look at it from a wider perspective. I am not really given to self-reflection, however. I am overcome by feelings of anger, fear, resentment and powerlessness. I take these lingering feelings with me to my next life. When choosing my next life, I am not truly aware of the larger perspective of my soul.

6. The Concentration Camp Victim (part I)

I die in 1944 in Auschwitz-Birkenau, and at that time I am literally reduced to nothing: there is no joy, no hatred, no human feelings, only the experience of my absolute *'nichtswürdigkeit'* (German for worthlessness). I am not a human being anymore, merely a shadow of a shadow. I wander around the concentration camp, past the rolled up barbed wire on top of the fences, on bare ground, through barracks, cold and hungry. I'm bald and emaciated, no more than a skeleton with bones that are jutting out. I am a woman, but I'm too lifeless to be raped, only fit to be kicked. I see myself lying on the ground in the dirt, and a high boot or shoe kicks my skull. Some blood appears, and it is very strange - this lifelike human color of red in a completely gray and dehumanized environment. I faint. I do not feel humiliated or injured because I'm hardly there anymore. My life force is like a very weak flame about to be extinguished.

I have come to the end of my journey through matter. I am now at the furthermost point away from my origin; to be further away is impossible, because in that case I would no longer exist. I'm at the farthest conceivable point away from God, and this creates a turning point. I am dead silent inside, and this absolute silence finally brings me back home, to the silence of God. After this life, nothing will ever be this bad; my fire is at the dimmest point, one small gust of wind, and it dies out. I can fight no longer, and I surrender; when I physically die, it is like slipping into a deep, still silence.

After my death, I am nursed and cared for on the other side by guides and angels, but it takes a long time before I show any intention to return to life.

Along with love and joy, my anger and passion have also been extinguished. I don't want revenge, I don't want to convince anyone; I just want to be in the silence of God, nothing else. The passion and aggression I had experienced in several of my past lives have disappeared, but so has all my life force. I do not want to exist anymore.

The Concentration Camp Victim (part II)

I see a section of a forest with a wide path between two rows of trees. I follow the path that is black (black mud?). It seems like autumn. The path leads me to a deep, large pit in the woods. In it are skeletons; white bones and carcasses without any flesh. I stand at the edge of the pit and look into it. As I begin to imagine who the people were to whom these bones belonged, I see them all in a row, with clothes, jackets and bags, talking with each other. The way they are dressed reminds me of the 1930s or 1940s of the 20th century. I see a middle-aged wife with a warm-brown fur coat and a hat on. She has black and gray hair in a low bun, blue eyes, and she talks with her neighbors; she is from a middle class environment.

Then I see myself, a young woman (about thirty five years), quite tall, slim, slightly curved back, with a small hat and long skirt, holding hands with two children, a boy of about twelve years of age, and a girl of five years of age. I am a Jewish woman and come from a well-to-do milieu in Germany. I have big blue eyes, which look helpless (in a slightly pleading way), black hair in a short hairstyle. I am somewhat fearful; I'm someone who adapts easily and does almost everything according to the social rules. I am afraid to stand out. I am married, but I don't have that much contact with my husband. He is somewhat distant, just as conformist as I am, and engrossed in his work. I keep myself mostly busy with our two children. I would like them to succeed. I am preoccupied with them and a bit fussy as a mother. I am quite fearful and nervous. I do not allow my true nature to be seen, and I avoid strong emotions -- I am thus somewhat of a *flat character*.

In the 1930s, when Hitler comes to power, we observe the political developments with fright, but we do not believe that we are directly at risk. We believe ourselves to be protected by our good civil position. We are gullible and not at all critical of Hitler and his regime. We are civilized and reasonably well educated, but when it comes to politics, we are very naive. At some point we, our family, are captured like many others had been already. We are on the train to Birkenau in Poland. On the train platform, I am separated from my husband. I see him disappear in the crowd. He and I are afraid, but we think we will see each other again. We think: 'This must be a mistake; we are such good, trustworthy citizens; this mistake will soon be undone.' I am with my children in the train.

I wonder where we are going, and then I see these words before me: 'Auschwitz-Birkenau', but when the regression therapist asks, I say: 'Birkenau'. When I look it up later, I see that there have been two camps, Auschwitz I and Auschwitz II (i.e., Birkenau) that were located close together. Thus, I was imprisoned in Birkenau. After arriving there, all of us women stood in a row with our children. Then men in green army suits with boots and caps came, and they took our children from us. My children shriek as they are pulled away from me. I freeze; I don't understand what is happening. This cannot be true; they surely will bring my children back to me later. I feel as if there is a large, sharp knife that rips right through me, from top to bottom through my entire body. When my children disappear from sight, I fall on my knees and collapse. But I can't really cry. It is more a desperate, dry gasp, as if I have been torn apart.

Later in the camp, the only thing the other women and I talk about and what runs through our heads is: where are our children and what is happening to them? All women who are mothers are obsessed by those questions, and our protective instincts somehow sustain us in spite of the miserable conditions in which we live (cold, hunger, vitamin deficiency, and drafty, cold barracks of dark brown wood). We must work hard doing forced labor - I don't know exactly what (something to do with naked corpses in a large, dark brown barn). We think only of our children. Different messages seep through to us, sometimes positive, mainly negative -- horror stories about abuse and fire ovens. My heart shrinks with misery and fear about what could be happening to my children. The thought that they are unprotected out there somewhere, amid all that, horrible, incomprehensible evil is intolerable to me. It is beyond my comprehension. We have done nothing wrong to them (the Germans); we have always been good and done our best, but after a while the idea that all of this is a mistake wears off. Apparently, there *is* such a thing as absolute evil, and we are right in the middle of it. As time goes on, the other women and I give up any expectation of an ounce of compassion or a scrap of humanity from our captors. We always assume the worst, the lowest. All that hate and aggression toward us; where does it all come from? It baffles me. I remain in the camp for quite a long time, during which many of my fellow camp-residents die around me, either from illness, or they are taken away and disappear mysteriously.

Rumors about gas chambers continue to circulate, until after a while we know for certain. Ironically I continue to survive - I the weak, frail coward. My constitution suddenly turns out to be tough and strong, even though I do not care about life anymore. Over time the hope that I will ever reunite with my children again is as good as gone. We know nothing definite, just as every other aspect of existence is uncertain in the camp. My feelings become too numb to still have hope. I die slowly inside. Every day those humiliations, those hardships -- physical: cold, hungry, always being unsafe; and mental: hearing again and again that you are nothing, scum, hardly worth to still crawl around; you could basically just be trampled to death. I walk around there appearing to be dead, with a bald skull, white translucent, empty eyes. I wander the barren plain in the camp searching for something edible, scraps of food.

Finally I am taken to the gas chamber, along with about thirty/forty other women who are still left over from the labor camp. We file naked into a white, half underground area. There is a dull sense of dread in my stomach. So now it is going to happen. I quickly go into a corner, so at least I have still some space to myself. Men in green army suits, dressed quite neatly, chase us inside. I am in the corner, a bare skeleton, and my elbows are pushing away from me; I am in a state of semi-consciousness, but still knowing that I'm going to die. Some women are now starting to scream, suddenly gripped by panic and agony. I concentrate on my own place in that corner, close myself off from their fearful screams, but at the same time I feel pity and sadness in my heart that it has come to this for us, that we reached this absolute bottom. But I know that death is the only way out. Existence here in the camp could go on no longer. There was no longer any way to stay alive. I feel myself to be superfluous. They are right, the Germans, I am *nichtswürdig* (worthless), and probably not one member of my own family is alive anymore, so why should I be?

At one point, the shower heads go on and the gas spreads, invisible, although I believe I can see it. The panic intensifies although many women are in the same dull state of consciousness as I am. Death may occur after three to five minutes. I can no longer breathe and become nauseous. For an instant, I feel the sharp agony of the fear of death in my stomach. Then I sink slowly away, through my knees until I fold up sitting on the ground in my corner, dead.

A beam of light falls on me from heaven, and through it I ascend to the other side. Along the way I see my children from a distance, in brown jackets. They look at me; they are in pretty good shape. But I pass them without feeling. I am inwardly dead, and I can no longer bring myself to go to them. I have no emotions anymore. I continue upwards and end up in a nursing room. I am provided with nursing care by guides, escorts and angels. I'm lying in a high, white hospital bed; I am completely translucent and weakened.

During a trance I see that, after a period of recovery, a special guide is talking with me. He stands before me in a long blue robe. The face I cannot see; there is a dark gray cloud around it. But he is called Bartholomew. He reaches out both his hands to me and I put my hands in his, as in a greeting. We embrace each other. I get a happy feeling in my heart. But I also feel very weak, so I lie back down on my hospital bed, and he comes and sits next to me. 'You have gone through a lot,' he says. 'Take your time to regain your strength.' And, referring to what happened with my children, he says, 'You don't have to understand everything in the moment when it happens.'

Then he takes me outside. We are on a path that leads to a mountain, a large, white, mountain, which for now seems to be covered by an equally shiny white shroud. 'That's the Promised Land,' says Bartholomew, while he points to the mountain. Suddenly I have to laugh because I see that it is on Earth! Who could have thought that?! The mountain: where heaven and Earth come together, there is paradise. 'We are going to build it together,' says Bartholomew, and 'We need you.' I react with disbelief. 'What should I do?,' I ask. 'Bring love among people,' says Bartholomew, 'and show them the way.' A soft, gentle feeling arises inside of me.

The jump into in my current life; fear of incarnation

Before I incarnate into my current lifetime, I see myself in an atmosphere of white light. I sit cross-legged, in a white robe, and before me kneels Bartholomew in a blue robe. He is encouraging me. Bartholomew appeals to my boldness, which is desperately needed because I still feel very weak. There are the events from the lifetime I spent in the concentration camp, and even before that that have depleted me -- the downward spiral of lives through which I gradually lost my fire and sense of self-worth. I am surprised - in trance - that I feel so weak and limp. I am entirely made of white light, with a white robe. I have a feeling that inside my torso, my heart and my belly - there is a kind of strength in the form of knowledge and insight. But everything beyond, and especially my arms and legs, is terribly weak and powerless.

Can I really incarnate in a state like this? It becomes clear to me now that it is only on Earth that I will regain my strength. That surprises me. I thought that I could recover also on the other side; that I could recover there slowly and completely. But apparently that is not so. I see that the purpose of my upcoming life is for me to regain my strength. I see a solid yellow color before me, a golden yellow that is both powerful and flexible. If I can develop this yellow energy of self-awareness and confidence, I will create a new foundation for myself. I see that yellow as an upright rectangular base from which all kinds of flowers can grow that spread around in a sort of cascade upon my surroundings. Flowers or color wisps of nice dark blue and blue-purple and also orange emerge. Warm, vibrant colors.

Now I imagine that I really proceed to incarnate. I am standing on the edge of that white, heavenly realm, and I have to jump. I realize suddenly that I actually feel so very tired. Bartholomew encourages me, but I am now overcome by great hesitation and with grief. Suddenly I realize that I really have to do this all alone, and that I should let go of his hand. It breaks my heart that I need to let go of his hand; I become deeply disheartened. But in the end I still jump and fall as softly as an autumn leaf gently fluttering down through a gray, misty atmosphere. I feel gloomy but not really anxious. Am I really present and aware of what is happening?

I see myself as embryo - I see the colors orange and yellow - in the womb of my mother. I see it all with a perspective of observation; I am not really engaged; it is more like a watchful waiting. As soon as I am in the womb, I am concerned about the next step: to be born. That frightens me.

7. The Roman Prince

I am looking down on a desert, a barren plain, in which are three large pyramids, sandy-colored like the ground. When I focus on the image, I see a caravan travel through the area, a group of people in long dress, carts and donkeys - and I see myself as a small boy in a cart behind, in an open box with some bags. I look in the distance towards our destination, and I'm in an expectant mood. We set up camp near some kind of settlement.

I see myself sitting there now at the edge of a deep, rectangular trench; my knees and lower legs dangle over the edge. It is a type of channel with grey, clayish soil. At the bottom are dead bodies, in the oddest positions. I look at them without emotion. I am a child, and no one explains what this is. I am curious and descend down to the clay ground level to walk among the bodies and to look at them. I experience this just as a curiosity, not as something shocking. These people were slaves; they died because of an accident, when a large body of water rushed through the channel while they were working. That tragedy does not affect my community and me. We do not see the slaves as human beings; they are not of our own kind.

When I look further into this life, I see myself as a young man of eighteen, in a white robe down to my knees with a belt around my waist, and sandals on my feet. I am a Roman prince in Egypt. I have a slim build, black hair that curls up at the sides, and almond shaped green eyes. I am vain and spoiled. I have never known suffering or poverty. I can see myself with a whip with which I lash the ground. I'm bored, and that makes me aggressive.

Now I see myself standing outside with that whip. Behind a low fence there stands a crowd dressed in rags; they beg for bread. Famine and disease are rampant. I lash out at those people with my whip. The sound of their pleading voices makes me mad - while I am also bored -and that combination of feelings is why I whip them. My whip hits the front of their bodies resulting in streaks of blood. The people back off screaming but cannot move away very well because they are all crammed so close together. Whipping them is my way of finding sadistic pleasure. I will teach them not to squeal like that.

Later I see myself entering the palace where I live. I enter a large space with a rectangular swimming pool in the middle with marble around it. It is a beautiful, abundant yet stark space (with steps and platforms and also white pillars). When I enter, the council of elders is waiting for me. I feel both caught and triumphant. They disapprove of the behavior that I exhibited outside earlier. They say that I have lost my self-control. Now I see what my position is in that palace community . I am a kind of heir to the throne, and because I am still young, I am under the direction of this council of elders, whose job it is to coach me to grow into being a worthy ruler. I'm not going to listen to their opinions, however. My throne is already assured, so they cannot make me do anything - and they know that. And so I ignore them and go my own way.

There are no ideals, values, or guidelines that I follow. My conscience has never developed. I'm pampered, and I live only for my own pleasure. Because everything here is about wealth and enjoyment, I am also easily bored. And that boredom makes me restless and aggressive. I never feel satisfied and fulfilled. At the same time, it is not in me to seek anything other than hedonistic pleasure. More fulfilling values have never been taught to me.

I enjoy myself sexually with a number of girls who walk around in the palace. They are slaves, but they look very nice and well-groomed, and at least they imply that they take pleasure in the small orgies that I organize. In my sexual experience power/cruelty and pleasure go together. And only my enjoyment is key to me. It is a question of how much pleasure I get out of it; the girls are the means, and it seems as if they also take that for granted. However, this kind of sex also does not fulfill me, except for some moments of pleasure, which often include a release of tension and aggression. I operate entirely from my lower abdomen (sensual pleasure in the form of food, sex and wealth) and solar plexus (aggression, cruelty, and desire for power). The centers of heart, third eye and crown chakra are almost completely closed. Therefore, I am always missing a sense of purpose and meaning in my life, and that hollow existence drives me crazy.

In the next image I see that I am a lot older, about fifty years old. My face is weathered and wrinkled. I sit on a kind of wooden throne in an abandoned, dark space. I am cranky and grumpy. Sometimes I walk around and kick against things that seem loose. I am somewhat calmer compared to the years of my youth, but this is not because I have come to my senses. Rather, I have seen it all, indulged in my aggression, and there is very clearly a void within me now. I have become even more self-absorbed, but I don't feel authentic loneliness, because I am unable to feel things deeply. I am somewhat depressed though, as if a gray veil hangs over me. I go outside sometimes now, which I had not done much in the past. I see myself standing on a balcony that is attached to my white palace. I have a very broad view, and in the distance I see where the three pyramids are situated. I stare at those pyramids; they awaken something in me, something from a distant past. Suddenly there is fear in my heart. I actually feel something in my heart!

Suddenly I wonder what I have done with my life. How did I get so perverted and violent, while earlier, much earlier...

8. The Priest-Scholar in Atlantis

When I concentrate on the pyramids, I end up in another lifetime, a much earlier life. I see many white buildings, and high quality technological equipment with red and green lights. My group and I run around busily. Located outside, in the middle, there is a great big round white disc lying flat on the ground, with six or seven long, straight roads running out from it. We are working on the disc, and we try to make contact with an alien civilization. Maybe the disc is a kind of receiving station?

I belong to a circle of adepts who are pretty far advanced. It is the ancient civilization of Atlantis. I am a tall, serious man with short-cropped dark hair, age forty-five or so. I am a kind of priest, as well as a scholar. We are fond of knowledge; we are completely in love with a certain type of understanding of the universe, which offers us a way to recreate society according to what are, to our understanding, higher principles. This knowledge is a combination of spiritual laws and state-of-the-art resources. For example, we can manipulate thoughts by using our equipment (something with waves, wavelengths, etc). The technology we have at our disposal is associated with spiritual knowledge, obtained through, among other things, meditation. We hope to enhance our technology and knowledge in the future through alien contacts. What I am observing in trance doesn't look anything like the current, materialistic technology of today.

We become immersed in our striving for knowledge and lose contact with nature (the natural rhythms of things). We do not pay attention to or appreciate the consequences of our actions. I do not have bad intentions; I am not driven by power, but rather by a strictly mental quest for truth. I am emotionally very underdeveloped, but mentally and spiritually (third eye), I am highly developed.

At one point, I see everything become very dark, murky blue and shadowy gray. At the bottom, I see a warm yellow, where I see simple people living and working on the farmland, but they cannot resist the forces that we have summoned. At the top right in the dark, I see a huge angel of white and light blue color. It stands on the horizon, pleading. It asks us something, but we are not receptive to the plea. I think it is pleading for love, as a counterweight to knowledge; the warmth of feeling as a counterbalance to clinical mental thinking. But we are not emotionally sensitive enough to receive this message. We are mentally over-developed, while our emotional center has hardly developed at all.

Now I see an immense tidal wave of dark blue-grey water that immediately smashes everything to bits. Everything crumbles under this force; and now, all I see is very deep dark blue and grey. People drown and are swept away in this immense water tide. I am drowning too. I am dragged away, and, at some point, I choke. I am baffled and do not believe at first that this is happening. After I drown, my body drifts lifelessly in the water; it is bobbing around, deep under the water. I keep floating around in my astral body. I cannot believe that what I thought was our crucially important project has come to an end so violently and suddenly.

Again, the angel appears at the now slate grey horizon. This angel is really gigantic; I do not even come up to her giant feet that are also very wide and earthy looking. The angel emanates something feminine. I imagine that I sit inside the palm of her large, calloused hand. She speaks to me: 'It was an experiment in duality,' she says. In some ways it is clear to me that we were not on course with our project. I can hardly believe it. 'You can't *overcome* duality,' says the angel, 'you can only *live* duality.' But I do not understand what she means very well. I have experienced too few emotions to understand this message. I do, however, see that my dark clothes turn into white now. When that happens, I suddenly feel as if I am a student who is open to learning something new. In that state of mind, I am humble, and I am receptive to the possibility that things may be fitting together very differently than I had thought they would. I am listening now to the angel, but because of my lack of development in my heart center, I am missing an important part of the message.

9. The Prostitute in Colombia

This life is set in Colombia. The first image I see is of myself as a baby in a hut. The surrounding area is shabby; the hut is in a humble settlement. My mother disowns me as baby, because I am a girl, and I am an excessive burden. If I had been a boy, she would have given me to a rich lord who had no son; that was actually the intent of my conception. Now, however, this intention has failed, and my mother no longer wants me.

She feels disappointed, anxious, and angry. If I had been a boy, she would have had a way out of her dire financial situation. Now she has to get rid of me; I see that her husband (who is not my biological father; that was the rich lord) stands by somewhat helplessly.

I am brought to a cloister of nuns. I see a rather large monastic community behind walls surrounded by grounds in a mountain setting. Here I have a quiet, peaceful youth, which is also a bit on the dull side for me. There is one dear sister who gives me special attention; she has sweet golden-brown eyes and a soft skin. But all in all I find my life there to be a dreary affair. In my adolescence, I occasionally go outside of the convent walls on errands or something similar. One day, while on the mountain road that leads to the monastery, I am held up by a group of men on a cart drawn by some horses. First they call out all kinds of provocative things to me. In a way, I do want to play their game. Then they kidnap me - not entirely against my wishes. I'm about seventeen years old. The men bring me to a brothel, which is also a community behind walls.

The madam overseer of the brothel takes me in and initiates me. My first sexual experience is painful and humiliating. The man who robs me of my virginity is not especially malicious, but I'm not at all prepared for what awaits me, and I feel dishonored when he removes my clothes. Also, the physical intercourse causes me much pain. I am appalled by the experience, but yet I know that I will have to remain in that brothel. Although I have to bite the bullet and accept my fate, I also find the experience to be exciting somehow. After a few years, I'm part of that community, and I acquire an increasingly more elevated position. I have a sound self confidence. I am a tall, well-proportioned woman with black hair and brown skin. I have dark brown eyes and full lips. I dress well. I have a natural beauty. I feel strong and confident. I take part in all kinds of intrigues and manipulations, both inside the brothel and with visiting guests, some of whom are gentlemen with power and influence.

At one point, I have contact with three or four of these politically influential men. One of them has my sincere sympathy. That's because this middle-aged man is so courteous and gentle. I'm not used to being treated with respect as an individual. I see this man before me dressed in white, with grey shiny hair, light blue eyes and slightly tanned skin. He is also a bit overweight. I do not so much feel attracted to him sexually, but his melancholy and courtesy move me. He is not a fighter (unlike me) and not macho. He does have influence in society, but that is based more on his intelligence and family background. I eventually fall in love with him, because with him I experience for the first time what it feels like to be seen and respected as a person. He is interested in what moves me emotionally. He is looking to me for a feminine sense of security and strength. He is not a cut out for all that political jousting and risks losing his position and prestige. I advise him and encourage him to defend himself. He is much more passive than I am and does not want to fight. .

There comes a time in that political conflict when action needs to be taken; the conflict is in the decisive phase. I decide to intervene to save my lover. I lose my typically rational and calculating nature, and I impulsively give a henchman the command to whip the two children of my beloved's arch-rival, who also is one of my visitors (clients). Later, these two children are found dead. I see blood streaks caused by a whip equipped with bullets, inflicted by a man who acted on my command. I pay him. I don't think I envisioned this result as a possibility. I believe that I only wanted to teach my lover's rival a lesson by threatening his children. The children are found dead, however, and I believe that I am dumbfounded by what I have caused. I have little direct experience with aggressive physical fighting that can take place out in the world. I'm really only familiar with craftiness and deception within the protected walls of the brothel.

My disproportionately bad deed evokes an overwhelming desire for revenge in the father of the murdered children (the rival of my lover). One day he comes to get me in my quarters, and he drags me outside. I am not aware of what is in store for me, but I know there is no turning back and that I am at his mercy. At some point, I realize that what I did could not be condoned by this man. My act was one of desperation as well as aggression. The man ties me up and takes me away on a cart. He locks me in his basement and tortures me.

I experience this torture, which is sexual in nature, as the worst thing I have ever gone through in my incarnations; even worse than what I endured in the concentration camp. The last time he tortures me, he brands me in the places of my body that are connected with female sexuality. Then I see myself shivering in a corner of the dark basement with a cloth around me. I am very sick and in a feverish state. Not long after that, I am tied to a wooden post and left to die. I see myself hang on that pole on an abandoned hill, somewhere in the mountains. I hang almost lifeless on that pole. I am thirsty because of the heat. Then I die. Afterward, there is only emptiness; a nebulous no-man's land. Dark shadows pursue me. I am scared; I have no resistance. I can no longer defend myself; my strength and self-confidence are broken.

In the final phase of this life, especially after the torture, my self-awareness and will to live were nearly extinguished. My prior confidence and self-esteem were shattered, leaving me no longer knowing who I was, and I had great self-doubt in everything that I did or desired. I have a feeling that after this life, there was a long period of stagnation and murkiness. Because my self-esteem had been destroyed, in subsequent lives I was submissive and fearful. I no longer made active use of my own passion and will, but rather exercised my will only in a passive way. For example, I sought out people with strong personalities with whom I felt recognized and loved a little bit, or social structures behind which I could take shelter.

Later in the regression therapy, I see that this life could have taken a different course. The key to that possibility lay in the relationship between my lover and me. He was lacking the courage to be visible and self-assured in the world. What I was lacking was the courage to show vulnerability. If I had let down some of my armor so he could see how vulnerable I actually was, he would probably have found the courage to move away from his family and live with me outside of the brothel. We would then have chosen each other, and both of us in time would have been able to step outside of the web of intrigue.

I see an alternative lifeline in which this possibility could have occurred. My lover and I live in a simple cottage far from the ordinary community. We are very happy together. We experience the physical love between us in a very tender and sweet way. I begin to cry when I see this. Through the experience of love in that relationship, I could have begun to heal the stigma that I carry with me as a prostitute. In this lifeline, he dies before me, but what we have had together continues to comfort me. I die a few years later, when I'm out walking on the road toward the village community; I see myself collapse (heart attack) near a few large stones where some children are standing.

10. The Medicine Woman in a Snow Landscape

I see a hut that floats in the air (?), but a steel-gray ladder hangs on it that I can climb and go inside. I see myself as a sturdy baby on the lap of my grandmother, an elderly woman in simple clothing. The cabin is surrounded by lots of white snow. It is in Lapland or something of the kind; it looks Eskimo-like. I see the face of a Siberian husky dog before me; he has white fur and expressive eyes. I see a path through a grove of dark green pines. When I'm older, I often take walks there; it is the road to the nearby community. My parents are absent -- I'm being raised by my grandmother, who dies when I am a teen.

I see an image of a ritual that we conduct in the forest. I am already a young adult woman. A group of about twelve people sit in a circle around a fire holding each other's hands. This gives me a feeling of warmth and unity. It is wonderful. I enjoy it intensely. I feel connectedness: horizontally with the people in the circle - and vertically with the sky. I have a feeling that we *become* the fire. I literally see a ring of fire, a perfect circle where the fire flares up and we are no longer separate beings; we go up into the fire. Participating in these rituals are the happiest moments of my life. Fire here means to me: inspiration, being together, connectedness, being attuned to each other and the cosmos.

When I am an adult, I fulfill a role in the community: I am a kind of medicine woman. I lead a humble existence. After my grandmother's death, I remain living in the cabin. I heal people, including children: I see myself sit in my cabin while children come to me, and I stroke their heads. As I stroke their heads, I also make certain gestures. I also do something with herbs and medicines. My role of medicine woman connects me with the community and gives me a sense of purpose and accomplishment. However, I guard myself against contacts of an intimate nature; for example, I do not have a family. I have a clear sense that I am different, and because of that I am always on my guard. I'm not truly spontaneous in how I express myself to others. My inspiration and joy in life flow mainly through the path of healing. I feel ecstasy at the rituals that I perform with my group of kindred spirits. When we are together, there is no need for extensive talk or an exchange of our feelings. During our rituals, we go about our work silently and intuitively, and then we depart from each other.

The caution that I always carry with me indicates an awareness of potential danger. As I wonder where that caution comes from, I end up in another life.

11. The Passionate Campaigner for Justice

I see the image of a funeral pyre, a pile with branches with a long, dark brown, wooden pole in the middle. I am being taken to it in spite of my angry struggle and opposition. I am sentenced to death for being a witch or heretic.

Prior to my execution at the stake, I had been locked in a cellar, separated from the other members of my group. I am a member of a group that is fighting for something and against the ruling authority, probably against the Catholic Church. I feel a deep hatred for that Church. My group and I have been meeting at regular intervals and listen to a leader in a white robe. Many of the attendees wear a white robe, but I am dressed in simple clothing. I am involved in politics; I fight for justice in a very passionate and angry way.

I see myself now in a humble settlement with huts. There is a group of people around me. They congregate and listen to me, while I am orating angrily. I want to make them aware of how much they are being mistreated and abused. I want to convince them of the bad motives of the authority figures and make it clear to them that they are being cheated and that they need to rebel. The people listen to me in a half-hearted way: on the one hand I confirm the suspicions that they also have, but on the other hand, my ferocity frightens them. They are afraid to revolt, because that may cost them their lives. While I am exhorting the people there, soldiers come to pick me up (because of my inflammatory language and rabble rousing.) I am transported to a prison cell in a wet basement.

As I am being dragged to the stake, I resist and I remain enraged. Only when the fire comes up to my thighs - I sit kneeling and bound - do I begin to panic, and I suddenly realize how alone I am. My group members have been separated from me. There are a total of three stakes (besides mine there are two to my right) surrounded by a rectangular square where people are gathered to watch the spectacle. I have not been able to contact the other victims. I feel overwhelming, burning pain; because of the smoke I can no longer breathe, and I lose consciousness.

After my death, I ascend and I meet two light figures in white. The names that come to me are Paul and Simon. Suddenly I realize that in this life, I had been inspired more by the political than by the spiritual. Now the political symbolically appears to me as a relatively small, sandy-colored globe. Then I see the perspective of the spiritual before me like a huge white-gorgeous globe, much bigger than the political sphere. It is clear to me that, from a broader spiritual perspective, issues are not so black and white, and everything that exists has its own purpose and meaning. This insight surprises me, but it also fills me with a kind of delight.

When I stand beside Paul and Simon, I find it hard to determine what it is that they are telling me. Eventually I make out that Paul says: 'The Light is inside of you,' and this means that I do not need to fight for it outside of me as much as I have done in this past life. Simon has a more humorous appearance; cheerfully grinning, he says: 'Lighten up!'.

As I am wondering whether Paul and Simon have more to tell me, they point to something behind them - a tunnel: a white, rounded tunnel with cloud-like walls. I'm going into it and all the way through it. On the other side, I come out and I fall into the universe: an immense dark space with stars in it. This space is empty yet full of anticipation. It is so big. I don't feel uncomfortable floating around there, but I do feel a bit disoriented. At one point I tumble down, towards Earth. I end up on a path that runs over the Earth. While I walk on this path, I see the round contours of the Earth (as if I am relatively large compared to the Earth).

I walk alone on this whitish path that leads to an immense sun. It is a huge orange disc that is two-thirds visible on the horizon. The sun is much larger than one can ever see on Earth. While I am walking towards it, an uncomfortable feeling arises in my heart, as if something is calling to me. I realize that this has to do with the fact that I am clearly *walking alone.* The words that come to mind are *settle down.* In some way, it is not right that I walk so solitarily and audaciously toward the sun. What is missing is a community with which to engage. I realize that I am meant to *settle* in on Earth, with others, and that we then can jointly turn our gaze toward this sun. That realization gives me a greater sense of understanding.

12. The Follower of Christ

In the last session of my therapy, I once again go back to the images of Paul and Simon, whom I met in the story of 'the passionate campaigner for justice.' I see Paul and Simon standing there again, now looking more like earthly people. That means, with Paul I see his lower body up to his stomach as an earthly body, and above it there is only white light. I concentrate on this radiant white light to feel the essence of it. It is a very crisp, clear and sober energy. It is not ecstatic, but very grounded and real. I ask Paul if there is anything he would like to tell me. He says to me that Earth is currently going through a time of transition, and that I could act as a guide in this process. I ask, 'What should I do?' At that point, Simon begins to make playful, joking gestures that make me burst out laughing. It is because I use the word 'should' (an old habit!).

As a further response from Paul, I see a type of caterpillar-like, moving, transparent tunnel before me through which people will find passage. This is the way my work as a guide would look. I would be able to form with my energy a kind of passage, or channel, through which people can travel to a more loving way of being. The energy I provide is translucent, transparent, and therefore almost invisible; nevertheless, it is clearly evident and present. It is a non-intrusive, fluid energy that radiates peace and safety and inspires self-love in a gentle way. I get the feeling that I have more to contribute to this time of transition than I usually assume that I do.

Now I turn to Simon. He is a more down-to-earth figure, and I see him completely as a physical person. He is middle-aged and almost completely bald, with an oval shaped face. He smiles in a comradely way at me, and as I am facing him I get such a sense of familiarity! I feel friendship for him. 'You were there also;' he says to me smiling, 'you do remember, don't you?!' I suddenly feel very self-conscious and barely dare to think that it is true. Was I really present when Christ was on Earth? I find it presumptuous of me to believe that I was there. But I allow myself to go and see, anyway.

First I see a rectangular white translucent square, a bit futuristic, like there are lights inside the tiles. In one of the corners, Christ stands in a white robe. I feel bashful. Then I go to him and see his face, framed with medium length dark hair. I see his eyes. These eyes contain something incredible. They reflect the whole universe. Everything is mirrored in them. I am overcome with awe.

Now I focus on who I was in that life. I see that I belonged to a group of followers of Jesus; I find myself a bit on the edge of that group. I was a woman. I am reminded of a story from the Bible. That story is about two women, Martha and Mary, who on a given day are told that Jesus comes to visit them. When Martha hears the news, she begins to clean the house in a frenzied manner, and she prepares her best meal, so that everything will be in perfect order when Jesus arrives. She is so busy that she doesn't notice that Jesus is already there. He sits in a corner and talks with Mary who listens to him attentively. I have the feeling I was such a type as Mary. I was open to the message that Jesus came to bring.

I now see before me that I sit in a semi-dark room and that Jesus appears in the doorway. On the one hand, he is a figure radiating intense white light, but on the other hand, he is an ordinary physical man. I get up and walk toward him. I have an indescribable sense of humility in his presence. I feel that I want to kneel in front of him with my head resting forward on the ground and that even if I were to lie flat on the ground, I would still be up too high compared to him. I feel enormous respect for him, but it has nothing submissive about it. He takes my hands, and he exudes a great inner light. While he stands in front of me, I focus on his energy and go inside of it. Seen from the outside, it appears as a shining, radiant energy of love. From the inside of it, I just feel deep, serene stillness. What strikes me in particular is that his energy is so *present*. It is a sacred energy, like the energy that you feel around people in their dying hour or when a child is born into the world. It is a strongly focused energy which is incomparably gentle at the same time. This gentleness has great power; I can imagine that it could be experienced as stern, because it is beyond compromise. The energy and love of Christ is radical.

I feel no urge to speak to him. I only want to be near him. Feel his light. Once you have felt the Christ energy, you cannot let go of it, and you will do anything to be in its presence. It is a kind of elixir that enraptures you, but not in an unbalanced way. It lifts you up, so that everything becomes less heavy and burdensome. Hope and trust return. He is always with us. That's the only thing he says to me, repeatedly: 'I am always with you.'

Contact Information

Pamela and Gerrit can be contacted through their website:
www.jeshua.net

Other Books by Pamela Kribbe

The Jeshua Channelings

In clear and accessible language, Jeshua speaks about the origins and destiny of the lightworker family. He offers a detailed account of the transition from ego-based to heart-based consciousness. In the second part of the book, Jeshua deals with several aspects of everyday life, such as relationships, work and health. He addresses the most common questions and problems we struggle with in these areas.

Some books are filled with shining wisdom. Others radiate great love. A few – a very rare few – are overflowing with both. The Jeshua Channelings is one such book. If you want to know who you really are, why you're here, and what your life is truly about, look no further. This book gently and compassionately guides readers toward remembering their magnificence as divine souls. Brilliantly insightful and inspiring, it is true gem and a blessing to our world.

- Robert Schwartz, author, Your Soul's Plan: Discovering the Real Meaning of the Life You Planned Before You Were Born - yoursoulsplan.com

ISBN-13: 978-1601456823
Paperback: 264 pages
Publisher: Booklocker.com, Inc.

Heart Centered Living

Heart Centered Living is living according to the calling of your soul. You can recognize the calling of your soul by the feelings of joy, peace and inspiration it brings to you. However, daring to trust your heart often involves a leap into the unknown. You may be confronted with deep-seated fears about your own worth and your ability to pursue your own path. This book is a loving guide on your way to heart centered living. It contains clear and informative channelings inspired by the Christ energy. They deal with different subjects, such as finding your true passion, how to create balanced relationships, parenting the new, sensitive children and emotional healing in the face of fear and depression. They also speak about the profound transformation humanity is going through, letting go of ego-based consciousness and evolving into heart-based consciousness.

This book is written for lightworkers, souls who feel compelled to go deep within and express their true soul's calling on Earth. The teachers who speak in this book (Jeshua, Mary and mother Earth) all encourage you to take the leap of faith and become who you really are. Their teachings gently inspire you to face and overcome whatever holds you back in listening to the voice of your heart.

ISBN-13: 978-1621412618
Paperback: 276 pages
Publisher: Booklocker.com, Inc.

The Christ Within

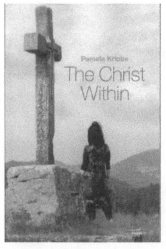

In each of us, Christ consciousness is waiting to be awakened. Christ consciousness is the awareness that behind outer appearance and form, all life is one and connected. As we enter this level of awareness, we gradually let go of our fear, our resistance, our need to control. We discover the reality of our divine essence, our soul. Life becomes less about struggling to survive, driven by the demands of the ego, and more about joy and creating from the heart.

Opening up to the voice of our soul involves taking a leap into the abyss: you are invited to rely on your inner guidance rather than the outer directions you are used to steering by. How do you let go of the worldly pressures and judgments that have become almost second nature? How do you know if you have truly connected with your soul? How do you deal with fear and trauma, which keeps you from surrendering?

The spiritual messages in this book, received by way of channeling, are meant to answer these questions and to assist you on your path of inner transformation in a loving and compassionate way. As you surrender to your soul, the Christ Within will awaken and illuminate your life as well as the lives of others.

ISBN-13: 978-1626469631
Paperback: 264 pag
Publisher: Booklocker.com, Inc.